Prairie Patrimony

Prairie

STUDIES IN RURAL CULTURE

Jack Temple Kirby, Editor

·SONYA SALAMON·

Patrimony

Family, Farming, and Community in the Midwest

THE UNIVERSITY OF NORTH CAROLINA PRESS · Chapel Hill & London

The paper in this book meets the guidelines for permanence and
durability of the Committee on Production Guidelines for Book
Longevity of the Council on Library Resources.

99   98   97   96   95   6   5   4   3   2

Library of Congress Cataloging-in-Publication Data
Salamon, Sonya.
Prairie patrimony : family, farming, and community in the
midwest / Sonya Salamon.
p.   cm.—(Studies in rural culture)
Includes bibliographical references and index.
ISBN 0-8078-2045-8 (cloth : alk. paper)
—ISBN 0-8078-4553-1 (pbk. : alk. paper)
1. Rural families—Middle West.   2. Family farms—Middle West.
3. Farm life—Middle West.   I. Title.   II. Series.
HQ536.15.A14S25   1992
306.85′2′0977—dc20   92-53622 CIP

Illustrations from P. L. Ardrey, *American Agricultural Implements:
A Review of Invention and Development in the Agricultural
Implement Industry of the United States* (Chicago, 1894).

For John L., who did not live to see this book,
and my mother, who did

Contents

Tables

Figures

Preface

My years of studying farm families began among student discussion groups in the cross-cultural family studies course I teach at the University of Illinois. When I began my first semester of teaching in 1974, I was initially struck by differences between students with farm backgrounds and those from suburban Chicago. For example, suburban students said they intended to leave for California (or a similar place with better weather than Illinois) upon graduation; farm-background students wanted to return home, if possible. Suburban students cited friends more than family members as intimates, while farm-background students spoke of the strength of their extended families. I became convinced, as the semester went on, that I was learning about fundamental cultural differences, and my curiosity was piqued.

When I turned to the literature, I was surprised to find little recent work on farmers, with the exception of the Canadian studies by John Bennett and Seena Kohl. No American research was evident since the 1940s, when fine anthropologists such as Walter Goldschmidt, Oscar Lewis, and Horace Miner, among others, had carried out ethnographic studies. But these were community studies, and as in most reports of the period, families scarcely appeared as actors. Only recently has anthropological interest turned to how culture is reproduced in the family context. Sharing a hotel room at a professional meeting with a colleague whose father was embroiled in a land dispute while breaking up a ranch partnership, and engaging in discussions with others having farm backgrounds, helped me to realize that, in the Midwest, obtaining, using, owning, and passing on land are of paramount importance to farm families. I decided to ask farmers about standard anthropological topics—inheritance and kinship beliefs—to explore the relationship between such cultural factors and the persistence of families in farming. Such issues had been virtually ignored by previous researchers.

The first farmer I met in 1975, whose family and I have kept in contact ever since, became the model for the yeoman farmer in this book. One fall morning we first met in the kitchen of the farmhouse where he had lived his entire life until retirement. He asked me three questions to decide whether I was acceptable even if a university professor: Did I own my own home? What religion was I? and Did my husband like "to beer"? It was important that I own my home. I thought being Jewish might be a problem, but it was more important that I was something than what it was. And finally, drinking beer, by definition, was a social act and important for a man to do. Although it was eleven in the morning, he invited me to join him for a beer—I had met with his approval. His offhand reply to one question that morning became the driving force of my research. I wanted to know why he had retired at age fifty-five when, clearly, farming was his whole life. "Why I'd met all my goals," he said simply. His children were farming, and he had acquired enough land to give them each a farm the size his father had given him. It took me a decade to unravel the full meaning of his answer and to understand the cultural significance of retiring before one personally might prefer otherwise.

Although he had only an eighth-grade education, this farmer was a highly intelligent man who lived fully committed to maintaining his heritage and an agrarian way of life. I was lucky to meet him first. My husband regretted our friendship when we attended a community beer fest with the farmer's family and he was pressed to drink too much. My two young sons giggled in delight when the farmer teased them about coming to work with him on the farm—he would have them shovel manure. "After all you have to take the bitter with the sweet," he commented with a sly grin. He was an anthropologist's dream informant who loved his life, and when he reflected on it, every observation was a quotable quote. Despite not acquiring the "bull-shit meter" that an acquaintance told me I would need working with the farmer, I learned a great deal about how farming can be a way of life one loves passionately.

This work was supported by a variety of funding over the many years I carried out the community studies. Basic funding was provided by the Illinois Agricultural Experiment Station, with funds allocated to Hatch Projects 60-302, 60-306, and 60-308. Critical and substantial support also came from the Agriculture and Rural Economy Division, Economic Research Service, U.S. Department of Agriculture, in the form of several cooperative agreements for field studies, and a year of sabbatical leave during 1988–89 as a Visiting Scientist in Washington, D.C., allowed me to prepare the first draft. A Rural Sociological Society Senior Fellowship in Policy Studies also supported my sabbatical. An early draft of this book (the wrong book, it turned out) was written during 1981–82 while I was on sabbatical in France with support from a fellowship from the University of Illinois Center for Advanced Study. It was that first draft that led me to develop the basic model for this version. Several University of Illinois Research Board awards also supported parts of the research. I am grateful to all these sources of financial aid.

I am also grateful for permission to reproduce here, in somewhat different form, portions of the following articles and essays that have appeared previously and are reprinted here with the permission of the publishers, journals, and organizations noted: Edward V. Carroll and Sonya Salamon, "Share and Share Alike: Inheritance Patterns in Two Illinois Farm Communities," *Journal of Family History* 13, no. 2 (1988): 219–32; Sonya Salamon, "Ethnic Communities and the Structure of Agriculture," *Rural Sociology* 50, no. 3 (1985): 323–40; Sonya Salamon, "Ethnic Determinants of Farm Community Character," in *Farm Work and Fieldwork: American Agriculture in Anthropological Perspective*, edited by Michael Chibnik, pp. 167–88 (Ithaca, N.Y.: Cornell University Press, 1987); Sonya Salamon, "Ethnic Differences in Farm Family Land Transfers," *Rural Sociology* 45, no. 2 (1980): 290–308; Sonya Salamon, "Farming and Community from the Anthropological Study of Families," *Rural Sociologist* 10, no. 2 (1990): 23–30; Sonya Salamon, "Farmland Auctions," *Rural Sociologist* 2, no. 2 (1980): 109–11; Sonya Salamon, "Persistence among Middle-Range Corn Belt Farmers," in *Food and Farm*, Monographs in Economic Anthropology, no. 7, edited by Christina Gladwin and Kathleen Truman, pp. 345–65 (Lantham, Md.: University Press of America, 1989), by permission of the Society for Economic Anthropology; Sonya Salamon, "Sibling Solidarity as an Operating Strategy in Illinois Agriculture," *Rural Sociology* 47, no. 2 (1982): 349–68; Sonya Salamon, Kathleen M. Gengenbacher, and Dwight J. Penas, "Family Factors Affecting the Intergenerational Succession to Farming," *Human Organization* 45, no. 1 (1986): 24–33; Sonya Salamon and Ann Mackey Keim, "Land Ownership and Women's Power in a Midwestern Farming Community," *Journal of Marriage and the Family* 41 (1979): 109–19, by permission of the National Council on Family Relations; Sonya Salamon and Vicki Lockhart, "Land Ownership and the Position of Elderly in Farm Families," *Human Organization* 39, no. 4 (1980): 324–31; Sonya Salamon and Kathleen K. Markan, "Incorporation and the Farm Family," *Journal of Marriage and the Family* 46, no. 1 (1984): 167–78, by permission of the National Council on Family Relations; Sonya Salamon and Shirley M. O'Reilly, "Family Land and Developmental Cycles Among Illinois Farmers," *Rural Sociology* 44, no. 3 (1979): 525–42.

Several people were important to the research and the writing of this book. Calvin L. Beale met me in 1979 when I gave my first talk on the research, and he has been a fine colleague, a source of immense information, and probably the only other person as deeply interested in rural ethnicity as I am. Frederick

C. Fleigel was a valued editor of my turgid prose, a colleague and adviser until his untimely death. Franklin J. Reiss, a land economist, helped me to understand the importance of soils and land values and assisted with my choice of communities in the early stages. Peggy Barlett has been a soulmate as well as an important sounding board during hours of talking data. John Hoffman at the Illinois Historical Survey aided my archive research on the communities. I wish to thank Nina Baym, whose criticism and advice guided me through the first two drafts, and Edward M. Bruner, whose critical reading helped my thinking toward the end. Many other colleagues provided insights, criticism, and encouragement that assisted me in refining and sharpening my ideas during the long process of twelve years of research and three of writing: Seena Kohl, Leann Birch, Carol Stack, Remi Clignet, Eugene Wilkening, Kathleen Conzen, Kate Cloud, Vernon Burton, Harry Schwarzweller, Linda Ghelfi, Jan and Cornelia Flora, Marty Strange, Gene Wunderlich, Charles Geisler, R. T. Zuidema, Tom Hady, David McGranahan, Sara Mazie, Paul Rosenblatt, Tom Lyson, Jess Gilbert, Pat Mooney, and Gene Summers.

In a special class are all the people involved in the field studies. Susan Carol Rogers was particularly important for her research with the German Catholic communities. In a year of working together at Illinois she finally convinced me that her Yankee heritage represented a real ethnic identity. Judith Lisansky carried out the Gray Prairie Yankee field study. Karen Davis-Brown, a master's student and research associate par excellence, worked in many capacities. Students whose master's theses were based on their field studies were Ann Mackey Keim, Shirley M. O'Reilly, Vicki Lockhart, Emily Rest (who worked with Susan Carol Rogers), Dwight J. Penas, Kathleen K. Markan, Katy Sherlock, Sue Mills, Marilyn S. Brengle, and Edward V. Carroll. Other students carried out studies in Irish and Swedish communities, which, while not part of this book, contributed to my thinking: Karen S. Jung, Barbara J. Kestel-Satrun, and Kathleen M. Gengenbacher. Rosemarie Zabel provided the very able computer analysis.

I owe a great debt to the more than five hundred farm families that were surveyed in the seven communities and the approximately one hundred families that were studied more intensively, though I cannot thank them by name. They invited strangers into their homes and opened their hearts and minds. I know they will not agree with nor like everything in the book, but I hope they feel the text conveys an honest picture of their lives.

Paul Betz, my editor at the University of North Carolina Press, patiently guided a slow and wordy writer through endless drafts and made substantive contributions. Jack Temple Kirby encouraged and guided several rewrites of the book to assure that this anthropologist dealt with the complexity of factors affecting the development of Midwestern ethnic communities. My sons, David and Aaron, grew up and left home despite their mother's obsession. Finally, my husband, Myron, taught me the importance of family processes, negotiation, and commitment by his generous giving of time, ideas, feedback, editing, and advice. Through it all he still kept his sense of humor and never told any farmer how I killed houseplants, although he always threatened to.

Prairie Patrimony

Introduction

Travelers crossing the prairie in the spring often see a lone tractor in a distant field, its trailing plume of dust marking the furrow as the farmer breaks the soil. This image, like that of the proverbial lonesome cowboy, leads many to regard the farmer as an individual working the land, self-reliant and independent. Scholars too fall into the trap, assuming that business decisions on a farm are made and implemented solely through the isolated farmer's individual effort. Nothing could be further from the truth: that farmer works that acreage by virtue of a family effort. Farming is rarely a solo occupation. Absent inheritance of or access to land through family ties, our farmer would most likely not be on that tractor. Each farm is in fact the product of a complex history of family processes, the result of which enables a farmer to work a particular tract at a particular stage of his life. Farm families transmit, along with access to land, a patrimony, a cultural heritage. A family's patrimony consists, in addition to an account of its past, of cultural beliefs shared with a community of families living in close proximity. Culture, history, and community shape a family's attachment to its land. Culture, in particular, mediates how kin groups manage, handle, and pass on land, processes instrumental to the production and reproduction of the gender and social relations in both family and community.

The Illinois countryside, where our farmer is toiling, has a certain outward sameness: a sweep of subtly undulating land divided into fields of row crops reaching to the flat horizon. Now and then the expanse is broken by a cluster of buildings signaling a family farmstead: a farmhouse with machine sheds, grain bins, and perhaps a silo and barn indicating that animals are raised. Trees planted to break the fierce wind that incessantly whips across the open prairie often demarcate the farmstead's boundaries. But while these farmsteads seem autonomous, the families that live in those households belong to communities at whose hub are the villages that dot the horizon. Farms and farming villages are both laid out in perpendicular conformity with the mile-square grid of country roads. At a distance one can discern the village by its grain elevator and at least one or maybe more church steeples reaching above an island formed by a canopy of trees. The village center typically includes a short main street with a row of stores, a post office, and a cafe. Running parallel to or jutting at right angles from the business area are a few tree-shaded residential streets lined with older frame houses and some newer bungalows. The village core is anchored by an elementary or high school at one end and a grain elevator at the other, the dominating structure on the horizon. In front of the main street's cafe, pickup trucks or later model cars are parked at midday. These regular, geometrically arranged farmsteads and rural village landmarks block out the social fabric of farm family life composed of kin, work, and community. The physical dimensions of the rural Midwestern family and community life present a simple surface that leads to a false assumption of homogeneity beneath.

Our farmer, his family, and his community symbolize for many the all-American ideals of family values, individualism, self-reliance, industry, and democracy. Yet the Midwest is actually an ethnic mosaic of farming communities, a product of rapid settlement during the middle and late nineteenth century by immigrants from northern and western Europe and by native-born farmers following the frontier west. In rural Illinois and throughout the Midwest, farmers are aware that the countryside is comprised of ethnically diverse communities. Each small community is unique, beginning from its original settlement and evolving through a process whereby culture interacts with environment (Ortner 1984).

In many ways these American communities resemble groups that anthropologists have always studied: they are small, homogeneous, discrete, and agrarian. Yet relatively few anthropologists have found rural America worthy of study. That the communities were founded by farmers from a variety of European countries during approximately the same period, however, provides an ideal benchmark in the study of how culture affects community and land tenure development. At the outset the populations were, because of their varied origins, culturally distinctive. Historical events such as the Great Depression and increased agricultural mechanization—the environmental factors each culture had to mediate—were remarkably similar for central Illinois. Under these circumstances, did the various populations evolve toward a single agrarian culture in response to environmental factors, or in other words, did the "melting-pot" operate in the rural Midwest (Epstein 1978; Glazer and Moynihan 1970)?

This book focuses on ordinary family practices involved in kin and gender relations, domestic organization, child socialization, and lifecourse development. For Illinois farmers these practices invariably directly or indirectly express a family's relation to land, most specifically, to control of it. As families enact these practices, while motivated to reproduce the family and farm, their actions are predicated upon cultural meanings of land and kinship. Although the cultural system changes when it is re-created as an entire community in each generation negotiates domestic micro-transactions with land, larger patterns for farming, land tenure, and community life emerge. Two cultural systems, I will argue, played a powerful role historically in shaping how Midwestern agriculture and communities developed.

Is it germane to refer to culture and ethnic differences for the rural social fabric when, to the observer making a windshield survey, American farming communities seem identical? To answer this question we must first consider approaches to analyzing culture and ethnicity, issues at the heart of current social science discussions. Anthropologists struggle to determine which aspects of culture have more stability, which aspects change, and the nature of the processes involved (Ohnuki-Tierney 1990a; Ortner 1984). Sociologists debate whether American ethnic differences are symbolic or real and whether ethnicity serves a function several generations after Europeans immigrate (Gans 1979; Waters 1990).

My view of culture is heavily influenced by recent work by "practice model" theorists in anthropology (Ortner 1984, 1990). Culture in this view not only determines action and shapes what people do, think, feel, and believe but also constrains options and inhibits people from alternative ways of doing, thinking, or feeling. More importantly, this approach is concerned with how the practices which constitute a particular system are produced, why and how a system is reproduced, and finally how the cultural practices that produce and reproduce the system also change it. Of much concern in this approach are practices of ordinary life enacted in the domestic order context. This focus arises because the myriad of small, repetitive, and seemingly trivial aspects of daily life embody and are organized by the fundamental concepts of the system (Ortner 1984). The analysis of basically asymmetrical relationships in a society—the negotiations and struggles of the cooperation and complementary relations among and between actors—is a major pursuit with the practice model approach to culture. These emphases are well matched to an analysis of processes operating in a culture dominated by family farming.

Though the typical emphasis of practice theorists is on the individual acting according to self-interest, I shift emphasis to the family as the agent critical to cultural production and reproduction. A precedent for this cautious extension is found in economic anthropology where the interdependence of family members establishes the family as the basic economic unit, particularly in the simpler societies anthropologists study (Johnson and Earle 1987). For agrarian societies, in particular, kinship considerations form the context of almost all social action. The social milieu which intertwines work and family makes it difficult to disentangle a lone actor—for example, the lone farm operator when acting within the farm family. Furthermore, because of the generational and gender asymmetries inherent to the family, the system of farm and land relations the actors seek to reproduce involves group interactions. Group goals take high priority due to the nature of family-land processes. Farmland's expense and the complex commitments required in actions pertaining to it assure that such actions involve the family group in negotiation and conflict along with reciprocity and support.

How the cultural system changes—develops over time—is another major emphasis in practice model theory. Agreement exists among anthropologists that not all levels of culture change at the same rate. Some levels change rapidly while others change at a much slower rate (Bloch 1977, 1985; Ohnuki-Tierney 1990a). Practical aspects of culture, for example, may be altered as people adapt their conduct to maintain households in the midst of changing environmental circumstances (Carter 1988). Culture constrains and regularizes the choices actors make, but this does not necessarily confine choices to only a narrow set of options. To probe change, practice theorists choose a strategic focus—an analytical window—such as a class of persons, a symbol, or an activity (Ohnuki-Tierney 1990b; Fernandez 1990). This window provides a mechanism to trace both change and the enduring structure of meaning that emerges with responses to historical events. Microprocesses are to some extent mediated by the structure of meaning in a given system. Through a focus on one issue, the results of the dialectic between culture and the environment are thrown into sharp relief. The window I use is land. How land is handled reflects what farm families want for themselves and value about the future or the past. By concentrating on the micro-dimension of family actions concerning land, looking through this window over time (because land transactions leave an objective record), we gain insight into the production of trends in rural society and agriculture—precisely those macrostructures which in turn influence the persistence of family farms and rural communities.

Now let us turn to the issue of ethnicity and the question of whether American farmers can be considered ethnics at all. Most contemporary definitions of ethnic identity best describe urban contexts. They depend on interactional criteria to handle settings in which varied and scattered people believe themselves to have a bond based on a real or imagined common legacy (Barth 1969; Gans 1979; Waters 1990). Consistent with these concepts is a collective, self-conscious, and articulated identity that "substantializes" one or more traits (such as religion, language, or skin color) and that is enduring and self-producing (Tambiah 1988). In contrast, the rural-agricultural context represents communities that are cohesive social entities with a physically and geographically definable locale and in which people not only share ancestral origins but an occupation, farming (Weber 1961). Furthermore, because Midwestern farming is most easily carried out on land within the geographic boundaries of a community and by families, interactions critical to identity perpetuation are vested mainly in the kin group and the local ethnic community. A shared culture rather than interaction with other groups, that is, through social structure, is used for self-identification and maintenance (Barth 1984).

My conception of ethnicity combines objective and subjective criteria. I must account for peoples who share origins but, because they live in separate communities, do not function as a group and never need act together. I use ethnic identity to refer to a sense of peoplehood that unites farmers in American rural society whose members think of themselves as akin by assumption of common ancestry and historical style (shared symbols, values, and standards) (Royce 1982). They recognize themselves as sharing that style, concretely, through land practices. I also extend ethnic identity in an unconventional manner to include those who do not consciously think of themselves as ethnically distinctive but who actually are. These are people who in fact share a common ancestry and effectively erect a boundary by means of consistently patterned behaviors, which results in their being classed as a group by others (McGoldrick 1989).

Being an ethnic without acknowledging an ethnic heritage may be unique to the United States. The choice of taking an "American" identity has received much attention, especially since the 1980 census, which asked for the first time about ethnic origin (Lieberson and Waters 1988; Waters 1990). Distinctive practices identified for the ethnic-denial group include a lack of emphasis on ethnic origins and genealogical connection, pride in being many generations from immigration, a priority for upward mobility, and a tendency to form loose kinship networks (Waters 1990:52-89). In combination such traits foster a world view that believes individuals invent themselves and that personal will, not culture, motivates actions. Collectively these practices, however, constitute patterned and routinized behavior, particularly in the domestic domain. In this manner a cultural system is reproduced in families, albeit unwittingly (Ortner 1984).

Those Illinois farm families who descended from the direct immigrants from various regions of what is now Germany are especially self-conscious about their collective identity and cultural heritage. They represent the type highly conscious of and articulate about a shared ethnic identity. They take pride in a common ancestral origin, readily apparent in shared beliefs, customs, and language (Royce 1982). They place high priority on ethnic endogamy and organize communities for the pursuit of ethnic interests. By contrast farm families descended from native-born Americans who migrated from the eastern United States have a British Isles ancestry in common, yet this group exemplifies the unself-conscious ethnic type described above. As members of the nation's ethnically dominant group, they do not regard themselves to be united by an ethnic identity, and they espouse beliefs about land without recognizing this as part of a cultural heritage. Individual families historically simply did things "the way we do," as "'Mericans." Choices made according to what was proper and moral did not seem to them distinguishing but, because others perceived a consistent difference, social boundaries emerged that marked them as a distinctive group (Barth 1969; Conzen 1980b; Gleason 1980). Such a distinctiveness may be more recognizable to others than to the actors themselves because their self-concept results in insensitivity to what actually communicates as distinguishing traits (Royce 1982). But these traits can produce a continuity of a world view, priorities, and regularities across generations, which could function to reproduce a culture as evident as that of self-conscious ethnic Germans (Royce 1982, 1974).

I focus on two distinct Illinois ethnic types, the German and those I call Yankees (a label I will defend in the next chapter). These types were chosen because they were and are dominant demographically in the Midwest and thus played a critical role in the development of the region's agricultural and social patterns. The Germans were from various Catholic and Protestant areas in what we now call Germany; the Yankees had ancestors from the Protestant British Isles (England, Wales, Scotland, and Scotch-Irish from Ireland), but their immediate forebears were native-born migrants mainly from the Northeastern and Middle Atlantic states who followed the frontier west.

Part I of this book centers on my argument that present Midwestern ethnic practices having to do with kinship and land have links to the past. In the century since Illinois was settled, a multitude of rural ethnic communities have maintained coherent cultures (Rice 1977). Each contemporary group has a culture different from that now evident in their ancestral homeland and likewise different from that brought by immigrant families founding the original community. From settlement until I observed them, a dynamic process took place in which culture, history, and context interacted to shape new ethnic types. Because some levels of culture changed more slowly, especially those behaviors vested in the family, the emergent structure retained continuity with the past (Ohnuki-Tierney 1990a; Ortner 1990; Sahlins 1981).

Among the farm-making ancestors of our lone farmer, agricultural practices underwent rapid transformation following settlement. Adoption of new technology soon made it difficult to distinguish a family's ethnicity by looking at a barn or a cornfield, and the farm population, like the landscape, appeared homogenized into a Midwestern mold. With the rapid change, what other practices remained more stable or changed more slowly? It may be that those practices not directly involved in survival had less pressure to change and undoubtedly involved taken-for-granted asymmetrical gender, generational, and social relations.

Chapter 1 is concerned with how the original intraethnic diversity within the German and Yankee types changed in the process of settling, farming, and making communities on the prairie. Chapter 2 shifts from ethnic variation to illustrate those practices of ordinary farm family life that typify Midwestern family farmers. Taken together, the typical family traits that crosscut the Midwest are sufficiently distinctive to constitute a subcultural family type in the United States. This profile of homogeneous traits serves as a benchmark against which cultural variation can be compared.

Seven communities, each studied for a year—three German, three Yankee, and one that combines Germans and Yankees—are described in chapter 3. Each community was surveyed in its entirety, and for a subset we constructed a kinship genealogy, gathered land and family histories, and observed everyday life. A community description is critical to the argument that cultural beliefs underlie patterned practices of Midwestern family farmers. Our lone farmer and his family are part of an ethnic community that acts as audience with a collective vested interest in the fit between household actions and the existing cultural system. The community monitors actions and reinforces or constrains family options using discussions structured by shared beliefs about land and informed by past accounts of "how we do things" (Bourdieu 1979).

An ideal typology of the enduring cultural structure maintained by Germans and Yankees is the book's framework, presented in chapter 4. Motivated by differing meanings attached to land, German and Yankee families practice distinctive land acquisition, management, and succession strategies to achieve distinctive goals. I term the German cultural pattern *yeoman* and the Yankee pattern *entrepreneur*. How yeoman or entrepreneur families, farms, and communities emerge as people act according to cultural themes embodied in a particular meaning connected to land, or a patrimony, is the subject of this book.

In Part II I focus on the nuclear family as the primary force reproducing cultural practices. Land transactions are inevitable as the lifecourse makes one generation yield to the next and ritually hand on control of land. Families are highly conscious of their motives, the meaning of their actions, and whether a transaction performance is flawed (Bruner 1986). However, because I found one family dyad more central to a particular process helping reproduce the family farm, the book is organized taking one nuclear-family dyad in turn to disentangle the family "black box" through land transactions over the family lifecourse.

In chapter 5 I discuss the husband/wife dyad and how it centers on farm management and ownership. Couples allocate family labor, resources, and time in accord with a fundamental scenario for the social ordering of the family, based on who should control the farm and land (Ortner 1984). In chapter 6 I focus on the father/son dyad, the primary actors in the succession process and the mechanism that assures persistence of the family farm and the farming occupation. Siblings, the subject of chapter 7, influence the outcome of the intergenerational transfer of family resources, the inheritance process. Networks, constrained and shaped by land acquisition goals and strategies, forge the link between the individual household and the wider community, as described in chapter 8.

In the final part of the book each cultural system is shown having implications for domains wider than the family. Chapter 9 deals with the land tenure consequences of culturally derived goals among yeomen and entrepreneurs. Chapter 10 considers how beliefs concerning land affect what families invest in their community and how these beliefs have consequences for its viability.

Farmers are eloquent spokespeople because they love the distinctive form of life that they lead and are fascinating to the anthropologist. They can graphically describe what they have in common with or how they differ from the family down the road or the neighboring community—only six miles as the crow flies but perhaps light years away in attitudes.

The anthropologist sifts the collected observational and interview data looking for repetitions in what people agree and disagree about, the way people converse and interact, what they cherish or detest, and what they recognize as flawed practices. Discovery of patterned processes in the flow of ordinary conversations, everyday activities, and family choices that show how people think, feel, and are motivated is the aim. Because informants share intimate life details, anthropologists traditionally mask their identities by disguising community names with pseudonyms and by making minor changes in distinguishing family facts. I follow this custom. The book is filled with the words of farm family members, spoken to me and my research associates in the course of conversations and in the midst of farming activities. Their words, recorded as closely to what was actually spoken as possible, should provide the reader with a sense of the experience involved in living, working, and cherishing a family farm, land, and the endeavor of farming.

PART ONE

Culture and
Midwestern Family Farmers

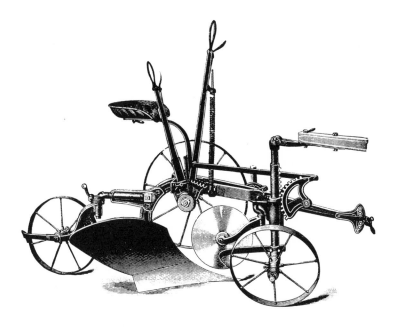

Historical Background of Ethnic Farmers

Practices of contemporary Illinois farmers are best understood by starting with the past, the source of cultural patterns that order action (Bloch 1985; Ortner 1990; Sahlins 1981). In just fifty years of the nineteenth century the Midwest was settled through one of the most extraordinary transfers of land and people the world has known. While the settlers were white and had Christianity, farming, and European peasant backgrounds in common, their cultural differences led the Midwest to be termed an ethnic mosaic. The Illinois piece of the complex Midwestern mosaic was richly colored by immigrants from various German states, both Catholic and Protestant, who settled in a densely clustered diagonal corridor between St. Louis and Chicago. Balancing the Germans was another group of native-born settlers who also had diverse dialects and religions. Three native-born migration streams populated Illinois: Upland Southerners, the southern part; Midlanders, the midsection; and New England Yankees, the northern third where Chicago lies (Meyer 1976; Swierenga 1989). Yankees apparently preferred Illinois as a Midwestern destination, causing this ethnic stock to eventually dominate the state's social, economic, and political environments (Holbrook 1950; Richard J. Jensen 1978). Each ethnic element carried beliefs about family and land as part of its cultural baggage.

The seven communities whose families this book describes were founded during the vast mid- to late-nineteenth-century peopling of the prairie. Wheeler, Emerson, and Libertyville were settled by native-born migrants; Heartland, St. Boniface, and Freiburg by Germans; and Prairie Gem by a mix of both ethnic elements. While immigrants from the German state of East Friesland established Heartland, St. Boniface's Germans were from Alsace, and Freiburg's were from Westphalia. Though sharing many traits, Frisians and Alsatians are sufficiently distinctive from other German states, such as Westphalia or Prussia, to warrant separate treatment by historians (Thernstrom 1980a). Language masked any cultural variation to native-born Americans, who tended not to discriminate among German immigrants from different regions (Conzen 1980a). It is likely that the Germans felt the same way about their American neighbors.

Early immigrants from the British Isles, like the Germans, originated in different areas with distinguishing dialects and ethnoreligious features: for example, the Puritans from East Anglia, the Royalists from Cornwall in the south, the Quakers from the North Midlands, and the Highlanders from the borderlands of North Britain and Northern Ireland. These groups settled in various regions in the United States, each of which served as a seedbed for regional cultural traits. Such traits were spread as the populations from the pioneer settlements moved across the continent, and according to a recent controversial argument, differences have persisted to the present (Fischer 1989). Another school of thought more widely accepted about American ethnicity holds that the original regional diversity had largely converged by the time of the Revolution, or long before the Midwest was settled (Greene 1988).

Unlike the contemporary Germans in this study, who are knowledgeable about their heritage, farmers whose surnames indicate British roots seldom had familiarity with their ancestry. Farmers of British ancestry had, of course, a greater number of generations since immigration to the U.S. than the Germans. Emerson and Wheeler farmers are descendants of migrants from a stream moving through Ohio and Indiana, but, because these people are unversed about family genealogical matters, whether they originated in New England or the Delaware Valley is unclear. Libertyville, in south central Illinois, was initially settled by families from the Southern Highland stream, but later a substantial contingent of migrants from northern Illinois, including some Germans, moved in. By 1982 many descendants of the Southern stream had left agriculture or were relatively marginal farmers, and thus Libertyville's farm population is now more like that of Emerson and Wheeler.

Throughout this book I apply the terms *German* and *Yankee* to the present-day descendants of the distinctive culture stocks from Germany and the Protestant British Isles that settled rural Illinois. Each term is used to convey a homogenized identity that eventually emerged within the initially diverse ethnic group; the generic label accurately reflects the view each ethnic has of the other. To non-Germans, all German speakers were the same; likewise, English speakers were all "Angles" to Germans. The term *Yankee*, when applied loosely to descendants of immigrants from the Protestant British Isles (England, Wales, Scotland, and Ireland), troubles historians who reserve the term only for descendants of seventeenth-century Puritans, or Southerners who use the term for Northerners during and after the Civil War. But labeling this group Americans, Old Americans, or British-Americans does not convey their unique historical position relative to the Germans. Thus, I use *Yankee* to capture how Germans identify native-born neighbors and because the label is sometimes used to refer to Americans in general (Handlin 1980).

Distinctive ethnic farming patterns identified early by historians, the evidence that these patterns were maintained over the century since settlement, and the social and environmental forces that influenced some culture change among Germans and Yankees are the subject of this chapter. Chapter 3, which describes the unique character that evolved for each community studied, addresses the current community-level variation among each ethnic element.

•

The Ethnic Distinctiveness of German and Yankee Prairie Farmers

EUROPEAN CULTURAL PATTERNS AT THE TIME OF EMIGRATION

Historians cast light on the European agricultural milieu from which the Germans and Yankees originated. Though in the nineteenth century neither the British Isles nor Germany were politically unified in the manner each is today, cultural commonalities did exist among loosely linked groups that shared a language stock.

During the eighteenth century, though small farms predominated throughout England, their numbers declined as a consequence of economic factors that favored farm consolidation (Mingay 1962). Large farms were run as businesses for efficiency and profit maximization, but even small farms of under one hundred acres were oriented toward commercial production. Tenancy was common on both large and small farms, and landlords demanded that tenants have substantial capital for start-up and operation. Several factors worked to the small tenants' disfavor and the decline of their numbers: tenants on small farms suffered particularly as rents rose after enclosure of common lands, and the capital constraints on tenancy made large farmer expansion easier than nonoperator entrance into farming.

The social consequence of farms being commercialized and capitalistic, undergoing concentration, and farmers being risk-taking entrepreneurs was a rural populace both stratified and highly mobile. By the eighteenth century, larger farms' use of a young, hired labor force produced a landless class that moved on a yearly or seasonal basis (Mingay 1989). The growth of the rural population had made possible the shift to hired workers, and because the work was seasonal, wages low, and housing scarce or overcrowded, this class was impoverished and the countryside at times in turmoil. Not just hired laborers were mobile, however. Nuclear families, such as tenants on large farms, moved according to opportunities for maximizing individualistic gains of wealth or social position. Prevailing inheritance practices also affected mobility. Impartible inheritance excluded all but the eldest son as heir, and younger sons went into professions, trade, or emigrated (Mingay 1989).

Transplanted to America, an ambitious Englishman without capital or inheritance had the possibility, with individual entrepreneurship, to attain the status of a large landowner—an impossible achievement in England. By the early eighteenth century, for example, New York already had about thirty capitalistic, great-landed estates farmed by tenants, a pattern common in all the middle colonies and similar to the large farm system left behind in Britain (Greene 1988).

Agricultural practices and settlement patterns differed widely from one part of Germany to another in the nineteenth century, but certain traits were widespread (Jordan 1966). Farms were rather small, family owned, and were worked intensively, typically at a subsistence level. These highly productive farms were operated by individual peasant families, and it was common for women and children to work in the fields. Most characteristic was a "locational stability" of the population in which families occupied land tilled by their ancestors and expected that improvements made would be enjoyed by their descendants. Germans emigrated to preserve cherished agrarian ideals that were increasingly difficult to achieve in Europe for economic reasons. Partible inheritance imposed by the Code Napoleon in Alsace and East Friesland had by the mid-nineteenth century left holdings in many areas too small to support families without supplementation. Similarly, where impartible inheritance dominated, as in Westphalia, nonheirs were unable to farm (Conzen 1980a, 1985; Berkner 1976). A combination of rural overpopulation, the Industrial Revolution diffusing into Germany, and dour fluctuations in weather, harvest, and grain prices, as well as required military service, pushed people to emigrate in the latter half of the nineteenth century (Conzen 1980a; Jordan 1966). The typical pattern was migration by family groups. Thus Germans were not destitute but sought a higher standard of living and to reproduce the permanent agriculture system they valued so highly.

Key historical and environmental factors in addition to culture influenced divergence between the two ethnic groups in the Midwest. The timing of their emigration meant that Germans and Yankees encountered different agricultural and social environments when they arrived. Yankees were the first to immigrate, and by the time they moved in stages to the Midwestern frontier, they were cut off from their European peasant roots by several generations. Germans came directly from Europe to Illinois and, because they arrived after the frontier had moved beyond the Mississippi, had little or no experience with pioneering life. For Yankees land was abundant, if they were willing to make the farm. By the time Germans arrived, land had become more scarce and expensive. Germans sought to establish villages that re-created their recently abandoned homeland, while Yankees sought to replicate Northeastern villages, already once removed from England. As these cultures interacted with history and context, farmers maintained some practices from the past though alterations in other practices caused changed forms of farming and community systems to emerge (Gjerde 1985; Ohnuki-Tierney 1990a).

MIDWESTERN SETTLEMENT

Railroads, begun with congressional land grants to aid in construction, were a key factor in Midwestern settlement. Through publicity campaigns the companies lured immigrants with offers of cheap land; the immigrants in turn provided the capital for railroad construction first as land purchasers and then as farm developers through shipments of hogs and corn (Shannon 1945).

Foremost among the prairie land-grant railroads was the Illinois Central, begun with a land grant in 1850. Completed by 1856, the line ran north to south through the state, and the company owned over 2.5 million acres of land in undeveloped areas. Trying to sell its grants as quickly as possible, the company employed such promotional and colonization activities as sending native speakers to recruit Germans and Swedes in Europe, in the belief that these groups would make good farmers (Gates 1960, 1934). Illinois, Wisconsin, and Minnesota, anxious to grow quickly and to develop a solid tax base of producing farms, also actively recruited in these countries and posted native-speaking guides at such ports as New York and Boston to aid potential settlers. The publicity spread by promoters and relatives was that conditions were most favorable in the Midwest, where there was no slavery and soils were richer than those long farmed, as in the Northeast. Handbooks for prospective peasant immigrants advised that already broken land could be obtained in the Midwest, which in the long run would be more practical than pioneering on new land (Saloutos 1976).

Letters from the first wave of immigrants who had arrived in the 1850s, the activities of the recruiters, and ultimately, economic changes in Europe were much more influential than the Homestead Act of 1862 promise of land in attracting immigrants (Dovring 1962). Given the recruitment efforts, economic woes, and the lack of land in Europe, it is no wonder people were spurred by letters from relatives already in America, such as this one written by a young son from Heartland to his mother in Germany, in which he tells her about the opportunities in Illinois:

God bless you at home, while we are happy, though heart sick in the new land. . . . You need not fear about the land. It is not likely in this country that the land be taken away. The government wants that we shall stay and improve the land. They fear that we will become rich and move to another place. It is not so, however. . . . I now have one hundred acres of land by a paper and it is all mine. Some of it is still full of water but we are working fast to get the ditches in. . . . When I am plowing I can shut my eyes and smell the dear land under me and say it is mine, mine, all mine. No one can take it away. I am king as you said. (Corner 1928:516–17)

Nationally, German immigration began in the 1840s and continued through the 1880s, with surges between 1840 and 1860 and again after 1880. The flow peaked in 1890, accounting for a quarter or more of all immigrants between 1850 and 1900. Among states receiving Germans to rural areas, Illinois ranked fifth after the other Corn Belt states of Wisconsin, Minnesota, Iowa, and Michigan according to the 1920 population census (Shannon 1945; Brunner 1929). Foreign-born inhabitants of Illinois peaked at one-fifth of the population between 1860 and 1880 (7 to 16 percent in the counties of our seven communities), and Germans constituted 40 percent of this group (Swierenga 1989). In central Illinois a flood of immigrants came after the railroad was established, with the largest growth, both absolutely and relatively, in the 1850s and 1860s. Among these newcomers the Illinois Central Railroad, particularly in the late 1860s, sold the most land to Germans (Gates 1934). The propaganda that so successfully lured Germans also attracted native-born farm families from the East. Northeastern and north central states experienced a net loss by Yankee emigration from 1860 until 1890 as farmers, beset by high land prices and soils that generations of exploitation had rendered thin and unproductive, moved west (Shannon 1945). By the 1880s the rural population of Illinois had stabilized (U.S. Bureau of the Census 1960).

ETHNIC FARMING PATTERNS

Immigrants, due to their diverse origins, represent variations on the themes of German and Yankee ethnic stocks that were transplanted to the fertile prairie of central Illinois. The process of adaptation to new social, economic, and environmental conditions in Illinois led to rapid change in those practices of culture directly entailed with economic matters. Where farming practices are concerned, many scholars have found little difference between native-born and immigrant farmers despite some "cultural rebound" among ethnics after a short period of time (Allan G. Bogue 1963b; Jordan 1966; Mackintosh 1990). Germans, however, resisted change in nonagricultural practices just as did other ethnic groups (Cogswell 1975; Ohnuki-Tierney 1990a; Mackintosh 1990; Ostergren 1986). Highly cohesive communities seemed particularly important to the maintenance of these cultural practices (Mackintosh 1990; Conzen 1990).

Germans and Yankees possessed unique resources to deal with the farming challenges of the prairie. The Germans were typically from peasant communities where the same family had farmed land continuously for centuries through careful stewardship (Netting 1981). Though unfamiliar with the farm-making process on the prairie, Germans were from a correspondingly temperate climate and thus could grow similar plants. The Yankees, also unfamiliar with the prairie, however, had previous frontier experiences and knew about the problems of farm making. Furthermore, Yankees had the advantage of membership in the ethnic stock controlling the political, financial, and educational institutions of the new region. From the outset ethnic farming differences were evident to observers as well as to the settlers (McNall and McNall 1983).

Native-born farmers generally were not considered good stewards of the soil. Though fertility-maintenance methods were known, the abundance of Midwestern land encouraged Yankee farmers to discard such practices as impractical and unnecessary. By the 1840s, because farmers neglected such practices as manuring fields, some of Ohio's soils showed the same depletion as those in the East that pioneers had left behind. Depleted soils were abandoned as farmers followed the frontier west into Illinois, with some eventually following it to lands beyond. Clearing forests and breaking the prairie sod were evidently more to a Yankee's liking than consistent land stewardship (Danhof 1969). Immigrant German farmers were considered to be from a contrasting mold.

A 1901 U.S. Industrial Commission report contrasts the farming practices between native-born and European immigrant farmers in testimony by a Mr. Oliver Wilson from the Illinois region where the seven communities in my study are located:

> Foreign farm laborers through central Illinois are usually Germans, Danes, and Swedes. . . . When they acquire farms of their own, they show a tendency to colonize. It is said that immigration has, in the main, improved the condition of agriculture. . . . German farmers . . . farm like the American farmer, except that they do not perhaps lay out quite so much money for labor, getting more help from wives and children. Their manner of living may, however, depress the local market somewhat. The Germans in Illinois are good farmers . . . coming here with a high idea of the necessity of keeping up the fertility of the soil. (U.S. Industrial Commission 1901:530)

Immigrant farmer behavior, described in a classic Wisconsin analysis of the Midwestern frontier, was explained as differing from that of the native-born Yankee as a consequence of contrasting cultural beliefs about land and family.

> The ambition of the German-American father . . . was to see his sons on reaching manhood established with their families on farms clustered about his own. To take complete possession of a township with sons, sons-in-law, and nephews was not an unrealizable idea. To this end, the would-be patriarch dedicated all his plodding industry. One by one, he bought adjacent farms, the erstwhile owners joining the current to the farther West. Heavily timbered acres of swamp lands which had been lying unused were prepared for cultivation by patient and unceasing toil. "When the German comes in, the Yankee goes out," was a local proverb that varied as Swedes, Bohemians, or other immigrant groups formed the invading element. But the American father made no such efforts on behalf of his offspring. To be a self-made man was his ideal. He had come in as a "first settler" and had created a farm with his ax, let the boys do the same. One of them perhaps was kept at home as a helper to his aging parents; the rest set out willingly to achieve beyond the mountains or beyond the river what the father had accomplished in the West of his day. Thus mobility was fostered by family policy. (Hansen 1940: 61–62)

The common adage quoted above, in this description of family and land practices, portrayed Yankee pioneers replaced by Germans. The "invasion-succession" process—in which, typically, German ethnics gradually bought out and eventually replaced those who had broken the land, especially the native-born—is widely documented for the Midwest (Hollingshead 1938). Practices by the first contingent of German peasants that reproduced a family and farm continued and produced persistent farms and farmers in subsequent generations. Indeed the descendants of German farmers remained distinctive from those of native-born farmers even one hundred years after settlement. Approximately seventy years later in the 1940s an eventual domination of Germans in a Minnesota county was attributed to their being the "most successful farmers: more diligent husbandmen, more careful in conserving soil and more frugal. Moreover, they are not interested in doing anything other than farming. They like farming, want their children to farm, and are buying land to make this possible" (Nelson 1955:15). It is estimated that Germans developed 672,000 American farms and by 1900 owned nearly 11 percent of American farms (Brunner 1929).

Following settlement, regularities that emerged across the various German and Yankee communities in part developed as families dealt with the same economic and historical events. Although people were aware they were, for example, Alsatian or Frisian originally, they came simply to call themselves Germans, and as they dropped German dialects with adoption of English, a key aspect of ethnic heterogeneity was lost. Yankees also had a variety of dialects, but as a highly mobile people who settled randomly, they had no commitment to maintaining their regional distinctiveness.

What caused Germans or Yankees each to emerge as a united ethnic element were those cultural beliefs shared across the ethnic group that did not change rapidly, resulting in traits also recognizable to those not of the same ethnic group and to historians (Cogswell 1975; Conzen 1980a, 1985; Jan L. Flora and John M. Stitz 1985; Friedberger 1984; Gerlach 1976; Hollingshead 1938; Miner 1949; Nelson 1955; Schafer 1922–23, 1927). Germans, plodding and industrious and committed more to continuity and preserving traditions than to economic progress for its own sake, were focused on the family. The farm was a joint enterprise in which, under the patriarchal authority of the men, women and children (who left school early) worked diligently. People lived in tightly knit ethnic communities (perhaps speaking German) and were organized around membership in a single church. The conviviality of beer drinking at ethnic festivals and taverns distinguished them to others. German ethnic identity was more a means to ends such as land access and network building than something preserved for its own sake (Conzen 1980a, 1990).

The capitalistically oriented Yankees approached farming as a business, viewed land as a commodity, and ran operations unsentimentally for profit and to increase the value of the farm. Rather than striving to cluster children on farms around them, parents worked to make offspring independent. Children were expected to leave and, through personal choice and drive, to establish themselves in the world (Calhoun 1918). While thrift and hard work were prized, risk taking and shrewd dealing provided almost a flamboyance to Yankee financial management. Yankees lived in loosely organized communities that favored materialistic priorities, multiple churches, and an emphasis on secular volunteer activities, which created the local social life and economic climate. As the cultural heritage of the dominant group, Yankee ethnicity did not need to be preserved or defended, and families did not as a consequence consciously regard their practices as traditional or seek to maintain what was customary (Handlin 1980; Greene 1988).

Because Illinois Germans and Yankees settled side by side, each element evolved fully cognizant of its counterpart. Each measured the other's farming and family patterns against its own standards. Germans were astonished at the autonomy of Yankee children and the seeming male deference toward women and women's independence. Yankees, who legislated Sunday blue laws and eventually prohibition, looked askance at entire German families boisterously drinking together in public, women working in the fields (Conzen 1980a), or adult males willingly obeying fathers about farm purchases (Corner 1928). The disregard of the counterpart's intraethnic variation contributed to the perception of the counterpart as an undifferentiated group, particularly in the case of the Germans.

In ideal form these two ethnic elements, the German and the Yankee, came to symbolize the tension, almost a split personality, existing in nineteenth-century American rural society. Germans represented agrarianism as a means to promote family welfare, and Yankees represented farming pursued for largely capitalistic and individualistic aims (Atack and Bateman 1987).

•

Factors Affecting Ethnic Group Homogenization

THE PRAIRIE ENVIRONMENT

Prairie pioneers faced conditions that forced alteration of traditional farming practices. The climatic extremes were harsher than most settlers had known previously. The high prairie resembled a grass ocean broken only by an occasional island-grove of cottonwood or oak trees. Much of central Illinois was swampy and required artificial drainage to make the land productive (one-half of crop-producing Illinois land today was artificially drained). In east central Illinois in particular, the glaciers left either gently rolling or flat soils with little natural drainage. From breaking the tough sod to installing drainage tiles, the cost of cultivating the prairies was high but was repaid in the resultant high productivity (Margaret Beattie Bogue 1959). Under the swamp lay some of the richest soils in the world.

In central Illinois family farmers were not the first settlers. Before the advent of large-scale drainage technology, vast tracts of the rich virgin grassland were used by absentee investors (generally Yankees) for cattle feeding (Gates 1932). In Wheeler, three such owners controlled over ten thousand acres in the 1850s and 1860s (Margaret Beattie Bogue 1959). After 1870 such large-scale farms started to break up as rising land values motivated the selling of the estates in small blocks to families who could then operate intensive, crop-rotating, efficient farms that made more competitive use of the land. This breakup occurred at a time when east central Illinois as a whole experienced its greatest population influx. The Yankee communities of Wheeler and Emerson and the mixed ethnic Prairie Gem were each established as a large-scale farm was divided and sold by the original investor (Margaret Beattie Bogue 1959; Gates 1932).

The Corn Belt label implies that central Illinois was always a specialized crop region, but that is only recently the case. Following the division of the large farms, small farms combined corn, oats, hay, wheat, cattle, hogs, and other minor enterprises. Gradually the variety lessened, wheat in particular diminishing in importance as it became evident that corn was well suited to the prairie. The pattern of corn and hog production, developed in the mid-nineteenth century, in which the corn produced was mostly fed to hogs, was so profitable it dominated until the introduction of the soybean in the 1930s (Allan G. Bogue 1963a, 1963b). It was only by the 1950s that much of central Illinois became a monoculture "grain desert," typically divided equally between corn and soybeans (Dovring and Yanagida 1979).

Owing to high costs, purely subsistence-level agriculture was never practical on the prairie; Corn Belt immigrants had to farm for market. Midwestern intensive row-crop agriculture benefited from early mechanization that reduced dependence on human labor and enabled the farming of larger tracts. High land costs and the improvements the prairie soils required, combined with the use of mechanized equipment, made capital and credit more important factors than in the East. Land prices rose steadily except in times of acute depression and linked high tenancy rates with the most productive soils. In each generation following the breakup of the large tracts, prairie farms have grown progressively larger and fewer in number, as a consequence of technological changes, crop specialization, market pressures, and operation consolidation (Strange 1988).

To accumulate the necessary capital to begin farming, settlers often required a period of tenancy. The fifty-fifty crop-share lease emerged in the late nineteenth century and is still the most prevalent arrangement in central Illinois, an area having the finest soils. Such an arrangement offers tenant and landlord mutual advantages, giving both, for example, a vested interest in caring for the land. Absentee owners, on the other hand, often use cash-rent leases, a system in which the landlord receives a set rent for use of the land whether the farmer has had a bumper crop or lost everything. Under this system the landlord obviously has no involvement in management (Reiss 1983).

Settlers in the 1860s, a common arrival period in our communities, were favorably positioned to ascend the agricultural tenure ladder from hired laborer or tenant to landowner. The decade enjoyed good weather, high commodity prices, and general prosperity. A scarcity of farm laborers made wages high relative to land prices. Conditions changed for the worse in the 1870s when prices dropped, the weather turned bad, and an influx of immigrants to Illinois created a surplus of farm laborers and tenants. Demand far exceeded the supply of rental farms for a twenty-year period from the 1870s to the 1890s, and high mortgage rates (10 percent) also prevailed. During the mid-1890s rates fell, and conditions were again more favorable for developing family farms (Margaret Beattie Bogue 1959; Allan G. Bogue 1963a).

By the late 1800s, the major structural features of twentieth-century central Illinois agriculture were in place. Family farms, steep land values, artificial drainage, a concentration in corn and hogs, mechanized operations oriented to the market, crop-share leases, and a high rate of tenancy associated with absentee ownership had emerged as characteristic of Illinois agriculture (Margaret Beattie Bogue 1959). The area was renowned as one of the richest farming areas in the nation, and the region was served by a wide system of railroads. The high cost of farming in the Corn Belt assured that the classical tenure ladder metaphor, climbing the rungs from tenancy to full ownership of farm land, could not be realized by a large proportion of Illinois farm families (Spillman 1919; Kloppenburg and Geisler 1985). Capital costs have never diminished; high land prices made high rates of tenancy inevitable.

The Jeffersonian ideal of the independent farm family on a fully owned farm became less attainable in each generation for much of the Midwest. Eventually, for economic reasons, the most common operator form throughout the region became the part owner, who farmed both owned and rented land. This process of agricultural change acted on and was responded to by the German and Yankee cultural systems.

THE COMMUNITY AND ETHNIC GROUP HOMOGENIZATION

Historical events such as the two world wars and the depression of the 1930s in addition to the institutions each group developed—schools, churches, banks—all contributed to the evolution of more homogenized ethnic identities among Germans and Yankees.

The checkerboard spatial distribution resulting from the railroad land-grant and homestead acts affected how villages developed. Germans tended to immigrate directly from Europe and in the Midwest attempted to reproduce the village life they knew best. By keeping their community exclusively ethnic through endogamy and language, Germans could maintain a segregation from American conditions, thus fostering the intergenerational reproduction of a highly cohesive and exclusive peasantlike community focused on the church (Ostergren 1981a, 1981b). Yankees, products of mobile ancestors, were not committed to exclusiveness of ethnic stock or community boundaries. Their settlement as individual families in communities for economic rather than ethnic motives led to less cohesive communities. Their communities mimicked not the peasant village of Europe but that of the Northeast they had left behind. In the early period after settlement, before good roads and easy transportation developed, people did not come into frequent contact with other ethnic groups. As land competition became more keen, it ultimately sharpened awareness of community boundaries and ethnic differences.

World War I was particularly critical in forging diverse German identities into a more uniform pattern. Prior to the war German communities were focused on themselves, perpetuating the dialect, religious practices, and ideals of the ancestral homeland. However, because the German American press was pro-German and pro-neutrality for the U.S., ethnic communities experienced public wrath once the nation entered the war (Ripley 1985). Such distinguishing traits as language were quickly dropped to avert public attention; rural enclaves became the last bastion of German subcultural identity in the country. Prohibition similarly negatively affected public German sociability in the context of taverns (Conzen 1980a; Dobbert 1967; Luebke 1974).

Schools were an important institution for altering the German identity, in particular. Midwestern school systems were locally controlled initially. This democratic structure allowed communities to select teachers that suited their beliefs, although German communities had to choose teachers from a pool dominated by Yankees. Teachers typically moved into the community and often married and remained. Starting around the turn of the century, educational professionals sought to centralize education with school consolidations, and Yankees, as seen previously, came to control the Illinois state system. Eventually they were instrumental in developing a more uniform curriculum better suited to the needs of the capitalistic society (Wayne E. Fuller 1982; Reynolds 1990). This Protestant and Yankee-influenced curriculum contributed to the convergence of ethnic identity within each group.

Because religious affiliation was along distinctly ethnic lines, churches were instrumental in the homogenization of ethnic identity. German consciousness was nurtured by church leaders as a mechanism for perpetuating the ethnic church in the voluntaristic U.S. society by invidious comparison with the Yankee majority (Conzen 1980a). Lutheran teachings preached against the siren calls of American Yankee mores represented as threats to Germanic ideals: individualism, antitraditionalism, work for cash rewards, and risk that called for the use of credit (Maurer 1924, 1925). Eventually, national leadership and training led to treatment of congregations according to denomination rather than ethnic origin as churches, just as schools, were consolidated for demographic and financial reasons. The Congregational churches, associated with the New England Puritans, were not as evident in central Illinois as Methodist and Baptist congregations. Methodists and Baptists reached for a wider group and had begun to spread among Yankees before they migrated to Illinois (Handlin 1980). Abstention from liquor was part of the teachings, and this tenet was a major point of departure from German neighbors. While Yankee schoolteachers were prominent in spreading cultural values among both groups, they married Germans in Prairie Gem, where Missouri Synod teachings ruled out drinking, but did not intermarry in lusty German Heartland (Corner 1928).

The physical environment combined with the economics of credit, market, and technology to pressure for a rapid adaptation of the customary practices among Germans and Yankees concerned with practical aspects of culture. Ethnic differences motivating choices in crops, equipment, or drainage were muted. Yankees, in the majority, controlled the schools, politics, banks, and other institutions. The German minority was set off, distinguished by linguistic differences and the exclusiveness of their communities. Yet each ethnic element functioned in a social environment that contained the other. Intergroup interactions contributed to forging within each element a common ethnic identity, premised on the dimensions of culture that were reproduced and thus had more stability. Cultural heterogeneity within each ethnic group converged into a hyphenated American identity.

•

Farmland Ownership in Illinois

Convergence into two major ethnic patterns would be of no consequence if this did not have ramifications beyond the family and the community. Land ownership patterns are concrete manifestations of choices made by farm families dealing with their most precious resource. Over time land handled in a similar way in communities sharing a common ethnic origin but with different religions, dialects, and regional derivation argues for shared cultural beliefs affecting behavior.

Land ownership records document choices over many generations when families participate in the farmland market. Territorial expansion by an ethnic group is required if successive generations are to meet goals of continuity or growth. Intergenerational persistence of landowner families demonstrates that family actions were taken to meet a continuity goal; its by-products are the persistence of the ethnic community and land fragmentation as estate settlements divide family holdings and heirs resist sales. Owner turnovers, however, characterize business motives for ownership, as land is valued as a commodity to be bought and sold according to market forces. A higher priority on profitability and efficiency leads investors to avoid fragmentation of holdings in family land transfers. Fluidity of a land market, associated with investment motives, provides land for internal community purchases and relieves pressure for outward community expansion to meet family goals.

A few important points must be understood about plat maps, which record owner names and the size of tracts and which were used for the analysis of ownership. Plat maps do not indicate whether an owner actually farms the land, nor does tract size reflect farm size, for a typical farm contains several tracts. While tract size has tended to decline over time, farm size has become larger. The making of plat maps is a commercial enterprise throughout the Midwest, and because a publisher located in the state began issuing maps in the nineteenth century, Illinois has a particularly good historical record. I chose a one-quarter sample of the total 640-acre sections within the boundaries of the modern ethnic community for analysis. Ethnic identification was determined from owner family names by local knowledge, with verification in a standard genealogical dictionary (Elsdon Cole Smith 1972). Analysis started with the earliest plat map available, but the date actually reflects ownership from at least three years previously, due to delays in recording land transfers.

I analyzed long-term land ownership patterns for the communities of Heartland (German Lutherans originally from East Friesland), St. Boniface (German Catholics originally from Alsace), Wheeler (Yankee Protestants), and Prairie Gem (Yankees and Missouri Synod Lutheran Germans from a variety of origins).[1] It is not necessary at this point to know the community

1. For the analysis of land ownership, one-quarter of the standard square-mile-sized

nor to identify the particular cultural belief motivating actions to see the large-scale ethnic patterns evidenced objectively by formal records, county plat maps.

Table 1.1 delineates the average tract size of land owned by Germans and Yankees in the four communities and the number of owners in the earliest, at the midpoint (around 1930), and in the most recent plat map. German communities have consistently experienced more land fragmentation than Yankee communities, having at least doubled in owner numbers and decreased average tract size by one-third over the century. In Wheeler tract size diminished by half. Yankee-dominated Wheeler is unusual because the Germans were consistently a few, large, absentee landlords. Yankee owners and tract size remain relatively stable throughout the century in all communities except Prairie Gem, in which Yankee owners declined as did average tract size. German pressure on the land market in this community perhaps affected Yankee ownership patterns.

---

sections that constitute the present four communities were randomly selected from the earliest plat map available (n = 12 sections, except St. Boniface, for which n = 9 sections, of 640 acres per section). For Heartland, St. Boniface, and Prairie Gem the earliest map dates from 1893; thereafter each available map (1913, 1925, 1929, 1943) was analyzed. In the 1950s, regular maps began to be issued at five- or three-year intervals, and one map per decade was examined (1956, 1966, 1978, 1986) for each community. A total of nine maps were analyzed. For Wheeler the earliest map dates from 1875; thereafter, available maps (1907, 1915, 1925, 1930, 1943) and then one map per decade (1953, 1966, 1976, 1985) were analyzed, a total of ten maps.

Owners designated "German" have family names verified as German and are presumably descendants of German immigrants to the Midwest. The label "Yankee" almost exclusively represents descendants of immigrants from the Protestant British Isles, and these are overwhelmingly English. Also included under the Yankee label are a few (ten or less) names for which no ethnicity was determinable. Other ethnic groups are present in several of the communities, but the amount of land they control is small. For example, in Heartland, Irish and Scandinavian owners together account for less than three hundred acres in each plat map data set analyzed. St. Boniface had a stable minority of Yankee owners despite a dominance of German farmers and an insignificant number of other ethnic groups. Wheeler had a dominance of Yankee owners, but a group of German owner-investors were active in the land market there, particularly during the Depression. In Prairie Gem, Irish owners continually accounted for a stable eight hundred to one thousand acres of land controlled.

Table 1.1. Tract Size and Ownership of Land in Four Communities

	German Heartland	German St. Boniface	Yankee Wheeler	German/Yankee Prairie Gem
1893/1907 Total acres	7,800	5,743	7,739	7,700
	Average Tract Acres (n)[b]			
1893/1907[a]				
German	124 (34)	105 (14)	273 (5)	118 (16)
Yankee	99 (30)	128 (33)	128 (49)	117 (43)
1929/1930				
German	112 (58)	115 (20)	396 (3)	108 (29)
Yankee	101 (12)	135 (25)	113 (57)	119 (30)
1985/1986				
German	76 (87)	84 (27)	152 (7)	79 (50)
Yankee	119 (8)	102 (28)	102 (64)	76 (35)

Sources: Adapted from Salamon 1987 and Illinois county plat maps, Rockford Publishing Co.

[a]1907 used for Yankee Protestant community because the 1875 plat map represents an early, large-scale farm period; the 1907 map, therefore, is more comparable with other communities for size and number of owners.

[b](n)=number of owners; multiple tracts listed for the same owner counted as a single owner.

Total landowners in mixed ethnic Prairie Gem increased by approximately one-third, attributable to Germans, whose proportion rose from less than one-quarter to more than one-half. The number of landowners in 1986 is greatest for Heartland and least for Wheeler, though these communities are equal in area. Where they dominate, Germans differentially account for increases in landowners through land purchases and tract fragmentation. Greater numbers are indicative of persistence, although Yankees might consider the average German tract size indicative of farms too small to be efficient. Tenants, for example, to put together a farm under conditions of land fragmentation, are forced to deal with numerous landlords.

Table 1.2, by comparing the persistence of ethnic landowning families over three or four generations, provides further evidence that differing family practices affect land ownership. Persistence is assumed when a family name appeared in consecutive plat maps of the series. If a gap occurs for a particular name, even if it reappears at a later date in another section, it is considered as two different families. Land inherited by women, who change family names at marriage, introduces a margin of error into this method of calculating persistence.

It is evident from table 1.2 that Germans have a higher persistence rate than do Yankees. For example, in German Heartland 46 percent of German family names appear in the longest plat map category in comparison with only 21 percent of Yankee names. Similarly, in German/Yankee Prairie Gem over half the German names are in the longest category compared with about one-tenth of Yankee names. In contrast, Yankee Wheeler reverses the German pattern: 13 percent are highly persistent whereas 42 percent of names are on only a single map. The few German owners in Wheeler acted like Yankees and differed from those in the German-dominated communities because they, except for one family in the longest category, are absentee landlords. German St. Boniface has more Yankee owners than German, despite being dominated by German operators (see chapter 3 and table 1.1). This discrepancy indicates that Yankees are more likely to be absentee, investor landowners. Of particular significance in Yankee-dominated Wheeler is the presence of the highest number of family names (50 percent greater). Though two other communities have similar acreage (table 1.1), the higher number of owners suggests more frequent owner turnovers occurred.

Consider the single plat map category for each community (table 1.2). A

Table 1.2. Persistence of Family Ownership over 3 to 4 Generations

		Occurrence of Family Names		
		6–9 maps (%)	2–5 maps (%)	1 map (%)
German Heartland				
Germans	(n=63)	46	30	24
Yankees	(n=39)	21	25	54
Total	102			
German St. Boniface				
Germans	(n=40)	23	50	27
Yankees	(n=66)	17	59	24
Total	106			
Yankee Wheeler				
Germans	(n=8)	13	38	50
Yankees	(n=148)	13	45	42
Total	156			
German/Yankee Prairie Gem				
Germans	(n=36)	53	33	14
Yankees	(n=78)	12	46	42
Total	114			

Source: Illinois county plat maps, Rockford Publishing Co.

lone plat map appearance implies that land was purchased for investment and resold quickly—inconstant ownership. In all communities Yankee names overwhelmingly dominate the single plat map category, and these names typically appeared in the earliest (1893 or 1875) plat map. In Prairie Gem 26 percent of Yankee names, compared with only 8 percent of German, were probably early land investors who quickly sold their holdings. In Heartland 41 percent of Yankees and 8 percent of Germans were also 1893-only owners. Thus, Germans were more persistent throughout the century and were particularly persistent through the early, volatile homesteading period.

Among the persistent Heartland and Prairie Gem German families, some achieved continuity in many family branches. To measure branch persistence, I sought three or more owners sharing the same family name but with different personal names. Prairie Gem had six German families present in all nine plat maps, and four of these had many branches. Correspondingly, two of four Yankee families were represented in all nine plat maps by a number of branches. Eight of the ten multibranched German families in Heartland, though not a single Yankee family, were present in the entire plat map series. St. Boniface had six German families and two Yankee families present in all nine plat maps; one German family qualified with many branches. Finally Wheeler had only a single family in all ten plat maps and five in nine plat maps; none had numerous branches. Germans thus can by characterized as more persistent landowners, implying shared cultural beliefs motivating land ownership actions.

Catholic versus Protestant religious affiliation, it might be argued, explains the consistency of German and Yankee economic behavior reflected in land ownership patterns (Weber 1958). However, St. Boniface Catholic or Heartland and Prairie Gem Protestant German landowners behaved more alike than did the Wheeler Yankee and Heartland German Protestants. Ethnic identity, thus, is more predictive of behavior than is religious affiliation. Despite varied backgrounds, the German farmers had the same proclivity to fragment land and to maintain ownership continuity. Similarly Yankees of differing Protestant persuasions, whether dominant in a community or sharing control with Germans, consistently maintained relatively stable tract size but were less persistent owners. Religion was not predictive of values, and many discount its effect on present American economic behavior (Greeley 1964; Johnstone 1975). It may be that the Protestant ethic, about which the German Lutheran immigrant church was historically suspicious, so pervaded schooling and national doctrine that hard work, individualism, and materialism were admired, regardless of religious affiliation (Catholic or Protestant). However, the ethnic consistency found makes land ownership appear motivated less by religious values than by family practices, a culturally derived factor.

An invasion-succession pattern, in which Germans gradually invade territory controlled by Yankees and replace them as owners (discussed more in chapter 8), occurred in Heartland, Prairie Gem, and St. Boniface, and has also occurred where Germans settled in Texas, Minnesota, and Nebraska (Jordan 1966; Conzen 1985; Hollingshead 1938). Yankees consistently declined as a proportion of owners and Germanic owners consistently increased. Characteristically, Germans tended to radiate outward gradually from the original core settlement by extending their ethnically controlled territory. Rarely have studies found that a Yankee bought out a German; this was a one-way displacement process. That this pattern appeared so consistently throughout the Midwest is further evidence that core cultural priorities were shared within ethnic groups, despite the regional variations at the outset. Persistence of German owners and a gradual decline in, or frequency of absenteeism among, Yankee owners exemplified by these communities are indicative of long-term demographic trends in the Midwest farm population.

•
Present Midwestern Ethnic Population Characteristics

Ethnic population concentrations today reflect the intersection of European and United States historical events at immigration time. Groups remain in 1980 where they originally settled in significant numbers. Germans migrating in greatest numbers coincided with the opening of agricultural opportunities in the Midwest (Lieberson and Waters 1988). In the Corn and Wheat Belt states west of the Mississippi, 40 percent of all residents report some German ancestry. The next-largest white group in the region is the English (a combination of the census English and Scottish categories that roughly corresponds to the Yankee label), which has less than half the German numbers.

The 1980 census (from which the above findings are drawn) was the first to obtain data on ethnic ancestry (U.S. Bureau of the Census 1982b).[2] Rural farm populations in the Midwestern states (eastern and western north central states combined) reflect the same dominance of German and English groups as the total population, but the German domination is more striking, as shown in table 1.3. Note that only in Missouri does less than half the rural

2. The data were compiled with the assistance of Calvin L. Beale.

farm population report some German ancestry, while the high of nearly 66 percent is in Wisconsin. Because the Midwestern rural farm population has a higher proportion of Germans than the 40 percent combined rural-urban regional population, Germans are disproportionately represented in the rural farm population. Yankees, as defined in table 1.3, are somewhat underidentified in the 1980 United States Census, and consequently here, due to several factors. First, the Scotch-Irish, an ethnic group that contributed to early Midwestern settlement, were not tabulated as a separate ancestry in the census and thus are missing from the Yankee group where they properly belong. Second, the nonspecifiers, a group giving "American" or other nonspecific responses for ethnicity in the census, are likely to be originally of British origin (Beale 1989c). Evidence for nonspecifiers to be of British origin is seen

Table 1.3. Dominance of Germans and Yankees in the
Midwestern Rural Farm Population

	Total Farm Population	Total Un-specified	Total Yankee	Total German	Percentage Yankee[a]	Percentage German[a]
Illinois	313,978	54,558	82,496	150,252	31.8	57.9
Indiana	276,154	65,769	72,980	122,656	34.7	58.3
Iowa	391,070	44,951	75,850	212,419	21.9	61.4
Kansas	172,901	32,482	41,078	81,832	29.3	58.3
Michigan	177,591	23,106	51,173	77,199	33.1	50.0
Minnesota	315,400	23,336	25,469	172,390	8.7	59.0
Missouri	282,074	65,225	83,826	106,598	38.7	49.2
Nebraska	178,113	19,745	25,096	101,301	15.8	64.0
North Dakota	103,881	5,670	6,519	54,116	6.6	55.1
Ohio	271,542	47,728	67,135	144,906	30.0	64.7
South Dakota	112,854	8,853	11,323	60,948	10.9	58.6
Wisconsin	282,782	22,305	35,352	170,940	13.6	65.6
Total	2,878,340	413,728	578,297	1,455,557	23.5	59.1

Source: 1980 U.S. Census of the Population (U.S. Bureau of the Census 1982b).

Note: The Yankee group consists of persons reporting English or Scottish as a single ancestry or English as part of a dual ancestry or of any of nine specified triple ancestry combinations. It also includes persons who entered their ancestry as British or Briton. Germans are those reporting German as a single or dual ancestry or as part of any of ten specified triple ancestry combinations. Because of multiple ancestry, the Yankee and German groups are not mutually exclusive (Beale 1989b).

[a]Total unspecified was subtracted from total farm population before calculating the percentage Yankee and German.

in table 1.3. Those states with lower numbers of nonspecifiers are those that contain proportionately more later immigrant populations of non-English-language background, people likely to have a greater awareness of their origins, and proportionately fewer people of old colonial stock (Beale 1989c).

Results from the 1980 census question, "What is this person's ancestry?" for Illinois (rural and urban combined) show that Germans account for 32 percent and Yankees for 19 percent of the state's population. Among the rural nonfarm population of Illinois, 48 percent are German and 32 percent are Yankee (English plus Scottish); the state's ethnic Yankee populations for farm (table 1.3) and nonfarm are about the same, but the farm population is more German. This contrasts with the higher ratio of Germans to Yankees among farmers in Wisconsin, the most German state. Wisconsin also has a higher proportion of the rural nonfarm population German (59 percent) and a smaller proportion of the rural nonfarm population Yankee (15 percent). These proportions show that a focus on German and Yankee farm groups in the Midwest includes the largest ethnic groups in the region; the German category accounts for more than half of the farm population.

Farming is particularly suited to preserving early ethnic concentrations. Why, in particular, are German ethnics so persistent in farming, an occupation that conceivably could preserve any ethnic group that originally entered it? A 1980 census study that matched present ethnic groups with immigrant groups in the 1900 census found those groups highly involved in agriculture then are still highly involved (Lieberson and Waters 1988). This occupational continuity is aided by an overall decline in farming as an occupation. People are moving out of, not into, the occupation, so that continuing groups are not diluted by new ones. The dominance of Germans in Midwestern agriculture is therefore a product of historical settlement patterns by, as we shall see, a population highly committed to persistence in the occupation.

Illinois is a rather typical Corn Belt state with a farm population of 1,341,104 in 1900 that by 1950 had declined to 772,521. The number of farms also declined from the peak of 264,151 in 1900 to 195,268 by 1950 and finally to 83,000 by 1988, a 60 percent drop since 1950 (Truesdell 1960; U.S. Bureau of the Census 1988; U.S. Department of Agriculture, Crop Reporting Board 1962). During the 1950s, a period when many small farmers left agriculture due to the greater capital investment required by more mechanization, Illinois lost 39,000 farms. While two-thirds of the farms present in the peak year of 1900 have disappeared, this occurred through consolidation of smaller farms, for acreage in production did not decrease until 1988.

Unlike the rapid shifts in some cultural practices necessitated by farming and marketing in the new prairie environment, those practices inherent to how families handled land could change more slowly (Ortner 1984). A novel situation could be met by family members responding according to their traditional positions. Heirs confronting environmental exigencies as they ritually passed on land to their children might alter some practices, but others could be transmitted relatively unaltered with the land. A Yankee farmer from Emerson commented on the consistency of his neighbors in German Heartland: "They will do anything for you, but don't try to do business with them. They watch out for their own. I don't think any of the land that is rented up there is rented to anyone outside the area. They'll buy you a beer or help you by loaning a piece of equipment or something, but don't try to buy their land. They want the land to remain in the family."

I speculate that other factors in addition to culture account for ethnic distinctiveness today. Historically, each group that came to the United States faced a very different environment. The British being much earlier immigrants encountered abundant land and a scarcity of farm labor. These factors promoted change in traditional economic practices because land was cheaper and labor more expensive, the reverse of the situation left behind (Gjerde 1985). When the Yankees came, they saw the prairie land as a commodity to be bought, used, or readily sold; for them farming was an occupation no different from any other. Yankees did not need or value building a cohesive community to meet these individualistic goals. By the nineteenth century when the Germans came, the Yankees were already experienced entrepreneurs on the land. The Germans came to the Midwest as direct immigrants after the frontier had largely moved past Illinois. Germans thought and responded as European peasant farmers according to their agrarian ideals of permanence, contentment with small size, and intensive agricultural practices. A highly cohesive community facilitated cooperation and interdependence in a strange, competitive new land. Compact, cohesive communities proved to be particularly crucial to maintenance of an ethnic identity (Conzen 1980b; Gjerde 1985; Mackintosh 1990). Thus the timing of immigration, plus the nature of agriculture and community life to which they were exposed before immigration, influenced how each group approached life on the prairie. As one generation managed and passed on the farm and the occupation of farming to the next, various factors—closeness to European roots, agricultural experiences, and community context—combined to influence the evolution of the cultural system.

Farm family ethnic diversity can be understood as varying around a set of common traits that arise from sharing rural American residence, occupation, and western European peasant origins. Before turning to cultural divergence in chapters 3 and 4, I describe in chapter 2 a common core of traits characteristic of Midwestern farm family life.

Family Farmers:
An American Family Type

Farmers say farming is the "best way of life" and regard their countryside as beautiful. Although they complain constantly about the government or about the bean and corn markets, farmers consider their work among the most desirable in America. Farmers' stories and self-deprecating humor capture this attitude. A retired widow said, "I go to the city and I just don't like it. I miss the quietness. It's lonely here, but there's always something to do." An active farmer commented, "You probably heard the saying: The farmer buys retail and sells wholesale, and pays the shipping both ways. . . . It's a good life. We wouldn't give it up for anything" (see Rhodes 1989).

Only those who love farming continue; the life requires commitment and is hazardous, demanding, and risky. Though farming is among the most dangerous of occupations, much of the risk is financial. "You just can't keep receipts in a shoe box like we used to. Farming is a big business now," commented a farmer about recent changes. Older farmers recall with nostalgia the days when farming was less specialized and every farmstead possessed a mixture of animals—a few cows, geese, and chickens. "Physically my life's a lot easier, but mentally it's more difficult. There's more pressure in farming today than there was then," said a farmer near retirement. The stress and gamble involved in farming make farmers today sound like modern pioneers.

Farm families epitomize what is truly "American"; farming and rural communities are closely associated with our Jeffersonian agrarian ideals. Advertising exploits the image of the farm family—authentic, virtuous, traditional, hard-working, self-reliant, and integrated in a close-knit community—to sell products to an urban society (Goldman and Dickens 1983). Though the image is used symbolically, farmers firmly believe their way of life actually to embody such ideals. "You're your own boss" is an oft-repeated adage of self-reliance that is clearly not the case (Mooney 1988). Farmers equate their outdoor work, free from the confines of an office or factory environment, another's schedule, or an employer-employee hierarchy, with independence. A son's return to the farm after abandoning a promising career is explained by his hatred of office routine and formal dress. According to a young farmer, back in farming after ten years away working in the city, "I like farming because I am my own boss. That's the aspect of farming I like the most. Otherwise it's a stressful job. It is in the top ten of the most stressful, you see. There is always something to worry about. Once you've finished the harvest then you worry about selling it; that's the hardest part of farming. I know farmers who won't play poker, but they risk more each day selling their crops than they ever would in poker." Farm families still hold the frontier ideal of self-reliance to be achievable, though this is, of course, generally illusory. Quick to criticize inner city families on welfare, they deny that, for example, their hefty government price supports also constitute welfare (Strange 1988).

Many features that in the past distinguished farm from urban families were demographic. Farm families were larger, marriages were more stable, and fewer women were employed outside the home. Recently urban-rural distinctions have become blurred as farm families have experienced a rise in divorces and a decrease in fertility and as farm women have entered the work force in numbers comparable to those of urban women (Beale 1989d; McCarthy, Salant, and Saupe 1988; Brown et al. 1988). Farm economies, historically unable to absorb all the children produced (except in the 1970s when many young people entered farming), have always forced young people to leave farms and rural communities. The resulting net outflow of the young has meant an aging of the rural population. In 1980 the census found the highest proportion of elderly (15.4 percent) in villages such as those studied here, with the lowest (10 percent) found in suburban areas (Clifford et al. 1985).

Though farm families have grown more like urbanites in some ways, they now seem more like their rural forebears in others. The continual decline in farm numbers has returned modern farm families to some of the physical isolation of their pioneering ancestors, albeit moderated by telephone, television, and the car. Farm families now see fewer neighbors in the countryside and have to travel farther for services than even their parents did. The relative physical isolation produced by the low population density of the rural Midwest, combined with other factors described below, has made farmers a unique American subcultural family type.

KINSHIP CHARACTERISTICS

When families farm, work and residence are merged, and workmates are also kinmates. Such families typified the nation prior to World War I, when the country was more rural, but most Americans now live and work in segregated settings and in particular need not deal at work with those for whom they have kinship obligations. Inevitably, because farm families blend home and work, family relationships cross a multitude of interpersonal domains. For example, business decisions affect family matters in ways beyond family income. In this way farm families and their communities have a great deal in common with other agricultural societies cross-culturally (Bennett, Kohl, and Binion 1982).

Despite their uniqueness, farm families are very American indeed. Their cultural beliefs about kin groups, descent, and the lifecourse resemble those of other mainstream Americans (Schneider and Smith 1978). While descent equally from the maternal and paternal lines is recognized among farmers and nonfarmers alike, most American families have a matrilineal emphasis (Schneider 1980; Colleen Leahy Johnson 1989; Newman 1986; Yanagisako 1977). A matrilineal bias is revealed by where families choose to settle, what children know about their relatives, and which side of the family is favored for holidays, among other factors. Farmers, however, are set apart by a patrilineal bias, caused by the circumstances of farming. The vast majority of farmers are the sons of farmers (Featherman and Hauser 1978; Lieberson and Waters 1988; Beale 1979), and the most common work team is that of father and son (Coughenour and Kowalski 1977). Men in families run the farm. Furthermore, land—the most valuable resource in farming—leads families to associate more frequently with, or to favor in other ways, relatives who are its source. Because sons succeed fathers and take over the home farm, land follows the male line, and families tend to live near the man's kin group. Daughters also inherit family land; but their husbands generally farm it, and a husband's work partnership is with his father. Therefore, unless more land comes from a woman's relatives, families tend to visit, interact, and feel more obligation toward the man's kin.

Farm families are male-centered when residence, work, and inheritance patterns act in combination. As a result of being male-centered, farm families maintain many asymmetrical relationships reminiscent of their western European peasant ancestors' male-dominated cultural systems (Goldschmidt and Kunkel 1971; Michaelson and Goldschmidt 1971). Older men control access to family land, the farm, and what is produced, allowing them to assert authority over women and children (Colman and Elbert 1984; Fink 1986). Though in theory women do not exercise power over men, a longer life expectancy means that women in actuality gain power when, as widows, they control family land. Female landlords are the bane of their male relatives, who are frequently their tenants (Salamon and Keim 1979). A pattern in which women become matriarchs in old age is often associated with a patrilineal kinship emphasis and with peasant agriculturalists cross-culturally (Michaelson and Goldschmidt 1971; Masuda 1975; Lebra 1984).

Midwestern farm families are residentially stable, whereas most American families are highly mobile (60 percent of the middle class moves frequently for jobs or changes of housing) (Fuchs 1983). Commonly a farmer can point to his farmstead as the home of his parents and of his grandparents before them. A family in Illinois can display a state placard with an official "Centennial Farm" label if the family can prove with legal documentation that the farm has been owned by the same family for over one hundred years, a span encompassing the lives of three or more generations. A number of these farms were found in each of the communities I studied. Being a centennial farm does not mean that several generations live together on the farmstead, however.

Farm families share the American cultural theme that the nuclear family is the most important kinship unit and should preferably occupy its own home

(Schneider 1980). While some of the currently retired generation lived with or on the farmstead with the husband's parents during the early years of marriage, that occurs rarely today. Couples who lived jointly say they "don't recommend it." Today's farm families prefer nuclear households, as do other American families, for reasons of privacy, intimacy, and independence from relatives. However, in contrast to more mobile American families, a Midwestern farm family is deeply embedded in a web of kinship. Stability of residence means that family life takes place in a multigenerational context, often with kin who share community, occupation, religion, and ethnicity. Though farm families live separately, related households often exchange meaningful labor, financial, and socioemotional services. Such a household coalition is termed a "modified-extended" structure (Litwak 1965). As a result, farm families must take into daily account members of their kinship network (Smith and Zopf 1970; Beers 1937; Kohl 1976).

An advantage of intergenerational stability is the ready availability of supportive relatives. Farm children see their grandparents, aunts and uncles, and other relatives around them in church on Sunday. Parents and married children have frequent face-to-face contact; families are expected to drop in, to have relatives drop in, or to eat meals together. Similar to extended families elsewhere in the world, Illinois farm families are able to pool such resources as farm and household equipment or garden fruits and vegetables. If a young wife works off the farm, her mother-in-law might prepare meals during busy seasons. Babysitting is accessible and lovingly provided by grandmothers so that a young farm wife can visit the nearby shopping mall alone or with her mother along to watch the children while she tries on dresses. If there is a divorce or a death of a wife, for instance, other family members are available to substitute. Thus a young farmer's mother observed that "there's no wife out here so I come out and cook when they're in the fields."

Proximity to relatives has social costs, as is well documented for extended families in other contexts. A special burden typically falls on the young wife in patrilineal societies (Le Vine 1965; Lebra 1984). She may be constantly monitored by a mother-in-law, with whom she is thrown into extensive contact as a by-product of joint farm operations. One young mother of two preschoolers spoke of having "too many mothers" to deal with. She endured the advice and interference not only of her mother and mother-in-law but also of an aunt whose land they rented. Those who provide goods and services such as babysitting and rent-free housing (a house is often provided to tenants with the farm) feel free to offer their opinions on childrearing or the extravagance of a young couple's lifestyle as well as on matters pertinent to the farm operation.

THE FARM FAMILY HOME

A person born on a farm calls it his or her homeplace. Some families more than others include actual buildings in their homeplace conception and seek to preserve them, but all identify with the land. If neither spouse is a homeplace successor, the couple establishes a new farm that becomes the homeplace for their children. The immediate area around the family home, the farmstead, contains buildings to protect equipment, store grain, and house animals if they are raised.

A farm family home is distinctly fashioned by its simultaneous functions as business office and residence; work requirements shape the use of domestic space. For instance, the front door and frequently the living room are rarely used. Some families never bother to build a walk to their front door; relatives and friends know the back door is the main entrance. To reach the back door a visitor must invariably pass inspection by the ubiquitous family dog. Dogs are seldom house pets; on the farm, animals live outside the home. Some dogs are kept merely to alert household members when a stranger is on the farmstead. Those living alone sometimes possess a guard dog for protection. One such animal named Bear was said by his elderly owner to be capable of "eating you."

Inside the back door entrance an area is reserved for removing manure covered boots and muddy overalls. A basement shower may be used in an attempt to contain the inescapable work dirt. The kitchen, into which the back door opens, is the hub of family life. The family gathers around the kitchen table for meals, discussions, visiting, and perhaps even bookkeeping. A radio, or more often a television set, is nearby so that the day's weather or commodity market reports can be followed during meals. Dinner, the noon meal, is truly a "businessman's lunch" where all grow quiet when the market news comes on (Kohl 1976). Unlike urban dwellers farm families eat their largest meal at midday, and women often cook much of the morning to have dinner on the table at noon. With the movement of farm women into the labor market, more men eat their noon meal at a village cafe.

Illinois farm families purchase most of their food at the supermarket. As recently as a generation ago women baked bread and pies every Saturday, canned fruit and vegetables from the garden during the summer, and canned meat during the winter. Women also milked cows and raised chickens that added to the family funds and menu (Fink 1986). But today, though farm women still have gardens and many freeze what they raise, most home production of food has been abandoned. Television images of charity food pantries in Iowa during the farm crisis of the early 1980s illustrate the loss of the self-sufficiency that helped earlier generations survive the Depression. Some skills were lost due to closer government monitoring of food production on farms. It is illegal to butcher your own cattle, for example, although some families still do. "Everybody used to raise chickens and trade the eggs for groceries in town. But now you can't do that because of all the regulations—the big egg producers took care of that," said a cynical Illinois farm wife (Fink 1987).

Farm families value privacy, perhaps even more than urbanites or suburbanites require. Most families try to give each child his or her own bedroom—a realizable goal since the decline in family size. Families are accustomed to a great deal of space between their home and a neighbor's. A farm family visiting my home in a small university town remarked about how crowded together the homes were. Our corner lot was superior because, from their perspective, we have a neighbor only on one side (although we actually have two neighbors at 90-degree angles rather than at angles of 180 degrees). An Oklahoma farm family commented on their annoyance at a new security light installed on their nearest neighbor's farmstead several miles down the road: "They're invading our privacy" (Reiss 1980).

Homes tend toward early American decor sprinkled liberally with family heirlooms handed down with the farm. A grandfather's watch, an old butter churn, or a rocking chair are typical treasures proudly displayed. Most families modernize rather than restore old farmhouses. One family pitched every fifty-year-old canning jar of their mother's out the attic window during remodeling. Even years later, they bemoan having smashed jars that now sell for $6 to $10 at flea markets. Family photographs generally cover a prominent wall or shelf, particularly in a grandmother's home. Many families also display a painting or a commercial aerial photo of the farmstead, with the corn colored green for summer or yellow for fall, according to their preference. Most kitchens in older farmhouses have been remodeled and contain up-to-date appliances. The microwave oven, a favorite Christmas present, is visible in most kitchens. While there is a great range of housekeeping styles, farm homes are usually clean and orderly, as are the buildings and land on the farmstead. Neatness matters when relatives and neighbors, potential land-lords, are apt to drop in unexpectedly.

THE AGRIFAMILY SYSTEM

An interdependency prevails between the farm and the farm family: business decisions are intimately connected with the lifecourse of family members and household management. Men are at the same time husband, father, laborer, and farm manager, and correspondingly, women are simultaneously wife, mother, farm partner, and household manager. Sons or daughters are simultaneously children, siblings, heirs, apprentices, and play- or workmates.

The interplay between the family and the farm has been termed the "agri-family system," a concept elegantly developed by Bennett and Kohl and heavily drawn on for this section (Bennett, Kohl, and Binion 1982; Kohl 1976). Regarding the family and the family farm as a system provides a mechanism for taking into account how the family negotiates between the demands of the business and those of the family to assure labor, capital, and management to the farm and nurture, kinship obligations, goals, and community integration of the family. Trade-offs in finances, time, and energy between the domains of farm and family are a constant requirement. Tension exists between the two domains, as, for example, when the financial demand of a new refrigerator must be balanced against the requirement of a new tractor. Correspondingly, a child's college education draws off capital available for enterprise expansion. The merger of a nuclear family kinship unit—a system—with a farm enterprise—also a system—translates into the agrifamily: "one system with two competing and reinforcing subsystems" (Bennett, Kohl, and Binion 1982:118). This agrifamily system is embedded in a community milieu, a wider system organized by social networks of kin and non-kin that link one household with others. An ethnic community aggregates many households sharing a similar agrifamily system. A community, in turn, is situated in the context of a national structure consisting of an exceedingly complex system of institutions, markets, and governmental levels from local to national.

Because the family is a dynamic system whose members age in concert, the family and the farm accommodation is a dynamic process. Household expansion through the birth of an heir can motivate enterprise expansion, just as lack of an heir can be the reason for decreasing farm size. The intergenerational cycle of the family farming and the farm business intersect if, as parents age and die, the farm and farmland are to undergo intergenerational transmission.

The succession cycle affects the farm enterprise beyond just the actual replacement of father by son. A farm enterprise follows sequential stages of establishment, development, maintenance, and redevelopment in each generation. To prepare for the succession by an heir, parents must expand the enterprise to support another adult or nuclear family. Often the expansion, whether through rental acreage or land purchases, begins in early family phases, in anticipation of the cycle. When a son's family is brought in, the farm organization is at its most complex, with more possibilities for task specialization and commodity diversification. However, not all families have a strong urge to reproduce the farm, and some never undertake measures that make succession achievable (Kohn 1988). Such families continue to develop, but the farm does not; eventually, rather than a farm cycle developing, the farm ends.

Merger of family and farm has held a competitive advantage for this operation form. For example, the motivation to assure succession creates periodic pressures for management innovations that militate against enterprise stagnation. These periods are countered by maintenance phases when management becomes more conservative, and indebtedness and risk are avoided. A development phase that spurs innovation comes later in the family cycle when an intergenerational succession is imminent. Because every farm is not simultaneously in the same developmental phase, the cyclical conservatism of some protects the survival of the form. The family farm form is also exceedingly flexible, able to respond quickly to forces in the community and national structure by exploiting itself, cutting costs, and altering management strategies (Reinhardt and Barlett 1989). The inherent strengths of the form produce a competitive advantage that accounts for persistence of the family farm in many national contexts.

The family and the farm subsystems, however, both have vulnerabilities with the potential to affect the family farm cycle. Within the family system these can be interpersonal issues—structural tension points—that, unless dealt with successfully, can prevent the cooperation required to meet farm goals. This cooperation can range from deferral of household spending to nonfarming siblings' support of the successor. Some system vulnerabilities are out of a family's control—external factors such as the weather or the fluctuations of the land and commodity markets—others, however, result from family management choices.

THE FAMILY SCHEDULE AND FARM TASKS

Aside from very regular meal hours, farm time is loosely scheduled when compared with that of a salaried family whose life is dictated by the clocks of other institutions (Kantor and Lehr 1975). Not the clock but the task and the season divide up the days and set the rhythm of farm life. Farmers say their mood is directly related to the season. A farm wife commented: "Before and during the busy seasons he's a different guy. He's tense and paces the floor—I can hardly talk with him." On grain farms, spring and fall are the seasons of tight schedules, work deadlines, and business pressures. Families tend to turn inward as they unite to get the crops in and out. For a family raising animals, the seasons are more uniform, as the grain cycle is integrated with demands tied to the life cycle of animals. Only a specialized grain farmer can take vacations or have a true respite from the daily grind of chores.

Farmers are churchgoers, and religion imposes a rhythm to their lives: six work days followed by the Sabbath as a day of rest. After church, families typically visit grandparents for a large meal and get-together. Other close relatives are often visited in the afternoon. However, during the busiest seasons a family might work straight through Sunday, although their grandparents' generation probably stopped. Farm work is considered a legitimate excuse, by some, for occasionally ignoring the Sabbath. One family tells the story of how a more religious aunt passed their home on her way to church Wednesday evenings during the Lenten season and would shame them into attending despite their exhaustion. "One time my dad said he was just too tired so we turned off all the lights and pretended we'd already gone to bed. After she drove by we turned them on again," recalled the daughter.

Winters are a restful and quiet time when farmers plan or perhaps take on part-time work, but social life is most active during this lull. Men and women often meet in gender-segregated groups during the day: women with relatives or friends in card groups or over coffee, men at the cafe, for cards at the volunteer firemen's garage, or at a tavern (Perkins 1987). Evening socializing, especially on the weekend, is done as couples, though the gathering typically finds the women in the kitchen and the men in the living room. Couples commonly belong to age-cohort card groups that meet regularly in the evening. It is also during winter that groups of older women meet for quilting and gossiping.

Around March, when a hint of spring appears, farmers become nervous and begin to tinker with machinery and to worry about the weather despite the unlikelihood of their "getting into the fields" soon. Couples often go out to dinner alone prior to the onset of planting or harvesting "because once we're in the fields we have no time for each other." When either the fall harvesting or the spring planting activities are under way, the entire family converts to a different and more rigid schedule than that followed during the winter and summer lulls. The morning rising time creeps up earlier and earlier as the days lengthen, and by April families are up and moving by five. A husband explains his day's plans to his wife as he struggles into his clothes. Breakfast is taken quickly, and children are gotten off to school. The wife tries to do laundry while preparing food for the noon meal, if she is not needed in the fields.

The family works like a well-oiled machine during busy seasons. As one farm wife explained it, "When we're in the fields I use this old truck to feed the men and the machines." The truck has a gas tank that can refill tractors and other implements in the fields. Women with young children pack them all into the truck as they make the rounds with food and fuel. A retired father often watches from his pickup truck or waits in a grain truck beside the field being harvested. He is there to haul the cut grain or as a gofer. If the weather threatens, combine or tractor headlights are used so work can continue far into the night. Heavier equipment, while increasing the efficiency of farmers, has made for tighter schedules because the machines require drier conditions than did the lighter equipment of even twenty-five years ago. Working larger farms comes at the expense of flexibility and resiliency, some say (Strange 1988).

Running a farm necessitates a combination of management, labor, and capital skills associated with any small family firm (Rosenblatt et al. 1985). Farmers must plan what is to be grown and where, taking into account the soils and slope of land on the farm. Seed and chemicals must be purchased, and equipment must be kept in working condition in preparation for going into the fields. Choosing the appropriate herbicides and fertilizers depends on knowledge of soil types and the timing of the application; these are expensive inputs and demand farmers to be aware of what is available in the changing menu of brands. Adjustments in these inputs provide the family with budgeting flexibility—trading lower yields for less investment in fertilizer is an example.

When families are in the fields, a variety of tasks are required by planting, cultivating, and eventually harvesting corn and beans. Typically corn is planted first and then soybeans. Fields must be prepared before each sowing takes place. Depending on conditions lime or other chemicals such as nitrogen or anhydrous ammonia are applied (farmers often contract for these applications). If minimum-till farming is being used, farmers do less preparatory disking and plowing of fields than needed for conventional planting. Herbicides and fertilizers can be applied before planting, incorporated during planting, or used after the plants emerge. Usually beans and corn are cultivated after they have come up and before they are too tall for a machine to pass over them in the field. The emergence of the new crop is exciting. "The corn's up," people say and comment on being able to "row" the optical patterns created by the small green leaves.

By mid-June, planting and cultivation are finished, and life quiets down, unless a family also raises animals. Some families "walk beans" to pull out volunteer corn (from the previous year's crop) and other weeds. July is county fair time. Particularly when children are teenagers, the family may be very involved in 4H or Future Farmers of America animal projects. Farm children show animals at their county fair as well as in the adjacent counties. Families enjoy the contacts they and the children make on the county fair circuit. Those who win their category of animal showing, sewing, or cooking go on to compete in the Illinois State Fair, held in August after all the local county fairs are over. Families then begin to think about harvest time.

To the uneducated observer the corn and beans look dead by harvest time, and they are, because the crops are dried in the field before being cut. Timing is critical, for though the grain needs to be dry, the plants can fall over if harvesting is delayed. Farmers are continually measuring moisture content to decide when to cut a field. Nonetheless more moisture is usually removed from harvested crops by dryers (à la laundry) either in a grain bin on-farm or at the grain elevator. Families prefer to artificially dry grain as little as possible because fuel is expensive. At harvest, first the corn and then the beans are cut with the combine, unless some early beans were planted. The moisture is so sensitive in beans that the dew that collects overnight must dry out before a bean field is harvested. The combine is emptied into a grain truck that hauls the corn or beans to be dried and stored in farmstead grain bins or at a local elevator. Men usually do all of the tasks described above—they plant, spread chemicals, and combine. Women generally only disk, plow, or cultivate with a tractor; they also drive grain trucks (Rachel Ann Rosenfeld 1985; Kalbacher 1982, 1985).

Farmers use citizens band radios in their trucks, combines, and tractors to keep tabs on family members widely scattered in fields and buildings. Several years ago a well-respected farmer, working alone harvesting beans, caught a leg in his combine and bled to death before anyone was aware of his predicament. This convinced many central Illinois families to adopt the radios. Families use a distinctive farm brand of humor, one that dwells on personality and physical features, in their choice of a CB "handle." A particularly overweight farmer uses the handle Teddybear—for he looks like one. A farm wife awarded a $5 prize to the family member coming up with the handle Teabag, "because I'm always drinking tea." On farms connected by a CB, the base set crackles constantly in the kitchen as locations are communicated, requests for a rendezvous relayed, or a wife directed to find a replacement for a broken part in town. The citizens band radio restored a sense of working as a team that, as farms grew larger, families felt was lost. Community gossips, unable to listen in on telephone party lines since the modernization of rural service, have found the CB a real boon.

The farmhouse is the setting for the business management of the farm. Most families now use computers for bookkeeping and recordkeeping. The gender division of business tasks is highly variable. Nationally, bookkeeping is a female task, with 61 percent of farm women regularly doing books (Rachel Ann Rosenfeld 1985). Marketing can be either a male or female task or a joint effort, although it is typically done by men. Some families contract with a marketing consulting firm with whom they keep in constant contact for the right moment to sell the grain they have stored. Farmers say they make all their profits through wise marketing. Central Illinois soybean and corn farming involves weather risks, like all farming, but is highly vulnerable because it is dependent on just two commodity markets. The trade-off for the farm family that also has animals is more market flexibility, but more work and more management skills are involved. Regardless of what they produce, at the start of the year many farmers must sell when their taxes are due. In January it is common to see large semitrailers on farmsteads being loaded to transport grain to elevators that in turn ship grain by rail, truck, or barge to port or factory destinations.

CHILD SOCIALIZATION

A consequence of the merger of home and workplace is both parents in constant proximity to young children. Parents consider this involvement a major advantage of farm life: "A farm is a good place to raise kids. Kids learn to take on responsibility." However, specialized grain farms generate fewer chores than did the diversified farms of the past. Older farmers recall having to shell corn by hand and to care daily for animals when they were young. Today, families frequently acquire animals for child training rather than for production reasons.

Families that want their children to carry on the family business consciously go about inculcating them in farm lore and practices. From the time they are toddlers, boys and girls probably have a toy set of miniature farm equipment. One father of daughters was delighted that his two-year-old grandson had taken to the farm machinery toys he had given him for Christmas. "Did you see how nice he plays with [machinery] and how neat he puts it away?" he asked his wife rhetorically. "I got him everything, tractor, plow, spreader, and combine. He's set."

Small children hear their parents talk over the day's events at meals and are quite capable of describing exactly the process or schedule that a father is involved in at any time. One grandfather, whose goal was to maintain the family's centennial farm, methodically bought his grandson a sow "with papers" before the child entered kindergarten so that by the time the grandson was ready for the county fair circuit, he would be accustomed to the animals. Each time the sow littered, this preschooler was trained in the process of feeding the baby pigs. Eventually when the animals were sold, the money earned was placed in an account for him, "So he'll learn about money too," his mother said. Explained a young farmer, "I was in 4H at age 10. My project was hogs. I started out with 12 to 15 hogs. I would purchase them from my Dad and then when I sold them the money from them went into the bank and that's the money I used to put myself through college." A long apprenticeship is deemed necessary because not only is farming extremely complex, but becoming proficient about the range of decisions made on a seasonal basis requires absorbing a broad spectrum of experiences.

Because a father is present for meals, and much of the day during the nonbusy seasons, he is immersed in child socialization. When a mother is involved in a demanding task or has visitors, she can say, "Go find your father and see what he is doing." A boy has a tool set to use alongside his father in the machine shed. Sons and daughters alike become familiar with running both the farm and the household operations. One father told of riding the tractor with his young son napping in his lap. Another said, "On a farm you can take your kids with you when you are working and running errands. You don't have to make a special effort to be with the kids." One mother commented on the early involvement of their three children in fieldwork: "I had to take the kids to the fields since they were just babies. I'd pack them up and put them in the truck. Going to the fields has been a part of their lives ever since they can remember. They've really gotten farming in their blood."

Farm children are accustomed to large machinery in their everyday environment and operate equipment at an extremely young age. Every family tells what they consider amusing anecdotes about children and machinery. For instance, a farmer related a story of watching a combine come toward him in the field with no one driving it. When the machine stopped, his three boys, ages three, four, and five, jumped out. They were all driving—one at the wheel, one at the gas pedal, and the third working the clutch. A typical reminiscence of a man "who always knew he wanted to be a farmer" was this:

I know that by [age] six Dad would let me drive the tractor as long as he was on it with me. I would have to let go of the steering wheel to work the clutch, but he let me do the driving without his help. By eight I was doing fieldwork—driving the tractor alone. I would do the little things that helped like hauling-in. Then the next year I did everything. I disked and plowed. Mom thought it was too dangerous. She thought I might fall off the tractor, but Dad convinced her it would be okay. I would say, "Let me, let me," and Dad would say, "Well we sure can use the help."

Farm children are eager to put forth extraordinary efforts for the farm. One farmer recalled that during high school "I was doing more and more all the time. I would come right home and go to the fields. . . . My parents would not let me stay home to work like some of the other kids." The process that culminates in teenagers anxiously rushing home after school to help in the fields starts when children are very young and involves more than mowing roadsides and driving the truck to the fields. A woman recalled that her son demonstrated an early commitment to farming: "[He] learned how to start the combine when he was only seven years old. During harvest he'd sit up there with his dad and ask all kinds of questions. Then he'd get the manual to the combine out and start looking at that. We *really* had to watch him so he wouldn't start the combine by himself and take off."

Involvement in farm activities conveys to children, from an early age, their importance to the family enterprise. Children as young as six spend summers "walking beans" checking the rows for weeds and volunteer corn, aware that what they do is needed and has economic worth. While middle-class urban offspring are regarded as costly obligations to the family, farm children not only make a substantial contribution but are essential to maintain continuity of the farm in family hands. Because children are the heirs who will carry on, they have a stake in the survival and success of the farm. Thus, farm parents perhaps have an easier time than other American parents in asking children to work rather than play.

Labor is divided by gender on the farm; fieldwork and care of large animals are almost exclusively delegated to boys. A college-aged woman described how her brothers had one set of tasks and the girls had another: "We were responsible for the baby pigs and the garden while the boys helped my dad with the fieldwork and hogs." However, the change in what women do in the wider society has allowed more farm girls to do what were previously male activities. In one community a farmer had given his granddaughter a forty-acre plot to manage as her senior Future Farmers of America project; this would have been unheard of a generation ago. Although women historically cared for animals, chickens, and milk cows on the farmstead, they typically did not have responsibility for production management (Faragher 1986).

Farm children spend most of their waking hours with fathers and siblings. The distances between neighboring farms militates against young children, in particular, casually visiting with friends. Frequently one's playmates are cousins or siblings in a large family because kin are in close proximity. One woman recalled frustration when her city cousin visited the farm because the cousin preferred to play with the numerous cats in their barn while she, who took the cats for granted, was hungry for a playmate.

Parental recognition of a child's contribution to the farm and the awareness that their labor is depended on has consequences for a child's development. Adolescent farm children are not as apt, for instance, to experience the rebellion of suburban teenagers. Frequently, the son designated as the farm successor is treated as an equal by his father; respect tends not to engender teenage resentment. This is not to say that rebellion is avoided entirely, for opposition may be delayed until later in life if a father prevents the transmission of management when a son thinks he has earned it (Salamon, Gengenbacher, and Penas 1986). Farm children sense that the family works together toward common goals, but they clearly expect that their investment will be reciprocated by land inheritance, an education, or financial assistance. For example, farm children assume that, should they choose to attend college, their parents will pay the bills, due to the children's substantial contributions to the family enterprise. Only when children feel that repayment is not appropriate or forthcoming do they express a sense of exploitation.

FARM WOMEN

Like their husbands, farm wives are primarily the products of farm upbringing, though not to the same extent. However, it takes more than a farm background to make a wife committed to the farm. A husband who involves his wife in decision making or keeps her informed about day-to-day management cements a wife's commitment (Brengle 1981). A farm wife with a farm background brings to the marriage not only the experience of her on-farm training but also potential access to information, labor, and land through her relatives. A wife also provides the heir to the family name and farm, thereby making intergenerational continuity possible. Providing an heir involves more than producing a baby, for a wife's continuity commitment influences the attitudes of children toward farming or eventual cooperation with the sibling who succeeds parents on the farm (Jung 1980).

No matter how much they do on the farm, women consider it "help" (Rachel Ann Rosenfeld 1985). Farm women feel indispensable and generally do not complain about exploitation by their husbands. Domestic work is viewed as critical to the team effort and therefore as productive as fieldwork. A woman does not feel scrubbing the toilets is demeaning when her husband is out in the barn shoveling manure—hers probably is the less burdensome task. A woman's contribution is largely domestic and also includes raising animals for the family's food, housepainting, and running farm errands. In hog producing areas of Illinois, women often control the farrowing process. The explanation for this management shift is that tiny pigs are like babies and women are better with babies. "What are you going to do today?," a question typically asked by women, may be asked by men as women take over management decisions in some domains. One young farm wife was observed inoculating pigs and cutting their incisors with the assistance of her three-year-old daughter, a job she had decided on and scheduled.

When the family is immersed in busy-season tasks, women understand that "the farm comes first." Because the farm is also theirs, they are in agreement with this priority. Men, because of the difficulty in finding men for hire, are now more reliant on wives for dependable and, of course, cheap field labor. The revolution in farm technology has made this possible. Farm equipment no longer requires great strength to use, as it did even twenty years ago. The result is more women now involved in field activities than were their mothers (Wilkening 1981b). Younger farm wives claim to prefer this involvement to "staying in the house cooking meals and minding the kids." With a mother or mother-in-law nearby to babysit and the local fast-food restaurant to

supply meals, farm women can participate in fieldwork as they or their husbands choose. Such involvement tends to diminish as soon as sons become
old enough to help or when operations are large scale and are dependent on
the sort of labor a full-time employee supplies, but a trend is certainly evident
for more equal gender contributions in the field on mid-sized family farms
(Buttel and Gillespie 1984; Rachel Ann Rosenfeld 1985).

FARM MEN

Farm men active in childrearing are quite capable of other domestic tasks, if
needed. But while women are more equally involved in the production domain dominated by men, a similar shift by men into the domestic domain of
women has not occurred. Accordingly, men are more satisfied with changes
from the traditional division of labor than are women (Wilkening 1981b).

Farm men are skilled in a multitude of tasks required by farming. They are
welders, machinists, electricians, plumbers, accountants, and market speculators. The relative isolation of the farmstead has made farmers adaptive, and
they master as many skills as possible. As the business side of farming became
more critical to survival, men were forced to learn new skills—marketing and
computerized recordkeeping—unless they designated the tasks as female.

As men age, their farming contribution changes. When a son is taken into
the business, a father gradually shifts from more physically demanding tasks
to those more mentally demanding. A key to the shift is who plants, runs the
combine, and sprays chemicals. Such tasks are typically kept by the person in
charge of daily management decisions. After a father withdraws from the
fields, his value lies in the information he provides for the operation. His
gathering of tips at the local coffee shop or from old cronies at the grain
elevator can provide the successor with leads on rental land or acreage up for
purchase (Salamon, Gengenbacher, and Penas 1986). Farm family members
can make a substantive contribution throughout the lifecourse; the mid-sized
family farm always can use everyone.

Midwestern farmers have faith that the family farm not only benefits those
directly involved, financially or as a way of life, but also benefits the nation
with efficient and economical food production. Commenting on the strength
of the family farm, a farmer said, "I do not think corporations will take over.
They do not have the dedication or deep interest like a farm family. When
your pigs are yours and they are sick you are out there trying to do all you

can to save them. But if they belong to someone else you're not going to go out with the pigs in the middle of the night." This sentiment probably would be agreed to by all farmers in the study, but whether a farm is diversified with pigs to manage, distinguishes farming patterns.

Shared traits emerge from Midwestern families having grain farms, a similar settlement pattern, and the heritage of northern or western European roots. Yet as we now turn to the distinctive cultural systems associated with Yankees and Germans, we see that actions motivated by a particular set of beliefs about land maintain different structures of domestic life. These contrasts have implications for how families interact with other families and how they relate to their communities. As a consequence the quality of community life produced and experienced by rural families varies as does the continued viability of the small villages at the community's center.

The Community Context

Railroad companies such as the Illinois Central created a uniform system for the location and design of Midwestern towns. Regularly spaced along the rail line, the towns were laid out in a grid on either side of the tracks. Even the names of village streets are the same along the Illinois Central route (Lingeman 1980). The pattern of a main business street, grain elevator, and residential side streets repeats itself throughout the Midwest. Some towns predated the railroads, but the eventual spacing was designed to extract profits efficiently from the agricultural hinterlands. Yankees, who were the primary town developers, viewed towns as a way to organize local trade and to attract real estate investment, which was a business itself (Hudson 1985). Although the villages initially looked alike, a unique community identity emerged under the combined influence of ethnicity, settlement, and environment.

In this chapter, we will take a close look at seven of these communities: Emerson, St. Boniface, Wheeler, Heartland, Libertyville, Freiburg, and Prairie Gem. Each was investigated during a year-long ethnographic field study between 1976 and 1987. My initial studies, from 1976 to 1981, were carried out in six communities in east central Illinois. Called the Black Prairie, this area is comprised of rich loam soils, produced by the latest Wisconsin glacier, that are among the most productive in the state. In these early studies, I found that German and Yankee communities, among a group including Irish and Swedes, showed the greatest contrasts (Salamon 1984). Therefore, in a study between 1981 and 1983, I focused on a German and a Yankee community in the Gray Prairie region, approximately seventy-five miles to the south. The Gray Prairie has less productive soils that were produced by the older Illinois glacier that reached farther south than did the Wisconsin glacier. The difference in soil types allowed me to vary a critical environmental factor for farming while holding constant the cultural factors of ethnicity and religion—German Catholic and Yankee Protestant. Consistency of ethnic characteristics in the Gray and Black Prairie paired communities would suggest that farming patterns are more strongly determined by cultural factors than by soils. Another Black Prairie Yankee community was included in a 1986–87 study that focused on the relationship between land tenure and community quality.

From these studies I acquired data on three paired sets of German and Yankee communities: one pair from the Gray Prairie and two pairs from the Black Prairie. Another Black Prairie community, fortuitously, has a half-German, half-Yankee composition. Because each community was studied by different individuals, the data obtained differs in quantity and focus. For example, three graduate students and I studied Heartland, the first community, for two years, and as a result it produced the most data. By the time Wheeler, the last community, was studied, my ideas about ethnicity, land tenure, and community life were well developed and could be the focus of study, as they had not been previously. Hence Heartland and Wheeler provide key data for the book.

•

Structural Dimensions of Community Variation

Rural communities can be compared by using a set of structural dimensions, outlined in table 3.1. In a particular community, the configuration of these dimensions accounts for the content of the intangible aspects of life: cohesion, attachment, cooperation, social support, and well-being. Implications

Table 3.1. Dimensions of Variation and Their Impact
on Community Quality

Dimension	Community Implications
Environmental factors	Set options or constraints on growth and maintenance of farms and community
Manner of settlement	Affects extent of linkage among households and shapes ideology for community welfare
Ethnicity	Influences homogeneity of values and religious participation
Religious structure	Affects integration of community
Demographic factors	Influence cohesiveness of population and potential self-sufficiency, especially between village and countryside
Institutions	Through involvement or support by population, indicate strength of identification, attachment, and value placed on cooperation
Social structure	Through vigor of networks, reflects mobilization capability, degree of household segregation, and social support available
Land tenure	Produces social stratification according to who controls local land and how it is divided

for community factors more accessible to the casual observer also stem from the organization of these dimensions: homogeneity, population size, social stratification, and religious affiliation. The unique arrangement of the dimensions constitutes a community's personality.

ENVIRONMENTAL FACTORS: GEOGRAPHY AND NATURAL RESOURCES

Soil quality affects agricultural production and, therefore, land values. An aerial view of farmland during the winter reveals a great deal of soil variation that escapes the eye at ground level. The way the glaciers deposited debris and the way soils were formed (by grass or forest) could build soils with very different productivity for neighboring areas. In east central Illinois, Yankee pioneers avoided swampy areas and instead chose land under trees or on rises. Once the swamps, with their rich soils, were artificially drained, however, the chosen soils of pioneers turned out to be the poorest in the area (Margaret Beattie Bogue 1959). Those farms on the best soils are consistently more productive and more expensive to buy.

Communities are also shaped by how close they are to other population centers, roads, and natural resources. For example, whether a community is close to a good highway system today or was next to a railroad in the past affects the economic flexibility of farms (Nicholls 1975). During the early period of farm settlement, access to markets was critical. The Black Prairie communities were originally settled next to railroads and are currently twenty to thirty miles from an urban center by interstate highways. The Gray Prairie communities are also near an urban center, albeit a smaller one. Having been platted earlier than the Black Prairie communities, they are about twenty years older, did not need drainage, and were therefore opened to settlement in the 1840s. Communities with easy access to railroads tended to thrive. Families tell how during the Depression they sent cream daily by rail to Chicago and used the cash for family staples. Today good roads follow the network established by rail lines and link farm families to nearby sources of supplementary income, medical facilities, and shopping. In Illinois, as in other Midwestern states east of the Mississippi, now most rural residents need to drive no more than an hour to reach a metropolitan area. Thus family members can easily supplement income with off-farm work.

MANNER OF SETTLEMENT

Rural communities evolved in response to differing imperatives. Railroad company agents and religious or social promoters recruited immigrants to the villages established along the lines. First-comers in turn recruited immigrants from their original area so that eventually ethnic groups settled in clusters. Heartland, St. Boniface, and Freiburg were formed by such a chain migration process. Other communities, such as Emerson and Wheeler, grew after acreage was sold by an original wealthy land investor. In another formation pattern, exemplified by Libertyville, a community developed when individual households chose to concentrate in one locale. Population homogeneity relates to the process of community formation (Conzen 1980b, 1990; Kollmorgen 1941; Beale 1989b).

The motive underlying the founding of a community affects the extent to which members share a world view. The historian Page Smith (1966) divided rural communities into two categories: (1) "covenant" towns founded on a philosophical agreement of purpose by a relatively homogeneous ethnic and religious group and (2) "cumulative" towns, which grew without a plan through gradual settling by individuals impelled by economic motives. People founded covenant communities to perpetuate a way of life typically based on an agrarian vision rooted in the Bible. Cumulative towns were committed to boosterism; growth, progress, and making money were indicative of community well-being. Success was measured by commercial achievements. Over time, according to Smith, covenant towns tended to remain small, true to the covenant of origin, and predominantly agrarian. Cumulative towns, shaped by individual entrepreneurial vision, either boomed into commercial centers or eroded. Heartland, St. Boniface, and Freiburg were covenant towns, while Emerson, Libertyville, and Wheeler were cumulative towns, although none of them experienced a real boom.

ETHNICITY

A community's settlement process has implications for its cultural diversity. Historians argue that a critical mass of ethnic families was both a prerequisite for community formation and a determinant for the persistence of ethnic traits (Conzen 1980b; Kamphoefner 1984). For example, German farmers were typically stable when clustered in a community but resembled highly mobile Yankees when they settled alone, as did the Germans who filtered into Prairie Gem from Iowa. Individual families were not subject to the same pressures as were chain migrants, and their adjustment to a community probably hinged on shedding ethnic traits rather than on maintaining them.

Before World War I, rural communities were ideal settings for perpetuating the cultural traditions of those ethnic groups that had continuity as a goal. Germans in particular used their relative isolation to preserve their language as a way of reinforcing group boundaries. Isolation placed enormous pressure on families to conform and also encouraged them to support one another against a foreign and potentially hostile outside world (Hawgood 1940; Conzen 1985).

The clustering of immigrant farmers promoted development of communal associations and church activities that reinforced community integration (Conzen 1980b). Similar activities were also present in cumulative communities but were not as easily premised on kinship and ethnicity. Yankee communities were founded and operated by families whose paramount concern was self-interest, which could militate against cooperating or mobilizing for the welfare of neighbors (MacLeish and Young 1942). Unlike the Germans, the Yankees feared neither assimilation nor the decline of community cohesion, for these were not paramount cultural values for them. Thus German ethnic traditions favored the formation of tightly integrated and distinct communities compared with those of the Yankees.

RELIGIOUS STRUCTURE

Rural churches integrate communities and help maintain ethnic values. Historically, Catholics and Lutherans were committed to establishing churches linked to an authoritarian, denominational structure in Europe. These churches consistently aimed at developing stable farm communities focused on the church, with congregations of northern and western European immigrants, sharing a cultural as well as a religious heritage. Most ethnic families clung to these traditional churches, which taught that salvation offered by other denominations was invalid (Hollingshead 1937).

The centralized churches differed qualitatively from those established by New World Protestant denominations. The Methodists, Baptists, or Disciples of Christ, for example, were more concerned with individual salvation than with the development of a permanent community around the church. Each of these denominations, within certain limits, recognized the validity of others. Members were recruited almost entirely from among those of Yankee heritage. Membership in a New World church fluctuated with the mercurial career of a charismatic leader. Ecclesiastical organization was subordinated to saving souls, so competition for followers—and souls—was great. Because these churches did not regard community stability as a high priority, they invested their resources primarily in their members' religious commitment.

A historical study of these two church forms in rural Nebraska found a striking difference in persistence over time (Hollingshead 1937). Once founded, the mainline centralized churches were stable, while churches from the New World group accounted for 90 percent of all closed congregations. Mainline church villages tended to have only one church; New World church villages tended to have competing churches—too many for small rural communities to sustain. Thus mainline, centralized congregations overlapped with community, and church membership equaled community membership. New World churches divided rural communities into community subsets; characteristics such as socioeconomic status took membership precedence over factors such as ethnic heritage.

Rural communities are aging more rapidly than the United States as a whole. The elderly constitute 13 percent of rural populations, compared with only 10.7 percent in metropolitan areas (Glasgow 1988). The relatively prosperous 1970s reversed the rural aging trend, but the 1980s saw a return to the pattern of young leaving the countryside. Furthermore, the farmers who started out in the 1970s were differentially forced out of farming by the economic downturn of agriculture in the 1980s. This age cohort contained families in their twenties and thirties—the group most actively involved in rural communities (Beale 1989d; Campbell 1985). Particularly in more remote rural areas such as Libertyville, those leaving farming must seek work elsewhere. Retired people, especially widows, are left behind. Almost a quarter of the people in the county where Libertyville is located are over the age of sixty-five.

Because elderly people represent such a large part of rural society, where they live has a community impact. In the past, farming communities were maintained by an elderly migration pattern: retired parents moved into the village when the successor married and took over the ancestral homeplace. Farmers saved to buy a house in town or, alternatively, children had to purchase the family farm to finance the parents' retirement. The move to town made it easier to attend church, go shopping, receive medical care, and visit with friends. But the town retirement pattern began to fade as roads improved and as rural villages lost doctors and other amenities. Elderly farmers can manage their specialized operations longer, using custom work by local active farmers, and higher incomes contribute to greater mobility. A new migration pattern known as "corn, beans, and Florida" emerged as the goal among wealthier grain farmers. Retirees can now summer on the farmstead and leave the community and an empty home in the winter to follow the sun.

When farmers no longer retire into town, the social fallout is great. A housing surplus produced by out-migration and a reduced in-migration of retired couples can alter a village's population base. Families attracted by low rents or by country living are lured to declining rural villages (Fitchen 1991). If residents not linked to farms increase substantially, the community loses the cohesion produced by occupational or income homogeneity. Farmers without relatives in the village have no vested interest in its governance, condition, or viability. Village and country clash over property taxes and similar matters that affect one segment more than another. Such a split—rural-farm versus village-nonfarm—can exaggerate differences among social strata and age groups.

INSTITUTIONS: SCHOOLS, BUSINESSES, AND COMMUNITY ACTIVITIES

A school fosters a community's vitality, identity, and loyalty. The ebb and flow of children at school brings people into a village to socialize or to spend money. Everyone knows or is related to members of the basketball and football teams, and people attend the games long after their children have graduated. School functions—sports, ceremonies, performances—bring the community together by forging a common history for children and their parents (Peshkin 1978b). Thus when faced with enrollment declines, communities wage battles to keep their schools. People say that losing a school takes away the heart of a community, while "school functions bring people together." A community without one unifying school or church possesses no single institution held in common. Conversely, in the past, St. Boniface, Freiburg, and Heartland had parochial schools that reinforced the shared religious identity, maintained ethnic endogamy, and fostered integration.

Voluntary social organizations, annual social events, and civic service also help integrate a community. Many communities have an annual homecoming or a service club committed to local improvement activities that benefit all; others are unable to maintain such organizations. The ability to constructively mobilize local energies indicates whether the residents share an identity and care to act as a group to perpetuate the community.

Communities vary in how successfully they preserve a central core—a school, a church, a grain elevator, and a restaurant—that marks a functioning social entity as opposed to a bedroom village. Local businesses have encountered fierce competition from regional malls or discount stores that lure families with cheap prices and simulated big-city life. Preserving a village business center despite this competition indicates that a community views this core as a high priority and that residents are willing to invest social and economic capital locally. Especially important is a cafe or restaurant where residents can meet and eat. Such a business provides a focal point for social life. Some communities have rallied to financially support core businesses, while others have let their business street die. Lacking a shared church, however, the school or businesses become more important to community vitality (Wilkinson 1986).

Midwestern agriculture has little corporate farming: the predominant enterprise form is the family farm, where the family makes the operational decisions, provides most of the labor, and seeks to generate income toward the support of the household (Reinhardt and Barlett 1989). Such factors as the size of farms, tenancy, the extent of absentee ownership, and whether land holdings are highly fragmented define the variables critical to the region's land tenure (Friedberger 1988; Kramer 1977). The nature of attachment to land, or land tenure—the complex of ownership, rental, farm size, and land transfers—provides the central logic for a rural community's economic and social systems (Bell and Newby 1971; Crocombe 1974).

According to Goldschmidt (1978), land tenure and farm scale account for differences in the index of quality of life—schools, infrastructure, and services. In two California communities where ownership was in moderate, family farm–sized units, by any objective measure the community was superior to the community where farms were larger than family-size, ownership was controlled by corporations located outside the community, managers ran the farms, and work was carried out by farm laborers. The complexity of regional agricultural patterns in the United States works against there being an inevitable negative community outcome from absentee ownership and farm consolidations (Swanson 1988; Friedberger 1988). However, advocates for the family farm use Goldschmidt's findings to argue that the trend toward farm consolidation is destructive of rural society and not conducive to sustainable agriculture or communities (Strange 1988).

As we saw in chapter 1, early mechanization and the costs of prairie farming made Illinois farmland expensive, causing tenancy—where the operator does not own the land—to become common (Margaret Beattie Bogue 1959; Allan G. Bogue 1963b). In the Midwest, tenancy does not automatically mean low social status and a marginal economic existence. In the communities I studied, most tenants and part owners farmed at least some land rented from relatives, who were commonly local or absentee landlords. In Illinois 43 percent of the landlords rent to tenants who are relatives (Bruce B. Johnson 1972;

Kloppenburg and Geisler 1985). Renting from a relative means that the relationship between owner and operator is fairly stable and is less likely to be exploitative. Some communities had many absentee landlords because outside investors' control of land was established early (Gilbert and Harris 1984). However, because of the great out-migration from farming between the 1950s and the 1970s, the number of heirs living elsewhere increased in all Midwestern communities. Absentee owners may be good citizens; although they do not use the community schools and roads or the water, sewage, and fire systems, they are often committed to preserving the infrastructure. But many absentee owners are mainly concerned with profit and resist having it siphoned off by higher taxes. For this reason, increased absentee ownership can negatively affect community quality (Mooney 1983).

Average farm size is correlated with the number of farms in a community. With farm consolidation, the number of independent farm operators declines and hired laborers tend to increase. Agriculture based on hired farm labor is associated with more stratified social structures such as the Southern plantation system or California corporate farm operations (Pfeffer 1983). The relative absence of hired labor and corporate farms has meant that the social structure is less stratified in the Midwest; nonetheless, how much land is owned affects a family's relative position in the status hierarchy (Beale 1989d; Pfeffer 1983; Hatch 1975, 1979).

Where farms are consolidated, a bimodal distribution occurs: at one end, a few farms too large to be operated by a family without hired labor; at the other end, many farms too small to support a family adequately. It is predicted that this distribution will eventually dominate the Midwest because middle-range, family-operated farms will be unable to compete (de Janvry 1980; Tweeten and Huffman 1980). In families on smaller farms, one or more of the adults works elsewhere and combines this income with farming. This form of farming, called pluriactivity or multiple job-holding, is widespread in Europe (Barlett 1986; Anthony M. Fuller 1984). Many farmers who operate middle-range farms have traditionally been pluriactive, but their farm income has outweighed other activities in importance. Family histories in the seven Illinois communities abound with examples of farmers who sold seeds and firewood, did custom work (using their machinery to help other farmers without the equipment), were carpenters or machinists, or drove trucks so that they could remain farmers. In Illinois, pluriactivity is often involuntary; a family cannot obtain more farmland even when they could easily handle it.

The distribution of farm size is an indicator of the social strata in a rural community. When farm size is homogeneous, the social strata are less divergent. When there are fewer farms, greater divergence exists between large and small operations, and greater social distinctions are also evident.

SOCIAL STRUCTURE

The distance between farm households, a result of the Midwestern homesteading settlement pattern, naturally isolates families unless space is overcome socially. Relatives are bound by kinship obligations, which assure interaction among households. A measure of community integration is whether households that are not linked by kinship also are close-knit. Communities differ according to the vigor of social networks linking households—whether support in nonemergency situations is generous, interaction is frequent, and aid is exchanged among nonkin.

Integration rests on the commitment of community members to maintaining group norms. Therefore, when a community is tightly integrated, an outsider moving in finds the atmosphere decidedly unfriendly. Barriers are erected because people are wary of intruders, and gossip is used as an effective social control mechanism. Boundaries are more permeable when households are loosely tied together; therefore, new people do not threaten the status quo. Loosely knit households ignore a great deal of social activity and proclaim disinterest about others' behavior. More diversity of social interaction is tolerated than in a tightly integrated community.

People highly committed to those sharing cultural practices and priorities are able to support other community members without regard to social status. Correspondingly, a more diffusely organized community produces a variety of perspectives and goals and social groups. Social stratification according to income differences segregates networks; people are more likely to interact with those in the same stratum. Aid to network outsiders is limited to a demonstrable emergency, which does little to reinforce community cohesion on a daily basis.

•

The Communities

For comparison, six of the communities are presented in three pairs. Each paired set consists of one German-dominated community and one Yankee-dominated community, which are matched for soils, geographic region, and approximate time of settlement. Two pairs are located in the Black Prairie region: the first is Emerson (Yankee) and St. Boniface (German); the second is Wheeler (Yankee) and Heartland (German). The third pair, situated in the Gray Prairie region, is Libertyville (Yankee) and Freiburg (German). Prairie Gem, located in the Black Prairie, is an example of the merged patterns because, as noted previously, half of the residents are German and the other half Yankee.

These communities represent the range of ethnoreligious variation commonly found among Germans and Yankees in the Midwest. Despite sharing many ethnic attributes with other communities, each community developed uniquely according to its origin, church, and time of settlement. These historic elements account for variation within the same ethnic group; culture accounts for the major contrasts between the ethnic groups, delineated in chapter 4.

PAIR I

Emerson: Black Prairie, Yankee Protestant

Emerson's main street, now almost an empty shell, shows signs of a once prosperous past. Standing empty or boarded up are a large bank, a gas station, a grocery store, and a restaurant. One converted storefront is a community hall. A garage, an automobile dealership, a grain elevator, and the post office still function. Emerson has not supported a cafe in years. Pickup trucks parked at one end of the main street where the farm businesses cluster are the only evidence of activity.

Several churches in need of paint are tucked among nicely kept homes on side streets. More older people than young are seen out and about. People tend their yards, but there are few gardens or trees along the sidewalks; some streets have homes that look abandoned. A well-kept ballfield suggests that some local organization exists; however, the village has no park. Emerson can evidently sustain the basic businesses that serve the prosperous-looking farms nearby, but the demise of other businesses indicates that community members did not support them. Despite some auto traffic and pedestrians, the sense of a village core is missing.

Settlement. Emerson bears the name of an Ohio professional who, between 1830 and 1870, acquired 4,500 acres (half of it from the government) for a large-scale livestock farm. After cattle raising became unprofitable, he tiled and drained the land to lease to tenant farmers. He attracted an Illinois Central shipping station by granting a right-of-way across his land and also donated land for a school, thus fostering the founding of Emerson around 1870. Between 1860 and 1870 his heirs began to sell half the land in small tracts to family farmers. Descendants of the founder still own large tracts as absentee landlords (Margaret Beattie Bogue 1959).

Ethnicity. Most of the families who bought the small parcels traced their ancestry to the British Isles and, more immediately, to families that headed west with the frontier through Ohio and Indiana. More than 80 percent of the heads of households living in Emerson in 1870 were born outside Illinois. In the early days, migrants moved from other Midwestern states such as Indiana, and many of these traced their ancestry to the Northeast (Penas 1983). Recalling her grandfather's migration from Ohio, an elderly woman explained why the Yankees came: "Why the land, of course. I'm sure they'd heard how fertile it was, so they came out to see for themselves." By 1900 Emerson was considered one of the more prosperous villages between Indianapolis and Peoria (Stapp and Bowman 1968). Its population and prosperity peaked in the 1940s, when nearby cities began to attract people for shopping, entertainment, and work.

Religious Structure. Churches were established early but lacked stability. At present, Emerson residents are divided among three churches (in two villages), and loyalty to any one church is tenuous. For example, the congregation of a local Baptist church grew dramatically during the tenure of a popular minister but diminished under subsequent leadership. Affiliation is chosen pragmatically: "With the kids going to school in Emerson, we felt it would be good to attend church there," was one farmer's reason for abandoning his childhood church. The community exerts little pressure for regular attendance or membership. As one farmer observed, "The Methodist church does not really serve to pull the community together. We go, but not regularly. When summer comes, lots of people go away every weekend . . . so the congregation dwindles." Because of church policy and for personal reasons, pastors tend to stay no more than five or six years. Short tenure precludes a pastor's sustained, intimate involvement with a congregation.

Institutions. Emerson farm families view schools as important "to pull people together." However, consolidation of their high school means that basketball and other sports events include people from nearby villages. Attendance and interest lapse once offspring graduate. In explaining why they lost interest, a farmer said, "It's more fun to have someone close to you involved." Similarly, serving on the school board is considered a mark of status, but the lure is strong only while children are in school. One farmer trying to raise a slate for an upcoming election complained that "civic responsibility doesn't exist anymore." Nevertheless, "Education is an important value of parents in the area," explained the daughter of a prominent farmer. Children are urged to achieve in school; even those who intend to farm are expected to prove themselves in high school and college.

Demography. In recent years the village has become a commuter bedroom town for nearby urban areas. One reason is that farmers are reluctant to retire there. As one resident explained, "Emerson has probably only four or five farmers at most. . . . There are some [farm] widows in town, but not many I know of." Because local retirees do not live in the village, outsiders began to rent empty houses. Farmers are critical of the new element: "I think when you have a lot of people working away from the town, they are not real concerned with how the community looks. They're only here to sleep. So they don't take much of an interest."

Because a rough gang of young people now hang out there drinking beer and racing cars, many farmers have turned against the village. Farm families commented on an initiative to allow a bar in the village. "It would be open every evening for drinking. . . . There's already enough drinking on the streets of Emerson at night. I think most people would feel that if a bar went in it would attract the riffraff from miles around," said one farmer. As country residents, some farmers with less social consciousness do not consider village affairs their concern. As one explained, "That's the nice thing about living here. You can watch the goings-on and not become involved. 'Course, if someone asks me directly, I say what I think. . . . But those of us outside the village limits don't have a vote."

Social Structure. Families recognize a sense of community among farmers, despite the village's decline. How the community functions as a social organization was explained by a farmer: "When [my son] was trying to get some land to live on we went to an auction and [my son] and someone else in the area were bidding on the land. Once that other farmer got word that [my son] was bidding for a home he stopped bidding against him. . . . Afterwards this neighbor said he was sorry to bid against him. . . . The neighbor said he was bidding on speculation, but a home for [my son] was more important. . . . People around here watch out for one another."

Farmers tend to evaluate the village critically according to boosterism criteria. That is, they equate expansion, economic vitality, growth, and increased property values with community well-being (Hatch 1979; Hofstadter 1955). Residents consistently pointed out two events that marked the demise of Emerson as a thriving commercial center. First, when an interstate was put through in the 1960s, Emerson rejected an interchange. Nearby towns that gained interchanges experienced some growth in population and business. Exactly who rejected the interchange is unclear, but farmers say a few absentee landowners did not want to lose acreage and some local businessmen feared competition. Individualism among Emerson's entrepreneurs apparently took precedence over the village's economic welfare. Although farmers feel that the interchange "would have been good for Emerson," one professional is delighted that the village has remained quiet and sleepy.

The second event cited for Emerson's demise was the loss of a farm implement dealership, which employed a dozen people. Some say local critics forced the flamboyant owner out; others say the business was in financial trouble. When the owner left, the community lost an active school board member whose business made donations to church and school. Furthermore, the amount of traffic the village could attract diminished, and the restaurant closed. One farmer attributed the village's gradual decline to apathy: "I don't think it's conscious. . . . All those complainers never offered anything in the lines of help or reorganization to boost the town. They've all just jumped on the bandwagon and frequent the businesses in [two nearby communities]." Thus by 1980 Emerson was a bedroom village that had few residents with any connection with agriculture.

St. Boniface: Black Prairie, German Catholic

Along the main road to St. Boniface, a large Catholic church stands alone in the countryside but within sight of the village. The well-kept church with its tall steeple dominates the horizon, and the bare grounds are immaculate. In the center of town, there is a hardware store and a small, well-groomed park complete with a train depot. A roadside table and sign welcome the traveler.

On the main street, houses are interspersed with businesses, one of them a busy tavern with a sign advertising lunch and dinner. At the far end of town, a large grain elevator overlooks an extensive cemetery in front of another Catholic church. Every morning streams of people attend mass at both churches and park their trucks for coffee at the cafe. St. Boniface has many new homes, including one small subdivision off tree-lined Church Street, alongside the cemetery. The village appears prosperous; the park, ballfield, and streets are carefully maintained, a sign of active involvement.

Environment. The land around what is now St. Boniface was first purchased by Yankees who wanted the flat, untimbered terrain for pasturing cattle, horses, and sheep. About the time a rail line was put through in the mid-1850s, the first drainage ditch was dug; before drain tiles were installed, only about 20 percent of the swampy land was tillable. Expecting the area to grow rapidly, the rail company built a large station, but development was slow until the Germans began to settle.

Ethnicity and Settlement. St. Boniface grew through the chain migration of Germans from several Alsatian villages. Although it is now French, Alsace was part of the German empire from 1871 until the end of World War I. St. Boniface farmers therefore consider themselves German. Like most nineteenth-century Alsatian immigrants, the settlers were Roman Catholics, many of whom left the region late in the century (Luebke 1980). St. Boniface began to flourish as a commercial center around 1865 with the arrival of the Germans, who tiled the land and established farms. Some early Alsatian settlers had previously lived in southern or western Illinois and were attracted by the land made available through advances in drainage technology. In turn, they lured other family members from Alsace with kin sponsorship.

Because most Germans arrived twenty years after the community had been established, they were too late to buy inexpensive land directly from the railroad. Later German immigrants had to work as hired laborers while accumulating the capital to begin farming; for them entrance was via the more expensive route of purchasing already developed land. By an 1870 county history, St. Boniface is described as a German settlement noted for its industry; the enterprise of the settlers was reflected in their organizing to drain their area of the township. Eventually Alsatians dominated St. Boniface, although they never dominated the ownership of community land.

Religious Structure. Community changes can be measured by the chronicle of the local Catholic church. According to one farm wife, "Our church is the center of the community." In 1875 the first seventeen families in the countryside erected a church, which was administered by Franciscans tied to Freiburg. Early in the twentieth century a second, smaller church was built in the village as increasing numbers of farmers retired, turned over the family farm to their children, and moved into town. This sustained retirement pattern has assured that ethnic farmers would dominate the village and has reinforced the original agrarian covenant between country and village residents. Religious commitment has produced five priests, eleven nuns, and one brother (St. Boniface Bicentennial Committee 1976). However, vocations were a product of the past, when priests with agrarian origins actively engaged the church in the farmers' lives. No longer, for example, are Rogation Days observed, when the priest ritually blessed seed and fields before spring planting.

Although the bishop of the predominantly Irish diocese has exerted pressure to close the smaller church, feelings run high to maintain the two parishes. The combined parishes, consisting of 140 families in the early 1980s, were already yoked by the service of a single priest. To assure that their church will survive the diocesan cutbacks and the shortage of priests, parish members take care of the bookkeeping, janitorial services, and cemetery upkeep: "That's how we keep the parish going—everyone pitches in and works. . . . We want something we can be proud of." Women are particularly religious, and they socialize children to be loyal to the church. A young farmer said that his mother watches his church attendance: "She'll call up and say, 'Would you like to come over for breakfast after Mass?'" He, like many younger adults, regrets the closing of the parochial school because his children will not have Catholic moral training.

Institutions. Large families, evidence of a commitment to Catholicism, supported the parochial school until the 1960s. But a 20 percent decline in parish membership, a diocesan shortage of nuns, and policy shifts forced the school's closing. The community has transferred its loyalty to the public schools. High school football games are particularly important. As many as two thousand people turn out for a game.

In the 1950s St. Boniface had five taverns, three grocery stores, two gas stations, three banks, both a hardware and an implement store, two grain elevators, its own water company, and a post office. Old-timers think "the town has gone down hill" because it now has only two restaurant-taverns, one grain elevator, a hardware store, the post office, one bank, and one small grocery store. A retired farmer complained about how the town had changed: "It's not like it used to be. There's not much here anymore. . . . The elevator office is out of town. When the store used to be in town, I'd see people all the time and we'd socialize. Now, I can go for a long time without seeing people. It's just different; not as farm oriented." During the day, farmers still meet and gossip outside the church, the grain elevator, the bar, or the cafe. The village has busy shops, and manicured lawns border well-kept homes. Older couples in particular support the local businesses. "I prefer to go to the local elevator . . . no matter what the price," explained a farm wife who argued that "small is better" when she expressed her opposition to the recent consolidation of two small, local grain elevators. Her son, however, trying to become established, favored the consolidation for economic reasons.

Social Structure. St. Boniface's location along an interstate about twenty miles from a city makes it attractive to commuters seeking a rural ambience. An early invasion of two small housing subdivisions on a farm next to town aroused the community. "It makes me upset to see the subdivision built on good farmland," commented a farmer conscious of the highly competitive farmland rental market. With the help of the mayor, a farm landlord, the community passed an ordinance to forestall further encroachments. The new residents are called "strangers"; they do not farm. Explained a fourth-genera-tion farm wife, "The real way we tell them apart from everyone else is because they're not related to everyone here, like the rest of us." An interstate exit nearby brought new business, and some residents feel that the advantages outweigh the loss of farmland.

A farmer in his thirties commented on the changes; he felt some regret about the decline in St. Boniface's agrarian foundations: "I remember when people would go from farm to farm to bale hay and shuck corn. It was hard work, but no one got paid but the person who owned the machine. Every-body helped everybody else. I don't think it's that people got less friendly or less neighborly, it's just that with the machinery they have these days, they just don't need the help. In fact, you should see it when someone is sick or dies during harvest. Thirty or forty combines show up, and get the job done in a hurry. I think people look for a chance to do things like that for each other these days."

The Catholic church, in addition to bringing people into the village for daily mass, is the pivotal force in St. Boniface. Those active in the church "belong to everything." The village converted land donated by the church into a heavily used ballfield. St. Boniface's volunteer service groups organize communitywide events, such as an annual pancake and sausage fund-raiser. An old grocery store, purchased by the village and remodeled by volunteers, is used for community meetings and wedding receptions. As a consequence, St. Boniface retains a sense of community identity despite the loss of its parochial school, some businesses, some population, and some farms.

Wheeler: Black Prairie, Yankee Protestant

Before entering Wheeler, a visitor is impressed by the large farms surrounding the village. Widely scattered farmsteads are located at the edge of huge fields extending to the horizon and undivided by hedgerows. These farms seem at odds with the village itself, where many small, run-down homes crowd together along several streets. One street, however, is graced with larger, older homes and a modern Methodist church.

Two brick-paved streets intersect at the village center, where businesses alternate with empty lots, marking the location of failed or burned-down establishments. Businesses directly connected with farming—grain elevator, fertilizer dealer, and bank—look the most prosperous and busy. A newly remodeled library, a renovated elementary school building, a newspaper, a grocery store, and a cafe indicate that Wheeler generates enough patronage to sustain the core activities that constitute a viable village.

Environment. In the mid-1880s, a Yankee investor bought a large amount of acreage and founded Wheeler, giving it his name. He used the acreage to run a large-scale cattle operation until an outbreak of disease in the herds forced him to sell off small parcels (at the same time this occurred in Emerson). Once served by a rail line, the village, although not on a main highway, has good connecting roads.

Settlement. A post-1875 wave of Yankee settlers bought the parcels that Wheeler put up for sale, and some of these families still have descendants in the area. Wheeler has retained its Yankee dominance; only a few German families moved in, and they eventually intermarried. From the outset there were clear social divisions in the community: those with money developed the area, and those without worked the land for them.

Demography. Today Wheeler is still divided physically and socially: most farmers live in the countryside. About two-thirds of villagers are involved in non-farm occupations; most blue-collar workers commute to nearby metropolitan areas. Some blue-collar workers are descendants of farm laborers; others formerly were tenant farmers. Nonfarmers that live in the country (28 percent of households) tend to have kin in the community and obtain cheap housing. Quite segregated from each other, farmers and blue-collar workers seem to live in different communities. The village also has a group of retired farmers, farm widows, and some business families and professionals who have purchased the few architecturally distinctive homes.

Religious Structure. In the early years of settlement, large landowners of adjacent parcels and of similar status kept to themselves, bolstered by intermarriage and the country churches where they worshiped together. Eventually, at Mr. Wheeler's urging, the Methodist church was built in town, thus tying the large landowners firmly to the village. Church membership in various Protestant denominations is still correlated for the most part with family social status, which is based on farm size and the amount of land owned. Wealthier families attend the prestigious Methodist church; those of comfortable means attend the Baptist church. For blue-collar families, the local church of choice is a Pentecostal church (founded in the 1930s), which draws more of its working-class members from outside the community. Several farm families attend church elsewhere, rejecting a local commitment mainly for theological rather than social or business reasons. Thus religion, rather than fostering community solidarity, divides Wheeler families.

Institutions. Many of the village businesses, including the weekly newspaper, are owned by non-Wheeler residents, women who purchased them relatively recently, hoping to find a market niche. Wheeler families, farm and nonfarm alike, however, do not feel especially bound to do their business locally. Some of the businesses, such as the restaurant, have changed hands and mission often in a few years' time.

The schools, vehicles for integration in other communities, have failed to unify Wheeler. When high school consolidation was being planned several decades ago, the three Yankee communities involved competed so intensely that the new high school was finally built in the countryside, effectively causing the deterioration of all three villages.

Nor does community participation serve to integrate Wheeler. Few farmers are consistently active in community affairs other than their church, and the blue-collar newcomers are seldom active at all. The prominent Old Guard, including the larger landowners and earliest families, participate only selectively. Less well-established farm families tend to encourage their members to become involved, and their participation in a wide range of activities keeps Wheeler functioning as a community. Once initiated, however, few communitywide activities persist or grow.

Social Structure. A recent school bond issue reinforced the social division inherent in Wheeler's landholding structure. Most of the larger landowners, especially those without children of school age, opposed new property taxes. The schism still existed several years after the tax hike was passed by the school board aided by a coalition of nonfarming villagers and rental operators. A board member was amused when three members of the opposition committee built new homes the year after they fought against the school taxes that they "couldn't afford." Asked whether surplus money should be appropriated by the community for the common good, Wheeler residents generally opted for individualism, which has reinforced the village's highly differentiated social structure.

Heartland: Black Prairie, German Lutheran

An exception among the study communities, Heartland is a community without a village. It is an unincorporated spot marked by a large Lutheran church and rectory, an elementary school, and a handful of homes. The church's substantial stone building with its tall spire dominates the countryside. It can be seen for miles and has been called the Cathedral in the Cornfields. Directly across the road, a dairy farm with large Harveststore silos emphasizes the agrarian focus of the community. Houses dot the landscape with a frequency indicating that small farmers and many nonfarmers live in the countryside. Heartland's lack of a village center can be attributed to its East Frisian origins. Frisians still live in dispersed villages in Europe (Zuidema 1978).

Environment. As late as 1867, much of what is now Heartland was still owned by the Illinois Central Railroad because the land was considered worthless swamp. The area was flat and low with sluggish streams. It was so poorly drained that early settlers described rowing a boat between villages after a rain. Swampy land did not deter three original German families from buying land for the bargain price of $1 an acre from the railroad, which was eager to sell its last remaining tracts. While accumulating capital by working as farmhands in western Illinois, the men heading these families had spent several years exploring central Illinois. Because East Friesland, on the border of Holland and Germany, was swampy, the Heartland families knew how to drain the land. Using spades, the men laboriously sloped their fields toward ditches dug with shovels and horse-drawn scoops (Corner 1928). Under the swamp lay rich loam soils, flat and almost entirely tillable—some of the best land in the state. Creating their farms from the swamp gave Heartland families and their descendants a special relationship to the land. Three generations later a farmer pointed to his farm and said, "I owe it all to this land out back here."

Because it was founded after the Illinois Central was completed, Heartland never had a rail line, although a nearby village had a station.

Settlement and Ethnicity. The community was expanded by chain migration from several villages in East Friesland. Most settlers came in family units, but in some cases a father or son would come first, work for a time, and then send for the rest of the family. By the late 1870s there were nineteen families, all but the original three coming directly from Friesland. That Heartlanders still speak German in the home indicates the strong commitment to their ethnic identity. People now in their fifties spoke only German until they began public school. As a middle-aged farm woman remarked, "Somehow lots of things I say to the kids seem more natural in German." Even one hundred years later, Heartlanders on "Luther Tours" return to East Friesland and visit relatives, although they are told their German is slow and old-fashioned.

Religious Structure. Heartlanders belong to a single Lutheran church, founded by the original families soon after settlement. Together they built the grand church around 1915. Community cohesiveness was reinforced during forty years of leadership by a single pastor, who insisted on speaking German for services until he retired in the 1940s. Because the congregation spoke only Low German, or Plattdeutsch, the pastor ran a church school where children learned the High German of the church liturgy in preparation for confirmation. The shared experience of "German school" confirmation classes three days a week and every day for two summer months cemented friendships among children otherwise split among three country schools. The German school also provided a context for choosing a mate, thus contributing to a high degree of ethnic endogamy (almost three-quarters of the marriages are German with German). The school no longer functions, but the church still dominates the social fabric of the community.

When the church held its centennial celebration in the 1970s, the congregation spent a year preparing for the two-day event. These activities produced two histories, a reenactment of the German school, and a service held by the three ministers born in the community. The celebration was capped by a traditional beer-drinking festival that no Heartland event is without.

Demography. While other rural churches have lost members or have an aging congregation, the Heartland church thrives. "Our church is young and growing. We have 275 kids in the Sunday school; most of them are from the original families too," said the farmer who is currently president of the 385-family congregation. Even when people marry and move elsewhere, "they almost always keep coming to church. . . . Our church will stay even if the young people aren't farmers," remarked the mother of a daughter who left but maintains her membership. She stressed that "the church is what holds us together." Families give land for home sites to children, who commute to work in nearby urban areas while maintaining a Heartland residence.

Institutions. Although the main street has no formal businesses, the congregation loyally supports businesses in three neighboring German villages. In the taverns and cafes, farmers gather daily for coffee, cards, a meal, or a drink. Heartlanders usually carry out business affairs within their own group. Houses are built, wired, and repaired by local craftsmen. Similarly, most of the community services are sponsored through the church. Some Heartlanders work with 4H youth groups, the volunteer firemen, or Cooperative Extension Homemakers' groups, but they are unlikely to be involved in groups outside the German area. For years, however, Heartland has produced excellent softball players, and when the local team plays, the community turns out.

Because the church is located at the juncture of three townships, Heartland children have always attended two different high schools. Thus schools were never depended on for community cohesion. Yet everyone loyally attends the high school games.

Social Structure. Church and community are synonymous. Through the pastor and the elected elders, the church dominates many areas of community life. Social support and economic assistance are arranged for needy or infirm members. Various ambitious projects, led by people from respected old land-owning families, have been undertaken by the church.

One past activity in particular, part of everyone's oral history, helped cement community solidarity. Early in the century, when a telephone company servicing the community failed, some leading households formed a new company to restore the deteriorated facilities; they installed phones for a fee (adjusted to income) set by common agreement. By the 1920s, all 82 Frisian families had phones. A line ring was used to announce church events, information, and calls for help and by those taking orders before a town trip. When a non-Frisian family moved into the home of a former community member, the phone was removed, and the family was told that no more shares existed. The tightly knit community did not welcome non-Germans.

Today, Heartland remains a farming-dominated community where agrarian values permeate the social structure. Family and community identity are inextricably entwined with the land. Although measured by land ownership, status can also be achieved by participation in worthy church activities.

PAIR III

Libertyville: Gray Prairie, Yankee Protestant

Once a trade center, Libertyville now has little commercial activity. When people "go to town," it is to the county seat about twelve miles away. At one end of the only street in the village are a grain elevator next to abandoned railroad tracks, a post office, a grocery store, a hardware store, and three churches, two facing across the street. At the opposite end of the street is a string of small homes. When farmers are not busy, a group of them can be found sitting on the steps of the hardware store during the day. The village focal point is the small, pickup grocery store run by a woman. In a few booths in the back, several men gather for morning coffee. The walls are decorated with Polaroid photos of the regulars' birthdays, celebrated without fail. Although the elementary school is in the community, the high school is in the county seat. A local cemetery is still used for burials.

Environment. The county where Libertyville is located was first settled about 1830. Forty-niners moving west on the Old Cumberland Trail had to pass near Libertyville, and some chose to stay. Because speculators quickly bought most tracts, the settlers could not purchase land directly from the government or the railroads. Like most pioneers throughout Illinois, the early settlers preferred timbered land. Settlers turned to general farming only after they had cleared the timber commercially from about a third of the community's area. Farmers first grew broomcorn for the commercial market. Later they diversified with cattle, dairy, chickens, and grain, and finally they specialized in grain farming after World War II. Today, small oil wells have added a new source of diversification to some operations.

Until a railroad was put through the community late in the 1870s, the region developed slowly, but by the 1880s all land except for some bottom acreage and remaining forest was "under fence." The village became a trading center, created by the railroad. Apart from one state paved road, only mud roads served this marshy area before the 1930s, making the railroad especially important to the farmers. After the WPA began graveling the roads during the Depression, people were more willing to pass bond issues to improve the roads. Aided by the present road system, activities shifted to the county seat, a change that doomed the businesses and ultimately the communal existence of Libertyville.

Settlement and Ethnicity. Residents who preserve family histories report that their ancestors migrated to Libertyville as individual families. Many were lured there from elsewhere in Illinois because of the cheaper land, but most came from Indiana, Ohio, or Kentucky and Tennessee. Historically the area was divided into two small, fiercely competitive communities only three miles apart. The two villages "got along like cats and dogs," according to a local historian. "Just why they got so at-outs with each other I don't know." Old-timers speak of literal warring when groups of rowdies traveled between the two villages. Eventually, school consolidation and the gradual shift of focus to the county seat muted the boundaries between these former archcompetitors. The historic rivalry, perhaps, prevented either village from surviving as a trade center.

Religious Structure. Churches have compounded the fragmentation of Libertyville. The community, like the county as a whole, has many churches—four within three miles. People agree that the churches do not integrate the community: "They couldn't have a united service [all three together] on a bet!" said a retired farmer. Each congregation numbers only eighty to one hundred members. "Everyone goes their own way. . . . We go to church in [the county seat], and people from there come out to the country," said a farmer. People either do not attend church at all or are very religious.

Affiliation is chosen for such reasons as age, vitality of the church, marriage, convenience, or politics. Because people take a rather pragmatic approach to religion, "they shop around" for a religious belief that suits them and do not feel compelled to support churches in Libertyville. The more religious families attend Wednesday prayer meetings as well as Sunday morning services and are teetotalers. An elderly woman commented on the importance of the church in her life: "Our church is our community. . . . Of course we are friends with our neighbors too, but we really don't socialize with them."

Demography. A shift in the makeup of the population has contributed to a decline in people's attachment to the community. Retired farmers now, for the most part, move to the county seat, and the countryside has become more diverse. Commenting on the newcomers, a farmer said, "There are lots of houses in the countryside, but there are few farmers." He sees few families that are full-time or "real" farmers: "Many work in factories and just live out here," he explained. If country residents own a little land, they typically rent it to the larger farmers. The full-time farmers are descended from the Indiana and Ohio stream of migrants, while most small or part-time operators are descended from the Southern stream.

Libertyville is an aging community. An elderly resident complained that they educate the young, who then leave: "Here's a sad thing about the entire county. We don't have anything, and haven't for a long time, to keep our children here. . . . The result of it is we pay through the nose to educate 'em and they go somewhere else. Now a lot of 'em will come back after they're ready to retire. We've got retirees all over here . . . [but] they don't add much to the county." The community that is rejected by its youth eventually becomes a retirement haven for some.

Institutions. According to early county histories, local critics complained that, despite the presence of prosperous landowners, little money was invested in schools, even though Yankees historically fostered education (Handlin 1980). For a long period the county had no high school and thus no unifying institution (Libertyville 1884). Now, after attending separate elementary schools, children from the two originally warring villages go to the single high school in the county seat. Other formerly separate activities such as Cooperative Extension Homemakers' groups and 4H are also consolidated at the county level.

People in Libertyville describe themselves as a community, and there are some vestiges of a structure at the pickup grocery store where they gather. People bowl together, hunting is a favorite activity of the men, and bingo is popular. The volunteer fire department functions as a social group for men; a hog roast was held to raise money for equipment during the study. Older women have a social club that has met monthly for years. In an emergency, such as when a house burns down, people unite to help the family. A town council operates and directs residents, for example, to clean messy property that offends local sensibilities. Through informal support, residents have cared for a handicapped man since the death of his parents. But social life is evident mainly among extended family members who visit each other frequently. Few are committed to formal voluntary organizations that might integrate a larger social unit. A woman volunteer said, "People here won't go to things much, and if they do it's always the same people." According to a civic-minded elderly resident, "We have a lack of public spirit around this place."

People know all about their neighbors and, for the most part, like them, but they are fiercely independent and private about their lives. The virtual lack of community cohesion in Libertyville is not bemoaned by its members.

Social Structure. Residents have difficulty defining the present boundaries of the community, perhaps because they have little sense of being a cohesive social entity. Said one farmer, "I never did think too much about that." Separated from Libertyville by a wide creek, a neighboring area developed as a thoroughly German Catholic community, socially oriented toward nearby Freiburg. Farmers in Libertyville are quick to point out the differences between their "loose-knit" community and the thriving German community, viewed as "closed," united by a single Catholic church. Commented a farm wife, "Those Germans across the river, their religion ties them together as a community. . . . Nothing defines us as a community. We're a hodgepodge."

An elderly woman referred to the community as egalitarian: "This is just one small town and one big family." Yet the favorite topics of conversation have competitive themes. A retired farmer commented about his work career motivation, which is inherently nonegalitarian and nonagrarian: "I spent my whole life trying to keep up with the Joneses. . . . I had one piece of equipment and the guy across the road would get a more modern kind. . . . I could never catch up with him. . . . I've been chasing him all my life, and that's a true story." People are preoccupied with money: ways to make it, what things cost, and how their neighbors got theirs. Loss of community is of less concern.

Freiburg: Gray Prairie, German Catholic

Most villages located five miles from a town of ten thousand tend to die or become bedroom communities, but Freiburg has survived as an agrarian entity. Its large Catholic church, located in the heart of the village, is the single most important reason for Freiburg's persistence. People come in daily for mass and then stop at a small grocery store or visit the cafe or relatives. When the farmers have a lull, they gather at one of the three taverns or at the Knights of Columbus hall. Although not suggesting great wealth, Freiburg's buildings and grounds are all well groomed. New homes are scattered throughout the village, an indication of renewal or expansion. Unlike the six other communities, Freiburg is large enough to support a family doctor, two dentists, and, recently, a new lawyer.

Environment. The original homesteaders came as a group and planned the layout of the community, which resembled a European village. Difficult conditions prevailed during the frontier period, but the community always supported endeavors that benefited all. Some farmers started businesses to provide a mill, dry goods, and other necessities. The community recruited a railroad, which after the 1870s transported farmers' products to urban markets. The land around Freiburg did not require artificial drainage and, typical of the Gray Prairie, had large forested areas. In fact, people still heat their homes with modern versions of the settlers' wood stoves.

Settlement and Ethnicity. Freiburg was settled around 1840, after a group of Westphalian immigrants living in Cincinnati formed a company whose goal was to create an agrarian, German Catholic community.[1] Working as artisans, the members each saved $10 a month until they had accumulated $16,000. A committee was then sent secretly to locate a 10,000-acre Illinois frontier parcel for the community. Secrecy was imperative to keep speculators from buying the land first and turning a quick profit at their expense. Each of the approximately 200 members paid $1.25 per acre and obtained a 40-acre plot and a town lot (town acreage was more expensive originally), all distributed by lottery.

Many settlers journeyed by water from Cincinnati to St. Louis and then traveled by wagon. Later settlers migrated directly from Germany by way of New Orleans and then over the same route from St. Louis (Perrin 1885). Perhaps because Freiburg was founded by Germans and has been dominated by them from the outset, people do not self-consciously talk about ethnicity—it is taken for granted.

Religious Structure. Freiburg at its height functioned as the Catholic mission center for much of downstate Illinois. By the late nineteenth century Freiburg had, in addition to its schools, a female academy run by nuns, a seminary for Franciscan fathers, and a convent. Old-timers feel, however, that the seminary did not directly advance the local economy and that little contact actually took place between locals and the seminarians. "They were fenced in," said a retired farmer. But the presence of these important institutions in the little farming village points up the mentality of a community that was willing to support activities of benefit to others. The Franciscan seminary functioned until 1965, when it was moved to Chicago. The building is now a museum run by a town group. Loss of these religious institutions has not

1. Cincinnati was a staging point for Catholic Germans who settled other rural communities. Cullman County, Alabama; southern Lawrence County, Tennessee; and Windhorst, Kansas, are similar to Freiburg, according to Calvin L. Beale.

affected church membership. The priest describes his parishioners as very devout: "They come to church even if they're mad at the priest. They don't take it out on God." Church activities such as daily mass structure the community's social life.

Demography. Many farmers still retire into town, but the stability of the community is reinforced by the nonfarm majority. Farmers have given or sold to their nonfarming relatives the land to build homes. The wooded areas around Freiburg have been built up in this way. Aside from farming, few jobs are available locally; living in Freiburg therefore means that people are likely to commute some distance to work. Farmers say that the children follow a pattern: they reject farming and small town life, leave when they graduate from high school, and after reaching their middle twenties come back to the area to farm or to bring up their own children. "This is a good place to live, though hard for outsiders because it's so tight," one resident explained. Such commitment to the community was evident when a small, local firm transferred operations to Indiana. Despite the financial hardship, most employees did not sell their Freiburg homes, hoping that they could eventually return.

Institutions. Freiburg once had five grocery stores. Today it has only one, used mainly for pickup shopping, because people have succumbed to the cheaper supermarkets in a nearby town. Several of the businesses started by original families still operate. The real reason Freiburg survives is that it remains the social center for nearby German Catholic communities. Because it was "a day's work" to travel to the nearest urban area, these communities traditionally shopped, sold hogs, went to church (if they lacked their own), and socialized in Freiburg. "We're all German, we stick together," explained a retired farmer.

From the peak of seven village bars, five still remain. Each tavern is associated with a particular group of men who stop daily for a "glass of beer, some bologna, and talk." The Knights of Columbus hall, built in the 1940s, gives the taverns some competition. Men who like to drink visit the KC hall two or three times a week. "When you spend all day with dumb animals you need to get out and socialize," commented a farmer. People complain that, unfortunately, teens do not use the village teen center much because no beer is sold there. Explained a teenager, "Freiburg is known as a heavy drinking town."

One focus of community spirit is high school sports. Residents say that sports "keep the community together." Even after children who were involved in sports have married, parents remain interested. "We all go to basketball games at the high school regularly. Our sons played and we still enjoy going," said a farm wife. The community is enthusiastic about all sports, including those for girls. According to one farmer, farm girls learn to play basketball with their brothers. Recently, backed by the entire community, the girls' basketball team repeatedly won the state championship for small schools; the boys' team won only once. One farm boy commented that sports teams bridge the gap between "town and country kids," a gap created by the many people who do not farm. Teenagers active in sports "all hang out together."

A high degree of integration and sociability is also apparent in the number and variety of communitywide activities that punctuate the year in Freiburg. In costume, a choir of adult men and women sing German songs. A group of men still visits homes annually to do a Twelfth Night pageant. Church picnics, down to one day from the former two days, usually draw about two thousand people. The Knights of Columbus also have picnics. Right-to-life groups organize social events, and there is an annual parade to celebrate fund-raising for cancer. Freiburg has blood drives and weekly bingo games; the KCs hold monthly stag parties and card get-togethers. Older women are active in quilting groups, which serve as the gossip arenas that complement the KC hall and the taverns for the men.

Social Structure. Varied informal and formal linkages maintain Freiburg as a tight community able to draw and keep its young people. One woman who, along with her husband, is a returnee feels that family is the main reason people come back to settle. Freiburg's integration is reinforced by frequent social interaction among the same people served by the school district, such as the men who come to the village KC hall. A farm wife commented that, although their area has four German Catholic parishes each with its own priest, "We back each other up. We go to each other's suppers, rummage sales." The process reinforces the bonds that join Freiburg (Rogers 1987).

MERGED PATTERNS

Prairie Gem: Black Prairie, Mixed German and Yankee

Along the main road, one sign welcomes the traveler to Prairie Gem, while another indicates the turnoff to a German Lutheran church situated among farms in the countryside. This split on the road symbolizes Prairie Gem. The Germans and the Yankees who constitute the population are about equal in number.

The main street looks cared for, and there is a small park across from the row of businesses. A substantial brick church in the village serves Yankees. Although some houses are shabby, newer homes on tree-lined streets give evidence that people still retire there. A large consolidated school building stands on the edge of the village, its parking lot lined with a row of yellow buses when school is in session. People, especially elderly residents, are out on the streets during the day. Retired and active farmers frequent the tavern or bowling alley in the afternoons. Prairie Gem also supports a grocery store, gas station, lumberyard, and grain elevator beside a rail line.

Environment. Prairie Gem was originally part of an unsuccessful, large-scale farm that failed despite the use of modern techniques such as mechanization and labor specialization. A single wealthy Ohio farmer, in all likelihood the most flamboyant large-scale landowner in central Illinois, made Prairie Gem Farm his first financial debacle in a chain of huge farming enterprises. In the 1850s he acquired more than twenty thousand acres in a single block, much of it from the Illinois Central Railroad, and embarked on developing his land with an army of hired men, machinery, and animals. Because he preferred operating the farm himself, he did not develop a tenant system, which proved disastrous. Within a decade his expensive improvements led to financial trouble with the railroad, and his mortgage was foreclosed.

A cattleman bought up the farm and added acreage, but by the early 1870s he too had lost his mortgage in the aftermath of lawsuits resulting from his having imported diseased Texas stock. Over a thirty-year period, the land was sold under the direction of a third set of owners, who also used a tenant farming system. Land sales were slow at first but picked up when a railroad was put through the area in the late 1870s. Tenants were still working some of the original large farm as late as 1900 (Margaret Beattie Bogue 1959).

Settlement and Ethnicity. Small landowners were settling in the area at the same time that the Prairie Gem Farm was being developed. Predating the Germans in Prairie Gem, some Yankee families had arrived as early as the 1850s, from Indiana for example. They farmed independently on poorer soils next to the moraine land owned by the farmer-investor. As a major employer, the large-scale farm allowed immigrants without resources to gain access to farming. Among these workers were Germans who, as late arrivals, began to trickle in after 1870, with a burst between 1890 and 1900. Like the Yankees, the Germans filtered into Prairie Gem as individual families from many directions and with only their ethnicity and occupation in common.

Several family histories contain stories about immigrant ancestors who worked as cattle herders, corn-shucker crew members, or tenants on the Prairie Gem Farm. One prominent German family traces its origins to immigrant farmers who had first settled in Iowa but whose children were attracted to Prairie Gem in the 1870s by land sales from the breakup of the large farm.

Religious Structure. From the outset, Germans and Yankees were segregated. In 1870 the Germans formed a Missouri Synod Lutheran congregation, a synod known for its conservative beliefs. In the mid-1870s the Lutheran church was established in the countryside to function as an exclusive community for German farmers, separate from the Yankee-dominated village. Their strict tenets cemented together a German community of families who, arriving individually like the Yankees, might otherwise have remained less integrated (Conzen 1980b). Strictures forbade members to drink and dance or to enter another church. Twenty years after the church's founding, the congregation was split when more liberal families resisted accepting the minister's word as law. In the late 1890s about twenty families formed a new church affiliated with a liberal Lutheran synod and constructed a church building on farmland donated by one family. In contrast to the Germans, the Yankees attended churches of various dominations in the village: Methodist if farmers, United Brethren if hired hands.

Today, with a relatively large congregation of four hundred, the Missouri Synod church is extremely successful in keeping its young people involved. The prohibition against entering other churches has insulated them from the rest of Prairie Gem because, aside from school activities, organizations meet in churches. Time and declining church membership have muted some of the community's former class- and ethnic-based religious distinctions. The disappearance of the ubiquitous hired man (all older farmers used them) changed the makeup of the United Brethren church, and it eventually affiliated with the Methodists. When the breakaway Lutheran church burned down twenty years ago, the members also elected to affiliate with the Methodists rather than rebuild. Persistent ethnic antagonisms are revealed in the comment of a Yankee Methodist about the liberal Lutherans' merger with his church: "Germans are always doing things like that. They don't like to spend their money."

Demography. Retired farmers from both ethnic groups have moved to town, and their presence has kept village and countryside unified. Children now farming and living on the homeplace pay daily visits to elderly parents. Critical community support, ownership and patronage of the stores, church activities, and volunteer service in the schools are provided by this large and relatively prosperous group of retirees. As elderly village residents die (twenty widows remain by local count), some housing has been filled by nonfarmers attracted to the school or to small town life. Longtime residents worry about the future because newcomers could become a significant presence in the village. "They're not part of the community because they don't spend any time in it, don't support it. . . . They spend their money elsewhere," said a retired farmer.

Institutions. Missouri Synod Lutheran Germans are thought to participate in community activities when "it is in their own interests." However, Lutherans are socially involved in the church. Old-timers remember being heaped with abuse as schoolchildren during World War I. At times, it appears, the tightness of the Lutherans galvanized the non-Lutherans into cooperation in opposition to the Lutherans' united, conservative stance. Once something is organized, the Lutherans actively support it in the interests of community welfare. For example, they cooperated to form a Community Club, largely dominated by farmers. The club sponsors Little League, holds an annual fall homecoming festival, and refurbished the village playground. Thirty years ago when the business district burned down, people joined together and rebuilt it; without businesses they felt the village would die.

People in Prairie Gem say that "the school holds the community together." They feel so strongly about their schools that the community taxes itself heavily to maintain a high school and an elementary school. Throughout the year "everybody comes" to activities, not just relatives of the participants. People are knowledgeable about school affairs, remaining involved even after their children graduate. Both Germans and Yankees serve on the school board. One German farmer's Yankee wife pushed him to participate, even though "he only wants to farm; that's his only interest."

A citizens' advisory group functions as a liaison between the school board and the community to express grass roots concerns to education professionals. For example, the advisory group negotiated a compromise between farm families and the school administration over the issue of excusing teenagers from classes to help during planting and harvesting. Such community involvement is exceptional for rural schools (Peshkin 1978a).

Social Structure. The underlying social division is between "those Lutherans," meaning the Missouri Synod group who hold themselves apart, and the rest of Prairie Gem. The Lutherans always insist that an in-marrying spouse convert, a policy that effectively sharpened differences between them and other community groups. The segregation has meant that Lutherans retained Germanic attributes in contrast to the breakaway Lutheran families, who mixed with Yankees and often intermarried. Several now-elderly German men from both groups married Yankee women who had come to the community as schoolteachers. As a consequence of these forces, Lutheran men are more uniformly German than are the women, and the men farm in a manner reminiscent of other Germans.

The united front presented by the Lutherans who resisted change has caused the rest of the community to unite to make change happen; the community has benefited from both processes. "My neighbors are Lutherans and you couldn't find better people; honest, good to do business with, but they're clannish. You can't get inside," said a retired farmer and community activist. The historically antagonistic relationship between "those Lutherans" and the Yankees has contributed to the divided yet paradoxically cohesive structure of Prairie Gem.

Within each group of ethnic communities, some historical, religious, and farming differences exist. Nevertheless, this variation is less pronounced than the contrasts between German and Yankee communities. One important structural dimension of variation, land tenure, was left out of these profiles. Because land tenure underlies all the other distinguishing community dimensions, it deserves and receives a separate treatment (see chapter 9). The next chapter contains the framework of the book: different cultural systems motivate family practices that seek to reproduce the farm and family. The practices of families in German and Yankee ethnic communities are distinct, having been organized by the fundamental differences in the meaning assigned to land. These family-based practices lead communities down divergent social and farming pathways.

A Typology of
Family Farming Patterns

A family cannot farm without land. Land is of such importance within an agrarian social system that whoever owns
it has power over family and community members, especially
those who want to farm. Control of land is the measure
of status within the farm family and of family status in the
community. In every generation, as owners age and prepare
to die, they must plan or carry out the ritual transfer of their
land. As land control moves through families via intergenerational transfers, or through communities via the land market,
the transmission is a vehicle for re-creating and reenacting
the cultural system. Land control is therefore a particularly
powerful analytic window on the organization of an agrarian
cultural system (Ohnuki-Tierney 1990a). While family practices are ephemeral, the traces left by land transactions endure

through legal records, maps, and family holdings. These chronicles permit us to concretely corroborate oral accounts and observations about family interactions.

Family land transaction practices are the mechanism that, by endorsing some options and excluding others, maintains the whole cultural system in its special configuration (Ortner 1984). The self-interest of those who control land, and who thereby dominate family and community relations, is to preserve their position and that of their successors (Bloch 1985; Ortner 1990). Practices that embody beliefs about land are therefore fundamental to maintaining customary asymmetric relations of gender (men over women), generation (elder over younger), and status (larger landowners over everyone else) in farm communities. Whoever controls land understandably has a vested interest in those practices that preserve the inequitable status quo.

My use of land as an analytic window on the dynamics of family and community organization is developed in the context of a comparative typology of ideal types, distilled from my field studies of German and Yankee family farmers. According to Weber an "ideal type" is an inductively arrived at construction that logically merges diverse elements that exist in reality into a "pure case." As a pure case, the ideal type is a heuristic device rather than a concept that entails evaluation (Gerth and Mills 1972). No one individual in a farming community, for instance, is likely to exhibit every ideal characteristic; though many aspire to fulfill the ideal, others depart from it. As constructed, my typology (table 4.1) portrays German and Yankee cultural systems as contrasting extremes of the same categories of behavior; actual behavior would fall somewhere along the continuum between the ideal types, with families from each ethnic group clustering toward either end.

The ideal typology corresponding with the control of land allows me to make an unambiguous case for farming patterns that are the source of variation in Midwestern agriculture and rural society. The ideal types correspond to the cultural systems that emerged among Germans and Yankees after original settlement. The respective cultural systems, European agricultural experiences, and timing of immigration shaped how the two groups dealt with the prairie environment and unfolding historic events. Of course, these cultural systems evolved as world events altered agriculture and rural life, but not every aspect of the system changed at the same rate. Although the systems were molded by multiple causes, no factor is likely to have more stability than

Table 4.1. Typology of Midwestern Farming Patterns

Yeoman	Entrepreneur
Cultural Meaning of Land	
Land is a sacred trust maintained by achieving continuity of family land ownership and an agrarian way of life in a particular ethnic community.	Land is a commodity, and farming is a business in which accumulation of land is a means to increase family wealth and power.
Implicit Social Order	
Whoever controls land dominates the system. Elders possess power in the family because they own the land, and elders from families with more land exercise more power in the community. As a man controls land through management, he can exert power over women and children involved in the farm.	
Relatively strong hierarchy in family	Weaker hierarchy in family
Less divergence in community strata	More difference in community strata
Goals	
Reproduce a viable farm and at least one farmer in each generation	Manage a well-run business that optimizes short-run profits
Strategy	
Ownership of land farmed preferred	Ownership combined with rental land to best utilize equipment
Expansion limited to family capabilities	Ambitious expansion limited by available capital
Maximize kin involvement	Manage the most efficient operation possible
Avoid risk such as heavy debt or costly expenditures	Willingness to take risks such as debt for business goals
Farms	
Smaller than average operations	Larger than average operations
Farms relatively similar in size	Bimodal distribution of farms
Diversification in operations	Specialized operations

the meaning attached to land, due to its centrality in farm family reproduction. We need to keep in mind that routine actions within the family are taken-for-granted practices that account for an inherent domestic conservatism (Ortner 1984). Even as they act within the constraints of their cultural system, however, families have a hand in shaping history just as history has an impact on the system (Ohnuki-Tierney 1990a).

•

The Typology

My thesis is that German and Yankee farmers have cultural systems that are based on fundamentally differing meanings attached to land. As a consequence family members have a particular repertoire of practices based on their conceptions about the goodness of a person, a farmer, a kin group member, and a way of life. Each practice has a connection with how land ought to be handled, which constitutes a schema that serves as an interpretive framework and a scenario for action (Ortner 1990). Specifically, such taken-for-granted beliefs as whether the family or an individual ultimately controls land owned, which generation is responsible for intergenerational land transfers, or how much land provides sufficient family support order interactions across a variety of lifecourse situations. As a consequence of German or Yankee families following a schema, a substantial array of kinship, farming, and community patterns are integrated into a whole system.

As presented in table 4.1, the typology outlines the links between beliefs attached to land and patterns of family life, farming strategies, land acquisition, and community involvement. Each link will be analyzed using the device of the window on land transactions to illuminate how land control operates and is transferred. This chapter delineates the core meaning attached to land among Germans and Yankees and how this culturally organizes a scenario of family actions with implications for farm structure. Other levels of the typology are explicated in the remainder of the book. Chapters 5 through 8 focus on how the practices organized by each cultural schema are played out in the domestic order. The specific interactional processes that result organize a household's relationships to kin and the ethnic community. Chapters 9 and 10 focus on how maintenance of the domestic order according to a cultural pattern underlies the development of the local land tenure system and the structure of the ethnic community.

The labels *yeoman* and *entrepreneur* (table 4.1), applied to Germans and Yankees, respectively, in the typology, crystallize the contrasting cultural systems. Each label derives from historical characterizations of the ethnic groups previously outlined in chapter 1. German (the archetypal ethnic) farmers were described in a derogatory manner as "yeomen" by agricultural economists in a fifty-year-old textbook (Ely and Wehrwein 1940). Yeomen were typified as concerned with continuity and tradition, content to plod along as their ancestors had, unconcerned with hurried economic progress, and slow to take up innovations or to change customary ways of doing things. These economists looked more favorably on the "entrepreneur" businessman-farmer, epitomized by the archetypal Yankee. Entrepreneurs were innovators eager to try newly introduced methods or equipment. An impatience with drudgery motivated a certain restlessness. An entrepreneur's planning horizon was short and dominated by financial concerns, unlike that of the yeoman, who seemed more concerned with providing for future generations than with profits for himself (Danhof 1969). Originally, these labels were applied only to the male operator as if he alone managed and worked a family farm. No connection between farm management practices and other aspects of rural life was even contemplated in economic discussions until after the 1940s (Goldschmidt 1978). In the past, scholars also failed to note that Midwestern ethnic groups farmed alongside one another, that interactions between Germans and Yankees in the public land market were motivated by cultural beliefs, and that these actions in turn shaped the land market.

Throughout the remainder of the book, I will freely alternate between the ethnic (German and Yankee) and typology (yeoman and entrepreneur) labels. Ethnicity is a good predictor of farming patterns even though a yeoman might be found among Yankees and an entrepreneur among Germans. In the fieldwork that I supervised, a phrase heard in one German (or Yankee) community was often repeated word-for-word in another, particularly when land or family practices were described. In chapter 1, I described a process of cultural convergence that emerged among initially diverse communities of Germans and Yankees after settlement in Illinois. Though the settlers were originally from a variety of locales in the country of origin, variations in dialect and customs became muted over time (Thernstrom 1980b). This historical homogenization process explains why features found in any one present-day German community in Illinois are likely to be found in any other German community, and likewise for Yankee communities.

•

The Meaning of Land

Land symbolizes what is most important to farmers: a means to do one's chosen work. For this reason families in all the communities believe that only land ownership provides real security and, by implication, real status. Germans in Heartland agree that "if you don't own it, it can be sold out from underneath you . . . you never know. If you own it, then it can't be taken from you." Similar sentiments are confirmed by an Emerson Yankee, who as a tenant farmer, considers his position insecure and has discouraged his son from farming: "Farming offers no security if you rent most of your land. Now it's different if you own land, but when you rent you always have to keep in the back of your mind that you could lose a piece." Because access to land is so critical, land's value is greater to farmers than its actual economic worth.

The way families handle land is important to the larger community. Land is salient to the maintenance of ethnic identity (Hollingshead 1938; Jan L. Flora and John M. Stitz 1985). If family farmers achieve continuity on land in a specific place, near others sharing an ethnic identity, then an ethnic community will persist. Thus land is a concrete and tangible symbol on which to focus personal and community attachment. As an indestructible and immovable symbol, land serves to reinforce the cultural beliefs associated with it (Simmel 1898).

Despite fundamentally differing meanings attached to land, as outlined in table 4.1, Germans and Yankees both seek to reproduce remarkably similar relationships of inequality between men and women and between major and minor landowning families. What distinguishes the ethnic groups are distinctive cultural schemas that order actions in the domestic setting. Such interactional processes produce family structures manifest in divergent practices for handling land transactions that also represent ethnic continuity. Such subtle contrasts in family processes as the timing of retirement produce variation in the organization of farms and the population of communities. For this reason, the typology outlines only that an implicit social order is shared by the groups; farm goals, family relationships, and community outcomes diverge. At the conclusion of the book I return to the shared notions of inequality with a description of a public land ritual common to both groups that crystallizes the reproducing process.

I begin explaining the typology by outlining current beliefs, goals, and practices of yeoman and entrepreneur farmers. It must be remembered that the cultural systems have roots in the past, brought by immigrant ancestors, though change, however minor, occurred in the course of each family intergenerational transmission of land. Farmers are pragmatic people who see themselves as adaptive. Yet family relationships linked with land practices are taken for granted, carried out in an unthinking manner because "that is how we do things." Maintenance of a specific family relationship to land, while other practices change, is the way farmers publicly reendorse the compelling and meaningful beliefs that order their lives (Ortner 1984).

YANKEE ENTREPRENEUR

Yankees today occasionally act in ways reminiscent of their highly mobile ancestors who settled the Illinois frontier. A man operating his parents' farm over a decade wistfully speaks about being restless: "I kind of plan on moving some time in the future—selling out here and going some place where the land is cheaper and setting myself up in a place of my own." This daydream derives from a meaning attached to land that is not bound by attachment to a particular tract or place and that emphasizes individual autonomy of control. Land is fundamentally used as a commodity. In this system farmers are committed to the business of farming rather than the family farmstead. According to a young farmer working with his father, "I'm not particularly tied to *this* land because of its history—even though that's nice and it makes it easier to get into farming, having it in the family. But I enjoy the challenge of farming. That's more important in my decision to farm."

Land ownership is an important measure of entrepreneur status and achievement; buying land demonstrates mastery of management skills. To remain a full tenant during an entire farming career, especially when running a large operation, signals poor business acumen. "We've never been known as tenant farmers," proudly explained a farmer. Actual land holdings, however, are treated unsentimentally. It matters little which tract is owned, only that ownership is achieved. "Land is a good investment, just as stocks are for me," explained this same farmer. During the year of a community study a Yankee farmer purchased a small tract from an absentee owner, then quickly resold it when offered a good price by a local businessman. This was a "smart move" in his view: "You don't make that kind of money selling beans."

Because land is considered a commodity, its symbolic value is inherently its financial worth. In this cultural context accumulation of land elevates families in power and permits expansion into ventures outside of agriculture. Yankee entrepreneurs admire ambition: the bigger the farm grows the better. A family of prominent landowners was amused by the comment "Your family owns everything down there." Decisions to buy or sell land are driven less by concerns for maintaining a family heritage than by financial concerns.

Yankees dwell on money in family and community discourse. Success, failure, goals, and motivations are all measured in dollars earned. Farming as a business is pursued for profits like any other business. The unprofitable farmer should not be in farming. An elderly Yankee bachelor, a self-styled self-made man who recalled working in the Depression-era CCC camps, epitomizes the entrepreneur–farm businessman. Although he has no children to pass land on to, he approaches the business of farming with relish. Over seventy, he remains involved in the daily farm operation because work is his diversion: "I guess I'm from the old school, and that means that I think you gotta produce. The whole point is to make it. For me work is a pastime. And it's a challenge; you try to make the most for the littlest cost. In a way it's like a game—but that's the way it is."

Their ethic of individualism and hard work, combined with financial risk taking, motivates entrepreneurs to seek the best return on their money; a bargain obtained overrides, for example, loyalty to community businesses. One crusty retired farmer, an owner of substantial holdings, personifies these traits: "Now my family and I we each own several thousand acres. We've got it scattered all over this area—in three different counties. We deal with seven elevators. It kind of spreads out the risk. You get different weather, different neighbors. . . . I never did go for insurance. . . . I never did hear of a fellow getting rich off insurance, did you?" Some, rather unrealistically in the light of government supports, consider farming positively as "the only true free enterprise left." Independence rather than the family heritage is what Yankee farmers rank high about farming. "You're like a little god; you choose what to do with that land."

Entrepreneurs, regardless of age, are seldom content. They energetically devise strategies, driven to expand, innovate, increase profits, or improve the family's social standing. "American farmers are profit-minded and inventive," commented a Yankee farmer approvingly. A farmer, almost ready to retire, still thinks about new ways to make money: "You know, there's probably a lot of money waiting to be made in compost, if you could think of some way to gather up all the stuff that's left behind after harvest, . . . clear off all the fields around here, and use some of the good cow manure from the barns. You'd need some device to keep stirring it . . . but that would be a good business for some young man to get into."

Efficiency is paramount in management. A young farmer, just starting out, imported a special Australian purebred dog to herd his beef cattle and hogs. In this way his wife can work off-farm, and he need not hire extra labor. Though the dog is as "ugly as hell, . . . he's as valuable as any piece of machinery, and does a better job than most people can." It is "good business" to manage an efficient match between machinery and size of operation.

When farming is a business, expansion by increasing land holdings is an end in itself rather than a strategy for getting children established. Available capital places the limit on possible expansion. Those that stay in farming are "good managers" and "good businessmen"; they are willing to gamble, to think big. A now-retired entrepreneur, successful according to other community members, explained: "Farming is not a way of life anymore. Anytime you think like that you are liable to lose your farm. All farming is, is a way to make money or go broke. . . . You have to have a business sense to survive in farming. Those that don't have it will lose out."

Entrepreneurs are risk takers comfortable with the gamble if high profits are attainable. A farmer spoke about losses in consecutive years that required loans taken on land owned by the family over a century. "How do you think I manage? . . . By borrowing against my equity. I pay $50,000 a year in interest. . . . I make it because I'm diversified, do some consulting, and have the oil business. . . . If I didn't have good equity I wouldn't have made it these past two years." Expansion into other endeavors is considered good business; farming is not just a way of life. "I'd go stark raving nuts if all I did was manage the farm," said a farmer who is also district manager for a seed corn company and runs an oil well drilling business. "I dropped my rental acreage a while ago. . . . I figured I could make more on seed corn and oil."

Larger family operations were typically recipients of substantial family assistance at the outset. "It's so hard to get started in farming unless you have some money behind you. Our family is different from others in the area, in that there is always some money somewhere, backing you up." Although he received generous family help, a farmer considers his becoming a large landowner a personal achievement: "When I got started, I had a brother who also wanted to start farming. Competition was worse [than for his one son], you had to make it on your own." Yankees who expand farms or businesses by taking risks consider themselves self-made.

Business principles govern the relations between family members. No entrepreneur expects otherwise. For example, an elderly Yankee farmer recalled negotiating a land deal with his in-laws. His future father-in-law wanted top dollar. "He wanted to sell it to me for $80 per acre, but I only wanted to offer him $70; but I gave in as I was marrying his daughter. Figure I got the better part of the bargain." At a later date another relative wanted 7 percent interest on a loan to buy land, and a local bank lent him the money at 5 percent. He did not express resentment over his treatment; business is business. When farming is business and kin believe they are treated and treat their own kin unsentimentally, then parents have no guilt about what they do with land and expect children to achieve independently. Though Yankee entrepreneurs are proud of being from multigenerational farm families, they feel their way of life must be sufficiently remunerative to reproduce the system. An oft-heard sentiment, particularly among smaller operators, was "It's too hard anymore, farming. It costs a fortune to start and buy machinery and . . . [our sons] can do better."

Consistent with business ideals that emphasize individual initiative, Yankee families are oriented more toward the present than the past. Children often knew little about ancestors or "weren't sure" how family land was obtained. History was evidently not a ritual theme in family conversation. Land long in family hands was treated the same or as no more remarkable than tracts more recently acquired. A typical successor to an entrepreneurial family farm reveals his lack of historical concern: "Most of the land I farm belongs to my parents. I know my mother inherited some, but the acreage my father owns, I just don't know a lot about it. I mean Dad hardly ever talked about who he bought it from or the circumstances. Dad liked to buy land—that's all I really know."

Few families studied displayed mementos or other artifacts. Old farmstead buildings are torn down when "no need" exists for them. One Yankee farmer offered to trace his family history "in just five minutes." History began only with his grandparents. Many had to consult the family Bible even for the names of grandparents. According to one woman, culture accounts for this lack of ties to the past: "We never talked about the past in my family. I'm not sure why. . . . So many people I think when they came here wanted so much to be American. They didn't talk about the places where they came from. They just concentrated on the here and now." When a Yankee—often an elderly woman—was knowledgeable about history, it was usually a personal hobby undertaken, for example, to prove membership eligibility to join the high-status Daughters of the American Revolution.

Because the past is not considered important to meet family goals, it is devalued. "Who cares about it?" emphatically stated an entrepreneur farmer. Entrepreneurs are eager for new experiences, to see the world and reach out beyond the confines of their farming occupation and the community where they live. Farming, family land, and community do not delimit the dimensions of their lives.

THE GERMAN YEOMAN

German farmers are obsessed with land; obtaining, keeping, or transferring it is the stuff of community discourse. Land control allows yeomen to achieve what they consider of highest priority: to own and work a farm. Yeomen are not averse to earning profits, for profits are required to stay in farming. However, profits are not the end desired but a means to maintain continuity of the family name in conjunction with a particular farm within a German community. A yeoman is likely to refer to money as irrelevant: "Money can't buy *this*," be it family land or a family heirloom. For family heritage is not measurable in dollars: "This land is worth a million and a half, but money can't buy this land," explained a yeoman proudly. Family-owned land is a unique, even sacred family trust not parted with easily. Unlike entrepreneurs, who measure status primarily by wealth and farm size, yeomen calculate standing as farmers by emphasizing ownership continuity, numbers of family members farming, and how much acreage is owned.

Traditional yeomen aim to give children an amount of landed wealth that reproduces the accomplishments of previous generations. A farmer said that he retired when he had reached all of his "goals," including "doing for my kids what my dad did for me." He was given two hundred acres to begin farming, as were two other siblings. His obligation was to give what he had received, "all paid for," to his children. Another father described aiding his son with a predeath transfer of acreage: "When he first started out on his own, the land I leased him he got the full profit off. That was just my way to help him get started. The land he inherited from us is all paid up in taxes—so he won't have to worry about that part of it."

Once land enters a family's possession, it becomes sacred. Families believe identity is tied to land. "Your land is really a part of you. Selling it would be like cutting off your arm." That generations of the family have farmed the same land is of great significance to yeoman families. "I've spent my whole life on this section," said a retired farmer proudly. Central to land's sacredness is that ownership assures the family security. An elderly farmer remarked, "My father never said much, but he told me to 'protect your family.' . . . My father was right. To protect your family has turned out to be the same thing as protecting your land."

Yeomen typically view their land goals in the context of a multigenerational family. Explained a retired farm wife, "When you get married two people decide what they want to do—things like owning land and farming it so we would have something to give the kids." Families therefore make an effort to assure there is a farmer to carry on, a process recalled by an eighty-five-year-old farmer: "I went into the service for four years and when I came back, I really wasn't so sure I wanted to be a farmer. But my dad told me that he'd raised me to be a farmer and that's what he wanted me to do. German fathers have a real influence on their sons. What else could I do?" Another farmer, in his fifties, never had any doubts about his life's work. "You know I never even realized that I could do anything else. I started working on the farm—well I can't even remember not working on the farm. I'm a farmer; it was never a question." Yeomen cannot understand why someone would expand a farm with land purchases without having heirs to provide an incentive: "It's too bad to work all your life and have no one to leave it [land] to. It must make you wonder why you did it," said a farm woman about a neighboring bachelor entrepreneur.

Yeomen credit previous generations, by their provision of financial support or a start with family land, for making possible the farming careers of their offspring. When a yeoman farmer now in his thirties graduated from high school, his father bought him a new tractor, plow, and planter and gave him the income from forty acres of family land. "He never planted another row. He said, 'It's your job now, and that's what my dad did when I was your age.'" This farmer emphasized the value of support provided in each generation. "I attribute my success to my father and my grandfather, we all started out the same way. When I was just getting started my grandad would lend me money. It was still a business deal, but at a lower rate of interest. . . . I want to set an example for my kids like my dad did for me and his dad for him." Another farmer referred to his brother-in-law's situation: "At age twenty-five he already owns eighty acres. . . . Now, I think he owes his dad some money, but he doesn't owe the bank anything." Yeoman families are bound by a meaning for land that links the generations through shared obligations. Parents help by passing on land in a manner that enables children to repeat the process and "do for mine what was done for me."

For yeomen the past is the guide to the future, and the present is part of that process. Families have a rich oral tradition that is continually recounted and reexperienced. Even young children in yeoman families know how ancestors settled in Illinois, how each acre of land came into the family, and how the land was farmed. For example, farmers often attribute reluctance to take financial risks to a father's admonitions. As one yeoman explained, "Around here people tend to be pretty conservative about taking on debts. You were pushed to get into debt there for awhile—credit was so easy to get. But the day of recollection [sic] comes finally. . . . I still have a hard time using credit even though that's pretty old fashioned. I grew up being taught not to buy anything you don't have money for—even if you need it." Cautionary tales are recounted about the Great Depression, when farms were lost due to families expanding by borrowing on land. To avoid risk, cautious management and frugality are hallmarks of yeoman management. "Being a good manager is one of the most important things to making it farming. Like when you borrow money, you've just got to be careful. You can't overextend your operation and borrow too much, so that you'll never be able to pay it back. Also, you have to know the right corners to cut when you're trying to save money." Yeomen are risk aversive because heavy indebtedness jeopardizes farm continuity. A farmer who set up all his children in farming proudly commented that the land he owned was "all paid for." According to his daughter, he was "very conservative with credit." The most serious failing is to be a poor manager and lose inherited land by becoming indebted. Land lost is still referred to as family land, even several generations later. A grand-father in one family had lost a large amount of inherited land due to a drinking problem. A neighbor commented that the man's grandson "really wants to farm, but with that land out of the family, it's not easy."

Ideally yeoman goals require expansion; to do for the next generation what was done for you necessitates more land than was inherited, if you have several children. Unlike entrepreneurs, yeomen have a lid on farm growth: expansion is not carried out for its own sake. Explained one of the more aggressive farmers in a German yeoman community: "I didn't start to really expand until I got married and had kids. I'm doing it for them. . . . You just have to go bigger than you used to." These days most yeomen acknowledge they cannot expect to attain the ideal of owning all the land they farm, as did their parents. More acreage to accommodate modern machinery has meant an adjustment in cultural notions about achievable goals.

Yeomen do not take lightly the lifetime process of reproducing previous intergenerational land transmissions. Accumulating more land requires wily skills. Family histories are replete with stories about the outsmarting of naive landowners (usually non-Germans) by obtaining bargain prices. A farmer proudly described his strategy of purchasing land "on speculation" outside the community boundaries and then trading it as parcels became available close to the family homeplace: "I never lost money on a land deal. I always expand, don't ever sit still. I always made money. . . . I trade when I find something larger." This expansionist philosophy had limits, however. When he met his goals, he retired in his late fifties and "stopped buying land," though he continues to help his children financially with land purchases.

An obligation is inherited along with family land: family welfare must be furthered. For this reason yeomen are critical of those who farm for a lifetime but never invest in land. For example, a tenant operator who farmed a large amount of acreage owned by relatives was termed a "fly-by-night" by his neighbor, who claimed with satisfaction, "I've never farmed rental land." He taught his children the same ownership goal. After a first purchase of land, his son said proudly, "My folks have always said land is the best investment."

Yeomen strive to own land within the family's community, and their lives are planned toward this goal. A young yeoman farm wife explained her sentiments: "We were both born and raised on the farm. It's love for the land and farming which keeps us at it; it's sure not the money. We want it to be here for our kids too. So if we both have to work off the farm, plus do all the farming after that just to make it, then it's worth all the hard work so we can stay here." Elderly yeoman farmers are content not to travel far beyond the confines of their community and feel ill at ease when they do. Younger generations cast their nets more widely, but even those that moved elsewhere often return later in life. A farm wife commented about her return after working a few years in a nearby city: "When I was in high school the last thing I wanted to do was go back to the farm, but you know the process of growing up helps you see how good your roots are." Yeomen who reproduce the farm and achieve continuity of family land ownership are content; there is no need to keep on striving. For yeomen successful farming is a way of life experienced within the nexus completed by family, church, and ethnic community.

•

Farming Patterns and Cultural Beliefs

Families farming in the same region with similar soils could be expected to have farms of similar size. However, operating with an entrepreneur rather than a yeoman farming pattern signifies differing land acquisition incentives. Cultural practices shaping enactment of intergenerational land transmission over generations have affected how farms develop among Germans and Yankees. Farm size is the concrete indicator of past family actions. I first compare the size of farms as outcomes of a family land acquisition strategy and then examine production strategies to illuminate the relationship between culture and agriculture.

Table 4.2 delineates the basic demographic and farm characteristics of the seven communities. The farm or operator types listed are U.S. Department of Agriculture categories for land ownership status. A tenant rents all the land in the farm; a part owner owns some and rents the remainder; a full owner owns everything farmed; and a landlord is a full owner who does not farm the land owned. As seen in table 4.2, and in accord with national statis-

Table 4.2. Community, Farm, and Family Characteristics

	Black Prairie				Gray Prairie		Black Prairie
Ethnicity	Yankee	German	Yankee	German	Yankee	German	German/ Yankee
Community	Emerson	St. Boniface	Wheeler	Heartland	Libertyville	Freiburg	Prairie Gem
Population	650	761	950	702	620	1,930	694
% Ethnic endogamy[a]	Y 75, G 25	95	91	97	89	100	G 60, Y 40
Religion	Protestant	Catholic	Protestant	Lutheran	Protestant	Catholic	Protestant
Farm household sample total	81	69	56	89	70	74	103
Tenure category (%)[b]							
Tenant	12	19	20	17	7	8	15
Part owner	43	46	46	42	37	43	34
Full owner	8	7	5	19	11	23	4
Landlord	36	28	29	22	44	26	47
Active operators[c]							
Mean farm size (acres)	514	397	839	309	502	274	616
Range farm size (acres)	35– 1,504	15– 2,033	152– 2,000	75– 1,053	50– 1,005	144– 882	191– 1,943
% Absentee owners[d]	73	52 (Y 55, G 45)	62	32	44	22	43 (Y 67, G 33)

Source: Community surveys.

[a]Proportion of both or one spouse in surveyed households having ethnicity of dominant ethnic group. Ethnicity is disaggregated where a significant mixture occurred; G=German, Y=Yankee.

[b]Numbers rounded, and therefore all do not add to 100 percent.

[c]Includes only tenants, part owners, and full owners.

[d]Calculated according to a one-quarter sample of owners present on a recent plat map and in the rural telephone directory for the area; G=German, Y=Yankee.

tics, part owner is the most common active operator type in every community (Schertz 1979). Landlords do not farm. However, they are frequently tenants' relatives who are retired or widowed but live in the community. Landlords, however, are also outsiders who are land investors. Farms were surveyed if over ten acres, despite whether farm income fully supported the family or was supplemented by off-farm work.

The term *family farm* actually masks a variety of business arrangements that families employ. Partnerships, family corporations, linked family corporations, and single proprietorships are as varied as families vary by developmental phase, size, gender composition, and, of course, wealth. When counting family farms, the Bureau of the Census in the census of agriculture obtains data for the farm and the operator's economic activities, a choice that has led farm women, in particular, to be termed the "invisible farmer." Although the USDA has recently paid attention to women's involvement in the farm, the agricultural census still considers a family farm one that is run by a single operator (Rachel Ann Rosenfeld 1985; Jones and Rosenfeld 1981). This ignores the very nature of a farm family: a kinship group that is also a productive unit. The farm family depends on the labor of male and female heads of household as well as the labor of children. Family members who farm together may not all reside in the same household, especially when a son or daughter involved in the operation is married and has formed an independent household. However, unless the farm is organized as a group of linked independent businesses, it is considered operated by a single nuclear or extended family.

I calculated mean farm size (table 4.2) of the active operators—tenants, part owners, and full owners—as well as the range of size. According to the mean size of operations, farms in the seven communities are comparable to middle-range farms in the Midwest. Establishing what delimits a middle-sized farm is akin to shooting at a moving target; the size is continuously redefined upward by economists and varies by geographic locale and commodity. The 1982 Census of Agriculture for Illinois farms with incomes over $10,000 included only farms that are commercial enterprises. In Illinois this yardstick yielded 71,000 farms with a mean size of 416 acres and a standard deviation of 398. I defined the middle by the Z value + .43 (middle third of a normal distribution). For Illinois this comprises farms between 244 and 587 acres. The boundaries for the middle hold for the county in which three of the communities are located. Mean farm size there is 413 acres, standard deviation is 361, and the range of the middle is between 257 and 568 acres. The means (table 4.2) of farms among the three German yeoman communities fall at the small end of the range of medium-sized Corn Belt operations, while the means of farms among the three entrepreneurial Yankee and the German/ Yankee communities fall at or above the large end of the range. Though the ethnic groups cluster at each end of the range, most farms in all the communities fall within the middle-sized range (Schertz 1979).

A component of land tenure is the extent of absentee ownership. A community's autonomy is affected by how much land is owned by nonresidents whose financial priorities may differ from those of a local landlord. The extent of absentee ownership varies according to ethnicity among the communities (table 4.2). The absentee landlord figure was calculated by cross-checking the local rural telephone directory with the owners listed on the most recent plat map (chapter 1, table 1.2). Because Illinois rural telephone directories cover about a county in territory, if the exact name of the owner was not found, he or she was considered absentee (not residing in the area). The Yankee communities of Emerson and Wheeler have the highest rates of absentee ownership, while the German communities of Heartland and Freiburg have low rates. St. Boniface, a German community with an absentee ownership rate comparable to that of the Yankee communities, has a farm population overwhelmingly German. It also has a majority of Yankee landowners (chapter 1, table 1.2). This discrepancy suggests that the absentee landlords in St. Boniface are likely to be Yankees. Prairie Gem, the mixed ethnic community, falls about midway in its level of absentee landowners, and because 67 percent of those landlords are Yankees (as in St. Boniface), absentee owners are probably Yankees rather than Germans. Only in Wheeler do the few (two or three) German landowners resemble the Yankees by being absentee owners of large land tracts.

•
Cultural Systems and Farm Size

Farm size results from land acquisition strategies developed in the context of a cultural system and the economy shaping local land markets. Consistency of behavior across ethnic groups living in different communities and farming a variety of soils but having similarly sized farms suggests a cultural patterning of behavior. Farm characteristics in the seven communities delineated in table 4.2 show mean operation size larger in the Yankee entrepreneur communities than in any of the German yeoman communities. The higher proportion of absentee landowners in Yankee communities accounts for much of the rental land farmed. Yeoman families say that present farms are larger than in previous generations, so gradual consolidation has occurred in yeoman communities since World War II. Rentals in the past twenty years have also grown substantially, though yeoman landlords are typically relatives (Salamon 1978).

Because land is so expensive, expansion for both types of farmers (as part owners) is dependent on rental acreage, but Yankee entrepreneurs are more dependent on rented land. German part owners (n = 32) rent significantly less acreage than do Yankee part owners (n = 26) (chi square = 19.094, 6 df, p = .004) in both Freiburg and Libertyville. When operations were compared between Libertyville Yankees and Freiburg Germans, acreage rented from others varied significantly. Rental acreage was broken down in eight increments from under 80 acres to over 560. Most Freiburg part owners renting acreage fell into the relatively small 80–160-acre range (72 percent), while most Libertyville part owners fell into the 400 to over 560 range (54 percent). Operation size is an important criterion for judging worth among entrepreneurs and an incentive to expand with rental land. As a Wheeler entrepreneur explained, "The first question people ask is how much you farm. . . . If it's 1200 or so then they want to know how much of it you own. . . . People have always rented in this area. So they assume you always rent some of what you farm; so they don't ask. . . . The size question doesn't bother people. It signifies success, prestige—shows you've grown."

The distribution of operations in all seven communities dramatically demonstrates the ethnic divergence in farm size (figs. 4.1 and 4.2). To determine the size distribution of operations, farms were grouped in intervals of 320 acres (which represents half the standard 640-acre section in the Midwest). In all the communities the distribution was positively skewed with fewer operations at the larger end. Note that the distribution of the yeoman communities (fig. 4.1) peaks in the smallest (0–320 acres) interval and quickly tapers to very few large operations. The largest yeoman operation (St. Boniface) is actually a three-family enterprise so intertwined that it could not be separated. In the distribution of the entrepreneur communities (fig. 4.2) the peak falls in the second interval, 321–640 acres. It is evident that a greater consolidation of farms has occurred where entrepreneurs dominate. In Wheeler, where consolidation has perhaps proceeded the furthest, the grouping of farms actually resembles a bimodal distribution. The lower peak of this distribution is not found in small or part-time farms but among operations falling in the middle and higher ranges for the area. Thus the mean shifts

Figure 4.1. Distribution of Farms by Size among
German Yeoman Communities

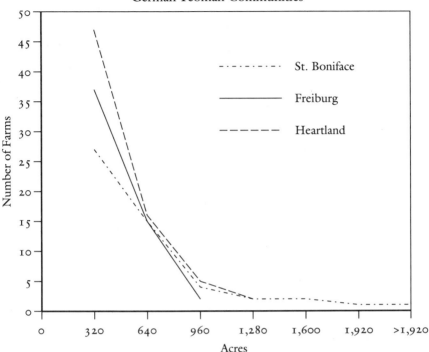

upward among entrepreneurs to bigger operations and a second peak for
Prairie Gem and Wheeler occurs in the large 1,281–1,600-acre range.

Contrasts in ethnic operation sizes are explained by cultural definitions of
the proper "fit" between family and farm. The more capitalistically oriented
entrepreneur forces out sons "because there isn't enough land," a practice that
fits the family (or numbers of family members) to the size of the farm. In
entrepreneur communities (fig. 4.2) the concentration of farms into fewer,
larger operations and numerous small operations coupled with higher levels
of absentee ownership (table 4.2) reflects a trend predicted as inevitable for
U.S. agriculture as the long-term consequence of capitalism and industrial
farming (Buttel 1983; Goss, Rodefeld, and Buttel 1980). The yeoman pattern,
which expands the farm only as far as is required to absorb children, fits the
size of the farm to family numbers. A new school of thought points to the
persistence of middle-range, full-time farms, because operators suit the farm
to family rather than capitalist imperatives, as the future of agricultural structure (Schulman, Garrett, and Newman 1989; Chayanov 1966). Yeoman communities (fig. 4.1) show a distribution that supports this perspective. Yeoman

Figure 4.2. Distribution of Farms by Size among Yankee and
Mixed Entrepreneur Communities

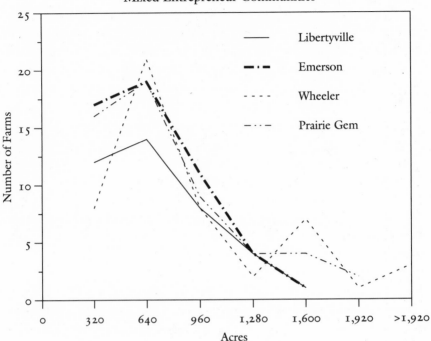

operations are clustered at the small end of the spectrum, and the presence of
less absentee ownership indicates control of community land by local residents. Thus, German and Yankee communities are representative of current
distinct farm-size trends that recall the themes identified historically between
agrarian and capitalistic motives for farming (Atack and Bateman 1987).

•

Cultural Systems and Farm Strategies

In all the communities grain crops are the primary income source, but farm
size suggests whether a family must supplement those earnings. A variety of
options can be tapped when grain crops provide an inadequate family income. Families can farm the land more intensively with other crops or raise
animals in a mixed grain and livestock operation, or family members can work
off-farm. However, the on-farm options require that families work longer
and harder than if they ran a grain-only operation. What strategies families
use to provide the income deemed satisfactory according to their notions of
adequacy further illuminate how the cultural patterns diverge.

BLACK PRAIRIE FARMING PRACTICES

Emerson and St. Boniface are located about thirty miles apart in an area of highly productive, expensive soils. The mean farm size for active operators is 397 acres in German St. Boniface and 514 acres for Emerson Yankees (table 4.2). Where larger German farms occurred, more family land had been inherited. (Smaller Yankee farms in Emerson resemble the St. Boniface pattern; size correlated with the size of inheritance.) St. Boniface families farm almost one-quarter less acreage than do Emerson Yankees and own a smaller proportion of their farms.

In St. Boniface, families were perhaps prevented from expanding by originally arriving later than Germans in the other communities, by having persistent Yankee owners dominant, and by being surrounded by land already in German yeoman hands. Their marginal farms force them to adopt compromise strategies to maintain farming as a way of life and yet meet yeoman goals. St. Boniface families express pride in their ability to survive in a context of competitive agriculture. They live modestly, and farmsteads typically have older buildings. Said a farm wife farming with married sons, "The figures they cite for how much land it takes to make a living are hogwash. Each of our boys started with only 80 rental acres. Even with a family they were each able to make it quite comfortably. It's just a matter of budgeting your money and spending wisely." The sons work off-farm in slack seasons, and hogs are raised; above all, this extended family cooperates in a manner characteristic of St. Boniface but more reminiscent of past farming patterns. The three families pool land, labor, and equipment: "Doing it together is the only way to make it work. . . . Living so close by . . . my husband and the boys can share machinery. Otherwise it would be too expensive for the boys." More than 30 percent of St. Boniface households mentioned joint equipment ownership as a component of their extended family cooperation. Cooperative farming strategies are rooted in yeoman cultural themes that advocate generational interdependence to promote farm welfare.

For secondary income, Germans in St. Boniface resort more to off-farm jobs than to on-farm production (table 4.3). No German part owners (typically working the larger farms) raised animals as a second source of income, while nine Yankees did (chi-square = 11.392, 3 df, p = .009). Nine Germans worked off-farm, however, while only four Yankees did. Wives in both communities account for more off-farm income than husbands but average a similar fifteen days per month. Thus it is husbands' off-farm work (Germans average 7.5 days per month in contrast to Yankees, who average 4.4 days per

Table 4.3. Active Operators' Second-Ranked Income Sources in
German St. Boniface and Yankee Emerson

	Grain Crops	Animals	Other[a]
St. Boniface (n=33)	7	3	23
percent	21	9	70
Emerson (n=42)	3	19	20
percent	7	45	48

Source: Adapted from Salamon 1987.

Note: Active operators include tenants, part owners, and full owners.
[a]Includes off-farm jobs, custom work, social security, and additional side businesses. For example, a German family raises worms; a Yankee household sells firewood.
Chi-square=12.546
2 df, p<.001

month) that produces the significant difference in off-farm income ($t = -2.52$ [37] p<.01). Several St. Boniface farmers work as janitors at night in a nearby city and farm by day. "Three out of four people work off-farm. That's how my dad got through," said one young German operator from a family of six children. Table 4.3 indicates that this yeoman made a highly accurate estimate of family strategies.

It seems surprising that St. Boniface yeomen, with their commitment to an agrarian way of life, chose off-farm work rather than on-farm production for additional income. The explanation lies in the small size of St. Boniface farms and in historical choices. A young farmer reflected that off-farm work is a logical strategy for St. Boniface families due to their land and financial constraints: "Animals take the capital investment. I think that's why more don't have livestock. It's just easier to find a second job." A retired St. Boniface farmer, who was the tax assessor for forty years, showed his 1979 work sheet with no local involvement in livestock. He indicated that a change may be under way: "Quite a few of the farmers are going into hogs—they don't take up as much ground as cattle." Since the survey was done, three or four St. Boniface extended families began new, labor-intensive endeavors. They grow produce or flowers and plants to sell in weekly urban farmers' markets. Such commodities diversify operations without requiring as much start-up capital as would animal production while making use of the dependable labor supply available in large Catholic families.

Another rationale for Germans' choosing off-farm jobs is the expense involved in raising large families. Off-farm jobs provide health insurance among other fringe benefits. Explained a farm wife, "My husband used to work off the farm and I still do. We did it so we could get the machinery paid off, and get the kids through college. It's been a long haul . . . and our youngest is in her last year of college. I think next fall I'll be able to quit." Work, as land, is sought to meet particular yeoman family goals; once goals are met, there is little incentive to pursue further accumulation.

In entrepreneurial Emerson, small operations are looked upon with some disdain; such operators are viewed as those inevitably forced out. One man boasted that six operators formerly farmed "what I do now." Emerson farmers are motivated by efficiency: "You don't want to have unused labor or expensive machinery that you're not working to full capacity." Emerson entrepreneurs try to use expensive machinery optimally on a single farm rather than share it. A son starting farming will share equipment with his father but attempts as quickly as possible to become more independent.

Families in Emerson evolved production strategies that combine grain crops with more on-farm enterprises (table 4.3). Beginning farmers working with their fathers show entrepreneurial initiative in mining every corner of the farm for "new things" with money-making potential. By choosing livestock, Yankee sons diversify with an activity that their fathers always avoided. "Dad never did really work at the livestock; now I've turned it into a money-making proposition," explained a young farmer. Emerson's animal production also indicates sufficient family capital available to finance a costly new initiative. Because sons commonly must repay capital used to finance these endeavors, they begrudgingly allude to the critical importance of family support. Entrepreneurial practices reinforce the search for autonomy and financial reward rather than farm reproduction.

GRAY PRAIRIE FARMING PRACTICES

Although Libertyville and Freiburg are located only twenty miles apart in the Gray Prairie (with less productive and less expensive soils), the mean operation size of active Libertyville Yankees is 502 acres, almost 50 percent larger than that of Freiburg Germans (mean 274 acres) (table 4.2). This is a highly significant difference. Yankees as a group farm larger operations than Germans as a group; almost half the Yankees but fewer than 5 percent of Freiburg Germans farm over 560 acres. Part owners account for the large Yankee operations and base their operations on more rented than owned acreage. Most Freiburg part owners rent in the range of 80–160 acres; in contrast over half the Libertyville part owners rent between 400 and 560 acres. Yankees are clearly aggressively expanding by renting rather than buying land. As an entrepreneurial Libertyville farmer commented, "Most people think bigger is better . . . think you must always expand." The significant contrast in average operation size indicates that Yankees are motivated by differing family goals than are the German yeomen.

The Gray Prairie paired communities reverse the Black Prairie income sources pattern, indicating that yeomen and entrepreneurs can choose different routes to achieve similar cultural goals. Most Gray Prairie Yankees (as in the Black Prairie) have grain crops as the primary source of income, although less than half the Germans do (table 4.4). However, a striking number of Freiburg Germans have mixed farming operations as their primary income source—either dairying or livestock—compared with only a single confinement hog operation among Libertyville Yankees. Almost half of Germans are also involved in livestock or dairy as a secondary income source.[1]

Freiburg and St. Boniface, as German Catholic communities with strong religious commitments, have large families (a trait not shared by Yankees). Families, thus, must accommodate yeoman goals with many offspring, but each community confronts different environmental constraints and opportunities. Because Freiburg has not had access to a city with many jobs, as has St. Boniface, dairying has been the logical choice to establish as many sons as possible in farming. Freiburg families regard dairying as "much steadier and better than anything else" and a rational strategy when a dependable, ample labor supply is assured. "You can't do dairying without enough people around to work, . . . otherwise you never get away," explained a farmer, who as a son and a father has worked with family members.

A number of Libertyville families exploit oil resources rather than animals as a second income source. (Freiburg families decided too much damage was done to farmland for the oil found to make digging wells worthwhile.) One Libertyville family had cattle and hogs in the 1960s, but as one farmer said, "It didn't make much sense because we could make more money from the land [with oil] and didn't have all that work." Animals would indeed be more work for Yankee farmers with smaller families, but in describing their decision-making process, Libertyville operators speak more commonly of animals "not paying" and of hog prices being too low to make them economical and less often of family constraints. If a son is to be brought in, Libertyville fathers

1. The Freiburg yeoman dairying strategy emerged similarly among a community of German Catholics in another otherwise uniformly grain-farm area, Mercer County in western Ohio, according to Calvin L. Beale.

Table 4.4. Sources of Income According to Percentages of Operations in
German Freiburg and Yankee Libertyville

| | First-Ranked Income Source | | Second-Ranked Income Source | |
	German (n=55)	Yankee (n=39)	German (n=44)	Yankee (n=36)
Grain crops	41.8	76.9	38.8	13.9
Animals	12.7	2.6	40.8	33.3
Dairy	27	0	6.1	0
Other	18	20.5	14.3	52.8

Source: Community surveys.

Raw chi-square=18.458   Raw chi-square=17.117
3df, p<.0004   3df, p<.0007

like Emerson farmers opt consistently for developing a separate enterprise
that the son manages, such as trucking, so that he can have independence
within the family enterprise.

Despite a variety of pathways to meet family goals, yeoman farms in both
the Gray Prairie and the Black Prairie are smaller than entrepreneur farms.
Modest yeoman farms are indicative of the limits on expansion dictated by
land practices that tailor farm size to reproduction goals. In contrast, entrepreneur expansionist practices are indicative of land used as a wealth genera-
tor or to meet a production goal. Farms among entrepreneurs at the high
end of the distribution grow too large for one family to operate and must
depend on hired labor, a pattern relatively rare among yeomen.

YEOMAN AND ENTREPRENEUR PATTERNS IN OTHER CONTEXTS

Researchers have found the yeoman and entrepreneur patterns evident elsewhere among Midwestern farmers. One study used a sample of approximately one thousand Illinois families who farm officially designated centennial farms, meaning they are lineal descendants of ancestors who originally
owned the farm at least a century ago (Foster, Hummel, and Whittenbarger
1987, 1989; Khawaja 1989; Salamon 1989). Those of German background were
more likely than those of British background to know about the founding
ancestors and to have increased farm size since founding, but they started
with smaller farms that remained smaller to the present day. Expansion was
at a modest level. British farms were originally, and have remained, larger.
The yeoman pattern was also documented for Midwestern farmers raising

crops other than corn and soybeans. A study of Kansas wheat farmers found higher farm persistence associated with risk avoidance by German ethnics (Jan L. Flora and John M. Stitz 1985).

Thus in various environments and different historical periods, cultural patterns have influenced farm size and the continuity of ethnic ownership. It seems certain that this typology explains actions of a wider population than the seven ethnic communities that served to define it.

During the agricultural boom of the 1970s and the bust of the early 1980s many Midwestern families lost farms. A year after Libertyville was studied, for example, a much-respected entrepreneur failed after using leverage equity too aggressively. Farm loss for an entrepreneur is serious, but it is considered a risk inherent to doing business. However, for a risk-aversive yeoman a small amount of debt is a heavy burden, and loss of family land is a betrayal of past and future generations—a shame one can never live down (Lash 1990; Friedberger 1989). Entrepreneurial energy and flexibility perhaps serve the family well under the circumstances of failure in the same way that the yeoman strategy has adaptive advantage in uncertain times (Salamon and Davis-Brown 1986).

Family relationships, shaped by cultural beliefs about who should control land, are central to the reproduction of a yeoman or entrepreneur farming pattern. Families cannot be assumed to act with consensus regarding this pattern; household members have personal agendas driven by generational and gender differences that bring them into conflict with even so basic a group goal as the continued viability of the farm. Farm households are, like all households, a "knot of individual interests" and make trade-offs between group and personal goals as farms and land are managed, passed on, or inherited (Laslett 1984).

Families have decision-making points at which they negotiate issues of transfer of control over land and at which the farm becomes particularly vulnerable to survival (Carter 1988). Each cultural system deals in distinctive ways with such lifecourse points and families; in the process of producing gender and generational hierarchies shaped by kinship practices, ethnic groups reproduce particular structures of family relationships. The resulting family network of relationships is the topic of the next four chapters, which focus in turn on a nuclear family dyad central to reproducing the farm and then on the connections between the farm family and the community.

PART TWO

Interactional Processes
and Reproduction
of Family and Farm

FIVE

Husband, Wife, and Farm Management

Land is of such importance to farmers that its handling may serve as a metaphor for those aspects of the family system—for example, the gender hierarchy—that are shaped by culture (Broderick 1990). Yeoman and entrepreneur couples share a similar gender ranking of men over women, structurally resembling farm families in the past (Vanek 1980; Fink 1986), that does not, however, translate into conjugal farming teams organized identically.

The conjugal role structure that ethnic groups share derives from beliefs about farming and gender roles, including marriage based on a love choice, the division of labor on family farms, and the structure of community institutions. The husband and wife dyad is premised on exclusiveness and sexuality, with males as providers according to American kinship beliefs (Schneider 1980). Gender inequalities also derive from rural religious institutions. Church teachings reinforce family practices regarding what work is appropriate for women and women's place in the church and the home (Flora 1985). Uniformly on Midwestern grain farms, men are acknowledged as *the* farmers; women are deemed unfit to be farmers, though men always say, "You can't farm without a wife." Men, in addition to being the farmers, also market the family grain and thus control distribution of what is produced (Friedl 1975; Rachel Ann Rosenfeld 1985). Because the producer-manager is the highest family status in farm communities, men control the means for maintaining a superior position in the family and in the community's political hierarchy. Although couples farm together as a team, a potential for conflict exists, due to men's and women's personal agendas and the inequalities of the team structure (Yanagisako 1984).

The kinship system, encompassing rules for obligations, priorities, and rights, is relied on to mediate the inevitable gender (and generational) conflicts that arise over the family lifecourse. The anthropologist Francis Hsu has a model for defining kinship systems that links practices with family interaction patterns (Hsu 1965). He argues that a single, primary relationship in the nuclear family—husband-wife or father-son, for example—is dominant by being elevated and relied on to perpetuate the group. Accordingly, the other family dyads are subordinated or viewed negatively. Great Britain and Germany were strongly patrilineal nations at the time of our groups' immigration. Land was handed down from father to son in much of Germany, although in areas such as East Friesland and Alsace sons and daughters inherited equally (Fischer 1989; Berkner 1976; Conzen 1980a, 1985). Farm families today retain aspects of their patrilineal heritage symbolized by the family name and a woman's name change when she marries, though the father and son dyad is not always the dominant dyad.

The typical kinship system among white, middle-class Americans, however, emphasizes the sexual bond between husband and wife and correspondingly deemphasizes the intergenerational bond between father and son, the reverse of what is central to a patrilineal system (Goldschmidt and Kunkel 1971; Schneider and Smith 1978). In farm families where the husband and wife bond is dominant, resources are considered theirs rather than family property, and children are expected to leave, form an independent family, and produce their own resources. Land is handed down after the couple dies. In contrast, when the father and son bond is dominant, land resources belong to the family line and are handed down from father (parents) to son. Ideally, in this latter (more patrilineal) system the son's hierarchical position takes precedence over the mother's after a father's death, though in reality widowed mothers can wield much power. According to Hsu's model (1965), the family line is inherently discontinuous when the husband and wife dyad is dominant, and the line is continuous over time when the father and son dyad is dominant.

Conjugal roles have a special salience for farm families due to the meshing of residence and occupation—relatively unusual for America. Such integration means family hierarchy is played out continuously between team members. Because the family home is the workplace, a man is generally around as observer of and participant in his wife's domestic domain, just as a woman is privy to the everyday work life of her husband. Farm men are significantly involved in socialization of children, especially preschoolers, particularly during the quiet of winter and summer, when fieldwork does not draw them off the farmstead. While older men are prone to eating breakfast at a local cafe, younger fathers eat all three meals with the family, and management of the farm is the main topic of conversation (Kohl 1976). Correspondingly, women (and children) are involved in farm work. Their availability provides a flexible labor supply, an advantage with the uneven labor demands inherent to a farm's seasonal production. This flexibility has enabled family farms to remain highly competitive with large-scale, industrial farm forms, especially in the Midwest (Reinhardt and Barlett 1989; Buttel and Gillespie 1984; Friedman 1980). Due to economic benefits, such as access to land, potentially gained from a network of relatives, the very survival of the farm can be dependent on a woman's maintaining important kin ties (chapter 8).

While men recognize a woman's input as critical to the enterprise, because the agricultural census is a census of farms, a woman's work was masked if she was married (Haney 1983). Historically, husbands and the agricultural census implied that a woman's work was "helping" because she was not paid and her work largely made the family self-sufficient rather than earned profits. Documentation of farm women's productive labor has, therefore, preoccupied researchers recently (Sachs 1983; Rachel Ann Rosenfeld 1985; Fink 1986; Cornelia Butler Flora and John Stitz 1988). Historically, women's egg or milk money, women's discretionary funds, paid the mortgage in hard times such as the Great Depression (Fink 1987). A recent nationwide study showed that women's production involvement was greater on the smaller farms (typical of yeomen) and less on the larger farms (typical of entrepreneurs), although bookkeeping is still generally a woman's task on all sizes of farms, now as in the past (Rachel Ann Rosenfeld 1985; Vanek 1980).

The connection between conjugal roles and the near social environment of kin and community was first demonstrated in a classic urban study (Bott

1971). Couples with "segregated conjugal roles" in which family tasks are complementary (women having responsibility for domestic and childrearing tasks and men for economic support) have social networks that are sexually segregated and close-knit. Women in these couples socialize most with mothers, sisters, and other female kin, and men socialize with workmates, who are often relatives, fathers, and brothers. All members of such a network know one another well. Couples with "joint conjugal roles" share family tasks and may be dual earners as well. Men theoretically help with housework and child care, although in fact much of such responsibility falls on women. Networks are also joint; couples socialize together with people met through work, church, children, or other links. Individuals in the network typically are dispersed and unacquainted. The close-knit network has been associated for the most part with working-class families who lack mobility and provide, therefore, a stable group of relatives in close proximity. The loose-knit network was connected in the original study with middle-class, mobile professionals who depend on friends for social support more than do couples with segregated conjugal roles. Such contrasts highlight how culture can constrain or open interactional options in the network that links a household to kin and the wider community (Fisher et al. 1977).

Labor is divided because of the complexity of family farming demands. However, theoretical disagreement exists about the basis for the gender division. One hypothesis proposes that the nature of the commodity and the structure of agriculture determine gender roles (Buttel and Gillespie 1984; Tigges and Rosenfeld 1987; Coughenour and Swanson 1983). In this view the class position of families in the local structure of agriculture—that is, operation size, tenure category, and level of indebtedness—accounts for the division of labor. The lifecourse factor, whether family labor is available and what operation phase the family is involved in, is also hypothesized to explain farm family gender roles (Bennett and Kohl 1981). A third alternative argues a consistent pattern of sexism in the U.S., where structural factors caused exploitation of women's labor for the benefit of men, agribusiness, and other institutions (Colman and Elbert 1984; Fink 1986; Sachs 1983). One historical manifestation of exploitation was a denial that women contributed to the farm by the disallowance of the inheritance tax for men whose wives died, although widows were taxed. In all of the studied communities no single denial of their contribution enraged women more than this tax, which has since been altered. These various views all ignore cultural beliefs as a cause of a gendered division of labor.

A farm woman has the potential to affect the farm through contributions of an heir, land, labor, and capital (including income-generating activities and management) (Flora 1981). Additionally a woman's ability to provide ties to a network of kin or community members can affect a couple's team arrangement (Joan M. Jensen 1985; Kohl 1976). Similarly, because the farming couple functions within the developmental cycle of the household, the imperatives of the lifecourse alter the team according to children's ages and their presence in the household (Buttel and Gillespie 1984). As a consequence of shared beliefs incorporating both family goals and strategies for meeting them, farming teams vary consistently within yeoman and entrepreneur families. How these farming teams differ according to a cultural explanation is outlined in table 5.1.

The husband and wife dyad is emphasized in Yankee entrepreneur families. This bond is dominant, according to Hsu, where beliefs emphasize exclusivity, or an unwillingness to share with others, and dedication to individualism (Hsu 1965). Deemphasis on the continuity of a lineal relation with family land is based on notions that connections are considered ended by death. Married couples in entrepreneur farm families see themselves as business partners and expect children to leave the marital household, to spurn parental authority, and to make their way in the world independently. Household and farm resources in this scenario belong primarily to the parents and are rightfully the children's only after parents die. A Yankee farmer calls his wife "my right-hand worker," and couples refer to themselves as a team. "We always shared money. There was never his money and my money," explained a Yankee widow who worked off-farm while her husband was alive. Because the farm is their personal property, parents are under no obligation to involve children in management; Yankee husbands and wives ration business plans shared with children. The father and son relationship may be competitive and acrimonious because the son is not the instrument valued for continuity. The parent-child bond is the less dominant dyad, creating a structure less patriarchal with respect to both same-generation and intergenerational relations.

Continuity, according to Hsu, is a component of a father-son dominant relationship; every son becomes a father and thus a relationship forms one link in an unbroken chain of father and son relationships. Continuity is the yeoman goal, and this priority favors dominance of the father-son dyad that provides a sequence or connection to others. Because of the intergenerational dependence inherent to the dyad, hierarchical lines of authority are clearly drawn and observed—parents need the son (or a child) to assure continuity of the family farm, and the son is dependent on the father, who controls the

Table 5.1. Husband and Wife Dyad and the Management Process

Yeoman	Entrepreneur
Relationship to Farm	
Farm a family possession	Farm a couple's personal possession
Subordinate dyad	Dominant dyad
Conjugal Roles	
Farming team hierarchical	Farming team egalitarian
Women involved in production	Women on large farms not involved, women on small farms involved in production
Women provide production support	Women work off-farm; on farm, women less involved in production support
Women do bookkeeping	Men often do bookkeeping
Lifecourse for Women	
Valued as the heir producer	Heir production not as valued
Subordination during marriage	More autonomy in marriage
Widowhood peak of female power	Widowhood a peripheral status
Lifecourse for Men	
Retirement according to son's timetable	Retirement according to personal timetable

entrance to farming. Authority is male centered, and the son, who embodies continuity by virtue of carrying the family name, is favored. Husbands and wives in this system, according to Hsu, are more reserved toward one another, and more emotionality and closeness may be expressed between father and son. Because a woman is peripheral to continuity, couples may segregate their resources. A husband agrees a wife should keep the land she brings to the marriage under her name and likewise should keep control of money earned from her personal endeavors. As the family instrument for continuity preservation, heirs to the farm may take relational priority over the spouse and be more privy to the father's planning than a wife.

Repetition of a dominant dyad occurs in successive generations as children learn to be adults from parental role models and socialize their children with similar practices. This intergenerational replication causes a rhythm in families, which if examined over the long term, forms a "developmental cycle" (Fortes 1969). The concept of a developmental cycle within the domestic group explains the way changes in residence and household membership are cyclical over time; personnel change, but the potential family slots remain the same. Cross-culturally and historically a characteristic developmental cycle form typifies a society; regularity is an outcome of family lifecourse developments channeled by particular cultural practices (Fortes 1966; Goody 1966, 1976; Laslett 1972). The timing of succession, obligations of one generation to the next, and the designated heir together produce the rhythm of the farm family cycle—observable in the intergenerational transmissions of land processes.

Farm families constitute the building blocks of farming-dependent communities: their conjugal roles are related to the network of relationships that integrates the community; and choices made as a consequence of inheritance practices are key to how the local land tenure system evolves. Heartland and Wheeler provide the illustrative data for the dyad most concerned with farm management.

•

Yeoman Husband and Wife as a Management Team

LAND AND GENDER RELATIONS

Yeomen are cognizant that land is the key to a woman's family status. Despite practicing a hierarchy based on male dominance, parents are committed to giving their daughters land (or its cash equivalent to help buy land) to assure them lifelong security and independence. Expectations are clear in this regard: almost without exception Heartland women keep land inherited in their own names. One husband who forced his wife to sign over her land to him was still critically judged in widespread ritual discourse even years later. "That was her land and it wasn't right," said her daughter emotionally. Though he farmed land inherited by his wife for over thirty years, a farmer still refers to "her land" as distinct from acreage owned jointly or by him alone. Land bought after marriage is typically in both names—symbolic of the couple as a management team. Perhaps parents realize that a male-dominated system has potential for female exploitation, and thus where control of land brings status, a woman is protected by owning her own land.

If a Heartland woman brings land or the promise of inherited land to a marriage, the dominance hierarchy of the team is less pronounced. A woman who brought no land to marriage with a man inheriting a substantial amount, for example, had relatively low status. Her husband expected to be waited on. When I visited, he asked, "Don't you have something to do?"

when she attempted to join our conversation at the table. He was comfortable after she began ironing nearby where she could converse but was kept busy with domestic duties. When I asked to collect her genealogy, she at first demurred, saying only his was important because "that's where the land comes from." Another woman of the same age cohort, however, who came to marriage with inherited cash that financed a large land purchase participated in a very different relationship. She disclosed that her husband had difficulty making decisions and that their purchases of land were at her urging. Her position was strong enough that, though her mother-in-law opposed it, she rebelliously started a Cooperative Extension Homemakers' group. In a single exceptional case where all the land farmed belonged to the wife, she dominated the family hierarchy. "It's her land and when she says something I jump," the husband told us. Our survey was completed only when the wife agreed to participate.

The male-dominated gender hierarchy in Heartland families is connected to control of land but also derives from other cultural practices. According to a retired widow the traditional residence pattern emphasized a young woman's lowly position: "When I got married we moved on [my husband's] homeplace and I had to learn to get along with his relatives because that's where the land was. He was the only son so he had to farm the land; so I had to learn to get used to it. . . . His parents lived just twenty feet from us and they wanted to keep their noses in." While young successor couples no longer share the homeplace, a husband's parents typically provide access to land, and with land comes advice, obligations, and constant monitoring of behavior. One must never appear ungrateful to relatives who are also landlords.

Having sufficient land is important because Heartland families prefer that husbands and wives work on the farm; yeoman goals involve making full-time farming possible for them and their children. A woman commented on why she quit her off-farm job at marriage: "I have a full-time job here. My husband is of the old school, he wants me at home with the kids. . . . He would be lost without me 'cause I keep all the records."

Heartland domestic practices indicate notions of a continuous or lineal relationship with family land. Parents share the benefits of ownership generously with children because land is the family's, not a personal possession. All young couples surveyed in Heartland either lived in family-owned housing, were given land on which to build, or provided a trailer beside the parental home. Those couples farming lived rent free: "The house goes with the farm" is the community attitude. Furniture, appliances, and home remodeling are also supplied by parents, as "our landlords." Though parents love the homeplace, they retire into town when the successor marries and is ready to take over. Couples use savings to finance predeath transfers of land, children's land purchases, and cash securities and insurance to help with estate taxes. Among active operators 20 percent indicated clear instances of gifts or predeath transfers by parents (Salamon and Lockhart 1980).

DIVISION OF LABOR

Couples in Heartland term themselves "farmers" and consider their farm managed by a team, but a team hierarchically ordered and headed by the husband. Women of all ages refer to the busy seasons as when "we're in the fields" and call their team contribution "work," as opposed to mere helping. When a young couple was harvesting, the wife hired a babysitter because it was "cheaper for us to hire a sitter than to hire another man." Heartland women, however, uniformly agree with a comment by a middle-aged woman that the husband "calls the shots," though each team member is understood as vital to the farm.

Heartland families have always employed all members, regardless of gender, in production, for the welfare of the farm. Early farm equipment that required cranking was considered too difficult for these now-elderly women to handle, so their labor in the fields involved nonmechanical work—walking rows of soybeans to pull weeds and detasseling corn. A couple in their nineties, retired prior to mechanization, were proud of "working side by side" through over sixty years of marriage. They related how she did the plowing the year he broke a foot. "Some outsider had come by and thought it was terrible to have a woman in the fields" and reported it to the local newspaper, which photographed her at work. The couple called it "the famous plow picture." The wife commented, "It was not one of our better years; while I was plowing he tried to cook." When daughters only were produced, "They all worked in the fields. I didn't have sons so everyone did what was needed," explained the father. It was such field labor by women that caused an elderly Yankee farm woman, whose land bordered Heartland, to remark with disdain how "Germans allowed their women to work in the fields like animals." Yeoman couples agree that women's involvement occurs because the farm always has highest priority. "When my Dad [now retired] was busy he'd just tell my mother to drop the work for the house and pitch in," explained a daughter approvingly. Production participation by all family members, regardless of gender, is validated by the goal of achieving continuity.

The busy seasons highlight the involvement of yeoman women in production. Advancements in farming equipment now permit women to be more extensively involved in actual field labor. She works under a husband's direction, explained a woman: "I do plowing, disking, and cultivating which are jobs where I can't hurt anything. He does the difficult work such as planting and spreading chemicals." Even young children may not keep Heartland women out of the fields. Complained a mother of two preschoolers, "I hated it that I wasn't able to work as much this fall cause I was pregnant. I could haul corn only about half a day and then I'd have to quit." The next spring she loaded the car with all three children, including a two-month-old baby, when she took food to the fields. This couple farms one of the largest operations in Heartland.

> Some days I'm on the road all day—getting parts, taking meals, and transporting men from one field to another. Our land is so spread out, they leave the machinery in the fields and I drive them to the next field. . . . I have to keep track of who's in which field and how many for meals. In the spring I have two or three men for meals, in the fall five or six. I also haul corn to the elevator in the fall and I get a sitter for the kids. I'd stop home and make the meal, then go back out and haul more corn. . . . I take out a big noon meal, and sandwiches and fruit about four or five, but I don't take out a big supper. No matter how late they work, they can eat when they get in. If they are working late and eat a big supper they might fall asleep and that's dangerous.

Farming patterns reinforce the gender hierarchy. Despite extensive labor involvement, a Heartland woman does not claim any management control unless she is a landlord. However, as bookkeepers most younger women are completely aware of every financial dealing; some even take out production loans for the farm. One woman described her role: "I'm his sounding board. He talks over things with me and I pretty much tell him what he wants to hear. If he really wants to do something, but is a little reluctant, I encourage him. If he has serious doubts, I discourage him. I don't make the decisions, I help him make decisions." A woman seems to be more involved in decision making, even as a sounding board, if the husband (for whatever reason) does not work with his father, as in the case above. Although one husband farmed land obtained mainly from his wife's father, the father consulted and negotiated with him; if the husband wanted something extra or a concession, he had his wife make the request.

Retired couples recall working together differently from the middle-aged and younger couples now actively farming. All older women were once involved in animal care, but few farms now have chickens and dairy cows to supplement farm income. A remarried elderly widow supported her three children from the previous marriage with an egg and chicken route. Another retired farm woman complained about her arthritic knees, ruined from the many cows she milked in earlier farming days. She also kept chickens, and the egg money was critical to the family's expansion even in the depths of the Depression. That a Heartland woman did not entirely control her own egg money testifies to the strength of the yeoman male-dominated hierarchy: "I had some money from my egg route and I wanted to buy some kitchen curtain material and [my husband] said, 'No, we had to save it for land.' I was looking at today and he was looking at tomorrow," she recalled with approval.

With the introduction of more extensive government regulations of egg and milk production in the 1950s, Heartland women terminated these domestic enterprises, though families still keep a few animals for home consumption. Animal production today is typically hog tending or cattle feeding and is done by men. Among active farm families new women's businesses have emerged to replace eggs and milk; cake making, hair styling, and sewing are representative of present productive endeavors. Most women also still tend a large garden, with freezing replacing the ubiquitous canning of a generation ago. Although women may have some command over their income-generating endeavors, the farm demands appear the rationale for their earnings to be absorbed into the common budget, which the husband controls.

Women are perceived as guardians of family consumption with responsibility for savings that allow the land purchases which assure continuity (Kohl 1976). A retired farm woman, part of a team that successfully established two children in farming, described the importance of a woman in household management in the enterprise: "A lot of the success is up to the farmer, how he operates. But he needs a wife to work. If the wife is spending it all, fixing up the house a lot, living too well, extravagantly, they can't save anything. You have to save to make it." Heartland women particularly monitor family expenditures because over half of them are responsible for the farm bookkeeping. Many women of older generations had more education than men, who tended to leave school after eighth grade, "to shuck corn." Boys were understood to learn most about farming by working with fathers. One farmer, functionally illiterate but an astute manager, commented about how fitting was a woman's bookkeeping: "I think women are better at figures, don't you?"

LIFECOURSE

Although as teenagers older Heartland women worked in the community a few years as mothers' assistants, marriage typically came before age twenty to a man a few years older. Women born after World War II spent some time working outside the community, but they stopped when they either married or became pregnant with their first child. Couples realize that farming and social mores have changed, but because as yeomen they value any work that contributes to the farm, they are surprisingly accepting of recent gender role changes. A retired couple are impressed with their granddaughter's team sports. "You know girls do everything now," the husband remarked. "It used to be that women got married, raised a family, and worked at home milking, caring for the animals and doing the gardening. But in town . . . [our married daughter] is working and really likes it," said the wife. The husband considers productive work inherently good: "That work brings more money into the family, and with prices the way they are it helps." Off-farm employment, however, is viewed as critical to the enterprise rather than as a choice for self-fulfillment. "My check put food on the table," explained a former secretary who worked early in her marriage while her husband was becoming established. During the busy seasons she took vacation time to drive a tractor when he needed her. Families at mid-life hope to make a full-time living from farming without off-farm work.

A couple's retirement is seen as joint, as was their previous work as a team. "[My wife] retired when I did because I was able to take care of the animals then [switched from dairy cows to easier feeders], and she could come back into the house," commented a retired farmer. His wife looks back on a lifetime of work with her husband and says, "I felt really good when the boys bought land next to my land. The farm is growing." Heartland women have tended to outlive their husbands. For example, a retired couple in their late fifties showing family photos commented that all the men who "stood up" with them at their wedding were already dead. As a consequence of women outliving men by ten or twenty years, women have the potential to dominate the family hierarchy in their old age by virtue of their control over land.

A widow's duty, as stand-in for her husband and implementor of his wishes, is preservation of family holdings for the next generation. Retired widows are not intent on expanding the farm, although if resources permit, widowed mothers contribute financially to children's land purchases. "What else is money for?" asked a yeoman widow. Younger men are needed to farm the land, and elderly female relatives without sons cede most daily decision making to tenants by essentially conferring a lifetime lease. But widows with landlord status are dominant, at least symbolically, because men depend on them for land. Tenants, whether sons or nephews, must be conciliatory toward female landlords. Consequently men find themselves subordinate to some women in the extended family while ranking above women in the community at large. A middle-aged farmer with three elderly female landlords was described as "very aware of all the women he has to please" (Keim 1976).

Commitment to continuity emphasizes lineal above conjugal bonds across the lifecourse. The man who ordered his wife about as a servant referred to his own father with great warmth and emotion: "I was his right-hand man. I did what my Dad said. When he died he almost took me with him." Yet when he died, his wife emerged as a matriarch. She, as the maintainer of the family farm, controls resources with her "life use," provided in his will. For the first time in her life she speaks expansively about "my land" while at the same time profoundly missing her husband.

•

Entrepreneur Husband and Wife

LAND AND GENDER RELATIONS

Wheeler women commonly come from tenant farm or nonfarm backgrounds and bring no land to a marriage: only one-fifth (21 percent) brought access to inherited or rental land. Such lopsided marital resources do not produce the pronounced male dominance associated with a landless woman's status in Heartland. As the spouse of the farm operator, a woman acquires legitimate ownership rights that take priority over those of a male successor. Contributions of labor, particularly during the establishment phase, also underscore that "we're a farming team," as one wife said. "He didn't marry land, but he married a worker," she explained. Providing a cash contribution to the farm is another way of entitlement to relative management equality. One-third (n = 13) of the women from active farms (n = 40) worked off-farm. When a young farmer spoke as if he had free rein to make financial decisions—"If I want to get some land I'm going to do it, my wife doesn't have a say in it"—he was admonished by an older, experienced aunt: "Oh, yes she does. If a woman's working, helping to pay for it, she has a say in what goes on." Despite limited involvement in the day-to-day farm work, an entrepreneur woman refers to "our" land and "our" equipment and what "we farm"; she assumes a jointly owned enterprise.

Yet entrepreneur women more than entrepreneur men refer readily to joint ownership, especially that land bought through their joint efforts. A semiretired farmer commented on the male conception of land control that ignored access he had to acreage inherited through his mother: "It's so hard to get started in farming unless you have some money behind you. . . . It was easy for me to start farming, because I had a lot of relatives in the area that I could rent land from. We don't rent to outsiders, but to each other. We pass the land on from father to son." Behavior toward children evidences an entrepreneur couple's conception of their land as a personal possession. Wheeler successors are treated as business associates by parents—entitled to enterprise admission but not to special financial considerations. Parents believe harmonious family relationships are premised on businesslike work arrangements. Though an extended family works together, sharing labor does not occasion the frequent "extras" routinely provided by Heartland parents. For example, Wheeler children do not get rent-free housing. One son, successor to a family operation, rents parental farmland and was expected to purchase acreage for a house site. Although the father helped build the house, the young couple footed all the bills. Parents are adamant that each household in the extended family maintain financial autonomy.

When parents bring a child into the farm business, each generation expects benefits from the arrangement. "We cooperate with the kids. We could separate, technically we could have a sale tomorrow . . . but it would be hard on the kids. . . . They wouldn't have some machinery [my husband] and I own. . . . We farm together, but we're not a partnership. . . . This makes us more efficient," explained a woman. Parents are proud of sons farming with them but only involve sons if the operation's size makes it feasible and expansion does not threaten the parents' financial well-being. Furthermore, an entrepreneur couple's perception of a satisfactory level of well-being is higher than that of Heartlanders. It may include winters in Florida, a boat, or an airplane. Profits are expected to be spent by parents first and then perhaps invested in land that will eventually benefit children. Couples feel that they do a great deal to help children, but their assistance is calculated very carefully. Explained a farm woman about their joint operations with sons, "They could get strict with each other and keep track of time . . . but they don't because it helps us if we all work together."

Even though parents intend to pass on their land to children unless a couple has incorporated, children are expected to bear the burden of intergenerational transfer costs. A father whose large estate combined a lifetime of purchases with a wife's substantial inheritance commented on each generation having this responsibility: "The kids will have to come up with a quarter of a million for taxes. . . . We had to come up with $50,000." Children expect that parents will use profits from the farm for themselves because each generation must look out for itself. A son working with his father on land in the family for four generations appreciated that his parents were doing something out of the ordinary: "If it weren't for us wanting to farm dad would have sold out and been in Florida fifteen years ago."

DIVISION OF LABOR

Couples in Wheeler think of themselves as partners, but farming is the husband's job. When asked about the operation, a farmer's wife said, "I don't know nothing about the farm so you'll want to talk with him." Rather than saying "we're in the fields," during planting or harvesting women say that "they," the men, are. In the large operations run by extended families found in Wheeler, "they" can be a father and sons, several siblings, or even cousins, with the kin team frequently supplemented by a hired man or men. Those Wheeler wives whose husbands run larger operations may not drive a truck or tractor even during the busy seasons, despite an active participation during their early farming years. Transformation of some operations into pure grain farms in the past two decades ended some female involvement, for prior to that time families raised livestock, and women were absorbed in their care. Wives of smaller or middle-sized operators are more likely, as among Heartland yeomen, to provide production support such as driving trucks to the grain elevator. One woman typified herself as the farm "go-fer."

Wheeler women who do fieldwork are the exception; one instance occurred when a couple had no children farming and a wife preferred animal care and fieldwork to housework. Commented another farmer on the atypical example of a woman working side by side with a husband: "She's a real hard worker. I don't think she knows how to clean on the inside of the house, though. She takes care of all the animals and kind of runs everything else too. She's kind of in charge up there." If a woman is involved in production, logically she must control management, because the operator is the manager in Wheeler. Though the housekeeping comment had some basis in fact, the judgment implies the inappropriateness of overlapping conjugal roles in production. Interestingly enough, among Wheeler's farmers is a woman who succeeded a father despite having a brother; this is a phenomenon unlikely to happen in Heartland. Not having an entrepreneurial management style, however, this woman is content to work her inherited acreage, too small an amount, perhaps, for an entrepreneurial man to consider viable. Alternatively, wives of larger operators, like urban women, sometimes choose to work off-farm for self-fulfillment, particularly after their children have matured. These women have nothing to do with the farm.

Wheeler women married to larger operators work but favor nonfarm jobs that contribute cash to the operation (average farm size of 13 working women is 748 acres). A middle-aged wife of a large tenant operator said, "I've always had to work." She has held a series of secretarial jobs in nearby communities; recently she became an entrepreneur with a home-based cosmetics sales business. Teaching and nursing are other typical jobs held by Wheeler women. Even extended family support can, entrepreneurially, become a cash-producing activity. A grandmother, whose sons farm in a cooperative arrangement with their parents, babysits for the grandchildren while the daughters-in-law work off-farm. Comments on her charging kin reflect the conception of appropriateness of cash exchange among entrepreneur families: "There are some people who would think it's crazy that I take money for watching my grandchildren, or, they would say I shouldn't give up my free time to watch them. But by watching them we are helping each other. It's important to protect ourselves." Providing extended family aid is important, but labor should be financially rewarded even among kin.

A consequence of many Wheeler women working off-farm is that even those without jobs do not provide the domestic support taken for granted in Heartland. Two nonworking women with grown children mentioned having been "the only ones around here who took dinner to the field." However, neither furnishes the noon meal any longer, although they might take out drinks and a snack in the late afternoon. Recently, two related families combined operations, which ended one wife's bringing dinner to the fields as she had when the couple farmed alone. Typically, family exchanges are calculated in financial terms: "[My cousin's] wife works part-time and she can't take food out to the fields. So [the men] decided I shouldn't either. Some days I'll go to the cafe and pick up something to take out to them, but that's all." Abdication of women from meal provision has helped keep Wheeler's cafe in business. The shift was noted by the oldest, retired farmer: "More men nowadays come to town to eat because more women are working." At noontime the cafe, except during spring and fall, is filled with men talking farming who do not seem unhappy about eating out with other men.

Retired Wheeler women, but not many younger farm women, reported keeping the family books. This lack of involvement means that entrepreneur women have only a general idea of the farm's economic situation and little knowledge of day-to-day finances. Women could not supply past or present details about acreage in the operation: "I'm not sure, you'll have to ask my husband" was a common response. Assumption by men of the previously feminine bookkeeping task appears connected with consolidation and the entrepreneur's growing dependence on rental land. Commented a farmer on the shift to more tenancy, "Just to be a good farmer is not enough anymore. . . . People want someone who does their work well, keeps good records. Landlords really want a good businessman." When engaged in rental-land competitions held by farm managers representing absentee landlords, farmers must produce the books and be conversant about all management details. "Used to be that . . . landlords wanted tenants who had the biggest and best equipment in the area. . . . Now, landlords want somebody who's a businessman, a thinker," said a young farmer. If a wife kept the books, a farmer might lack familiarity with details and be handicapped if forced to ask her for information in negotiations with potential and actual landlords.

LIFECOURSE

During the establishment phase of farming most couples referred to women working alongside men by providing field support, running errands, and, of course, caring for the home. The cultural scenario is clearly aimed at men running a sufficiently successful enterprise that woman's labor does not have to be depended on. Even tenant farmers employed hired men. The absence of women in production can be explained by recalling the Yankee woman's equating fieldwork by Heartland women with treatment as animals.

Once the enterprise grows and sons mature, women can become almost extraneous to the day-to-day working of the farm. During the busy seasons it is striking how little women are involved on large Wheeler farms, especially women with mature children and no off-farm employment. While her family harvested, a woman attended her weekly Christian women's group meeting in a nearby city. Another was preoccupied during planting season with re-decorating the house in anticipation of a family event. A third said, "I've been going to the coffee shop a lot in the afternoon out of sheer boredom." In each case, sons worked with the father full time; additionally, these large operators relied on full-time hired men rather than use a wife's available, free labor. Despite women's participation during the establishment phase, on the whole a wife's contributions are not cited as invaluable to the farm. A man without a wife can farm in Wheeler, although he would have more difficulty keeping house. Because a woman does not work directly under her husband, she controls her own time; she can be quite independent.

The status of widows in Wheeler differs greatly from that of Heartland widows; this difference is related to diverse conceptions of land ownership. Although several tenant operators in Wheeler have farmed the same land for three generations, each time the land is transferred to a new generation of owners, the family's situation becomes unpredictable. As the widow of a tenant, a woman is particularly vulnerable, for the house goes with the farm—even if she has lived in it her entire married life. A tenant farmer's wife complained, "You never know in farming. . . . If you don't own your house you don't know, if you don't own your land, you don't know." After being effectively shut out of management, widows of large landowners are ill equipped to run the farm. Dependence on a son to manage the farm prevents a widow, despite being the landowner, from exercising the power usually connected with control of land.

Though gender roles among entrepreneurs appear less hierarchical than those among yeomen, over the full lifecourse, control of land is what ultimately defines a woman's status. During the active farming years yeoman men control land and are dominant, but among entrepreneur families partnership and ownership ideals, superficially at least, involve more egalitarian roles and provide women a great deal of autonomy. Retirement and widowhood point up the reality of the gender hierarchy among both groups, after the son-successor takes over daily management of the farm.

Yeoman beliefs emphasizing a continuous relationship of family with land carries with it status implications for a woman. A woman is important first by producing an heir. As widows Heartland women come into their own as more powerful personages in families that have achieved yeoman ownership goals. The key to their status is their assumption of control over land as widows and their previous involvement in farm management. With life use provided in a husband's will, a widow cannot sell any land, but she can control full management of the farm. As the maintainer of the family patrimony a widow represents her husband's (and her own) wishes, and she is a force to be reckoned with. Women in their eighties also live independently in Heartland due to their retaining at least eighty inherited acres in their own name. Land bought with a husband might be transferred to children at a husband's death, but land inherited from her family is retained by a woman. Commented a widow who felt "degraded" by others as she struggled to manage the family holdings, although eventually she was highly regarded: "I've learned to ignore things because I own land, and people respect that regardless of what they say."

The entrepreneur beliefs that shape a discontinuous relationship of family with land essentially make a woman extraneous to the enterprise once she is widowed. Because each generation attributes success to personal endeavors and parents expect successors to pay estate taxes, a son is not beholden to a widowed mother. Furthermore, the emphasis on tenancy as a strategy to expand farms or simply as a way to farm places a woman in a particularly peripheral position as a widow. If a couple farmed as full tenants, once a husband dies, a widow controls no land. A son, not his mother, must deal with the landlord to maintain management continuity. Thus, widowhood in Wheeler is not the peak of a woman's status, which is possible in Heartland. The next chapter is focused on the succession process, with emphasis on the developmental cycle formed by yeoman or entrepreneur cultural beliefs about which generation rightfully controls family land.

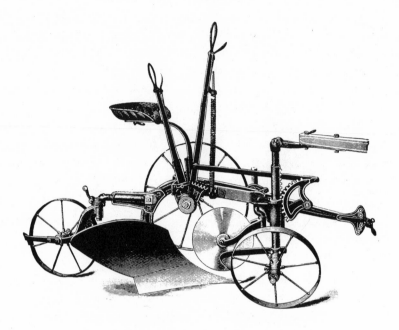

Father, Son, and Farm Succession

Agricultural folklore says that for a man to enter farming he must either inherit land or marry it. The grass roots wisdom about farming entry acknowledges that a family farm is produced by multiple generations and that succession of a father by a son forms a single link in a chain of intergenerational transfers. Without substantial family support that provides access to land, use of equipment, and time to apprentice, a farmer is disadvantaged (Mooney 1988). Clearly, folk wisdom assumes a model of succession by males with farm backgrounds (Beale 1979; Lieberson and Waters 1988). Where grain farming is dominant, as in the Midwest, farmers indeed are almost all male, and succession goes from father to son (Rachel Ann Rosenfeld 1985; Kalbacher 1982; Scholl 1983; Ross 1985). Whichever dyad dominates the nuclear family affects the succession process. For example, how a potential heir is viewed—as one's "bread and butter," according to a Heartland yeoman, or as an interloper, according to an Emerson entrepreneur who feels that "kids today think they should have immediately what it took some thirty years to acquire"—shapes the changeover of the farm's management. Though the process emphasizes the relationship between father and a son, the mother, brothers, and sisters are crucial to the eventual outcome of succession.

Continuity, according to Hsu (1965), is implicit to the father-son dyad, because every son becomes a father. Due to the intergenerational dependence inherent to the father-son dyad, hierarchical lines of authority are clearly drawn: a father needs the son (or a child) to assure continuity of the family farm, and the son is dependent on the father, who controls his entry into farming. Yeoman families are thus male-centered, with the son, who embodies continuity by virtue of carrying the family name, being favored. Intergenerational discontinuity, in Hsu's model, is inherent to the parental dyad being dominant; accordingly the successor does not receive favored treatment among entrepreneurs. With dominance of the husband and wife dyad the entrepreneur family structure is less obviously male-centered with respect to both same-generation and intergenerational relations.

Cultural schemes determine which generational hierarchy and which gender hierarchy is enhanced by succession, when management transfer occurs in the lifecourse, and whose rights to land are favored. Yeoman practices that elevate in importance the father-son dyad above that of husband and wife ideally transfer control of the farm in conjunction with a timely and orderly parental retirement. For example, in a yeoman Heartland family the father doted on his successor and confided in his son more than he confided in his wife. In contrast, entrepreneurs emphasize the parental ownership of the farm and family land and deemphasize what they regard as a child's premature claims. Early succession is not of highest priority, and parents plan estates and land transfers according to their own concerns. Parents in Prairie Gem, for example, say, "I'm not going to leave my money to my children because I intend to spend it all." Considering the farm as their personal property, parents are under no obligation to retire or to involve children in plans; those who control family land are entitled to spend the profits.

CRITICAL DIMENSIONS IN THE SUCCESSION PROCESS

Entrepreneurs subscribe to a kind of "credential" system in which a son must earn succession, proving his worth by accruing what parents consider appropriate achievements. Yeomen have a "sponsored" succession in which the parents aid and guide a son in acquiring the means and skills to enter farming. Final responsibility for succession, therefore, rests with a different generation in each group. This and the other dimensions of the succession process are outlined in table 6.1.

Transfer of the farm to a successor varies along a set of common dimensions for yeomen and entrepreneurs. First, a family context for the process is cast by the end goal. Yeoman socialization to create a commitment for continuity is similar for all children. By inculcating all children with the same goals, yeomen aim to assure support of the successor by other siblings. Continuity ideals are translated into yeoman parents' embracing responsibility for realization of the goal. Succession in this context is assumed. A middle-aged Heartland farmer said, "We always stayed at home, a part of the family. We didn't know anything else. The parents stressed the farm. They didn't want us to leave. They wanted to keep them in farming." A yeoman successor is also welcomed. A fifty-two-year-old Heartland father remarked about his twenty-two-year-old son who lives at home and works on the farm, "I wish he'd get married so I could retire." Another spoke about his retirement at age sixty-five being linked to maturity of his successors: "I knew when my kids were ready to take over."

Entrepreneurs socialize all children to value individualism and autonomy. A son's having begun to farm does not make his succession a foregone conclusion. Entrepreneur sons must enter a rigorous apprenticeship that produces enterprise-tested successors who have proved themselves aggressive. Even so, the successor may be resented if entrepreneur parents are not ready to retire and share control. For example, it is relatively common among entrepreneurs to keep a son on a salary, as opposed to the independent operations set up for yeoman heirs. A young Emerson farmer, after graduating from college, worked away from home, but after six years he returned to farm, discouraged by parents from returning before that. His father before him had also been refused permission to farm after graduating from high school; the parents advocated more education. In defiance, the father set up an independent operation on a neighboring farm. "He never did own any land until his father's death," said the son, "but eventually he showed his dad he could do it and they started to farm together."

Retirement is a form of family support; its timing either bestows or withholds aid for a successor. Timing of succession, a second dimension that separates yeomen and entrepreneurs, is connected to a father's retirement

Table 6.1. Fathers and Sons and the Succession Process

Yeoman	Entrepreneur
Family Context	
Farm tailored to family	Family tailored to farm
Sponsored system of succession	Credential system of succession
Succession assumed by parents	Successor must prove worth
Succession a family concern	Succession a personal choice
Parents encourage successor with support	Parents do not actively encourage successor
Who Is Favored in Family	
Male successor obviously favored	No specific heir favored, son expected
Siblings can be exploited in favor of successor	Potential exploitation of successor by parents
Succession	
When son ready	When father ready
Early retirement	Delayed retirement
Outcome is predictable	Outcome is ambiguous
Results of Process	
Successor usually produced	Successor often absent
Young remain in community	Young out-migrate early
Informal business agreements	Formal business arrangements
Easy access can make unambitious successors	Apprenticeship hones aggressive successors

from management control. A father's delay or acceleration of his retirement affects his successor's autonomy. Continuity implies that the farm belongs to the family, and as a yeoman goal favors an orderly retirement, as early as age fifty-five in Heartland. The motivation to retire is not strong among entrepreneurs because the farm is considered a personal possession. Retirement for entrepreneurs is tailored to when the father is ready (which can be never, but seldom before age sixty-five) rather than when the son is ready to farm independently. According to an Emerson farmer, "Almost all owners are actively engaged with the business until their death. Let me put it to you this way: What are you going to retire to?" His wife added, "If you retire you die. It's as simple as that. And most of the people around here would rather work themselves to death than rest out." For yeoman successors, parental support is predictable and assumed. Entrepreneur successors eventually receive support but seldom feel secure about counting on it.

Which heir is favored for succession, a third dimension of variation to the process, is linked to the dyad made dominant by the kinship system and beliefs about land. Ideally, all children in yeoman families should be set up in farming, but this has proved difficult to achieve with expensive Illinois land and the increase in farm size. A male child always takes over the homeplace because the family name must be preserved with the land. But the yeoman practice is not a "stem family" system because, as described in the next chapter, all children now inherit equally (Brooke 1970). The successor, however, is a favored child among equals. Those now farming in yeoman communities were the recipients of family support; those not chosen for reasons of birth order or ability are not around to tell their side. One bitter Heartland oldest son, farming elsewhere, commented sarcastically from his perspective about the favoritism given the successor: "Yeah, the younger one rode along while the older one worked and then the younger one got the land and homeplace because the older one left to get married." Although ideally yeoman daughters marry farmers and are established by parents on farms equal in size to the homeplace, a Heartland daughter married to a nonfarmer outsider, as the product of yeoman socialization, expects her brothers to receive all the family land. "I haven't put anything into the farm for years; why would I get anything back? Even when we were kids it was the boys who did the work."

Because for entrepreneurs the profit motive is primary, business goals dictate family choices. Moreover, entrepreneurs are reluctant to fragment farms to help set up more than one child. If one son begins to farm, typically the oldest, a father is disinclined to involve another. In one Wheeler family with three sons, the oldest chose to farm, and this precluded involvement of the other sons. A second son working at a full-time nonfarm job was permitted to join the family enterprise only after independently obtaining sufficient rental land to support his family. Because chances of further land acquisitions were slim for the third son, the parents encouraged him toward another career. This easing-out process affected this son's involvement in the farm, as he explained: "When I was in high school I saw the writing on the wall. . . . I used to help Dad when I was little, but then I didn't even help him because I knew I wouldn't be able to farm. I couldn't come back here now and farm by myself because . . . I wouldn't know how." According to an eldest Emerson son working with his father, another sibling's desire to farm cannot affect good business decisions: "It goes back to that problem of having your equipment, labor and acres farmed all mesh. Dad and I have reached the efficiency point now. . . . I'm all for giving [my younger brother] a chance to get in, but . . . I'm not going to just roll over and play dead on account of [my brother's] wanting to farm."

Entrepreneur parents do not actively encourage sons to succeed, and they insist on a long apprenticeship; they do not communicate whether succession is certain by signaling the end of the testing period. "Farmers, though, never suspect that there won't be someone to take over," commented an Emerson daughter about the problems with this process. She went on: "Sons feel held back and periodically they have to vent their frustration. There's a lot of conflict in the families over that issue." Entrepreneur sons speak as if it is the job of farming, its challenges, rather than family pride that motivates them to farm: "I love to farm. . . . The rewards are hard to explain. . . . But there's time to look and see. When things get too much, you can go out and dig in the dirt. And the isolation—that's a different trip. I guess the big thing is freedom—the freedom to do what you want, when you want it. . . . You're on your own, with no one to guide you, no one to tell you what to do and when to do it." Individualism as the strongest motive attached to farming allocates family factors to secondary importance in parental decisions about succession and retirement and in a successor's commitment to farm.

Differences between entrepreneur and yeoman succession processes are explored in Libertyville and Freiburg, with the focus on one child, the successor. These two communities present a great contrast. Freiburg has larger families with potentially more sons to deal with and the smallest farms of the seven communities. Libertyville, with larger farms and smaller families, keeps fewer of its sons. The succession process is part of the explanation.

LIBERTYVILLE: THE ENTREPRENEUR SUCCESSION PROCESS

Fathers seem to think succession just happens, rather than being planned to happen. Libertyville couples frame the farming team as "her and me" or "it's us," meaning the husband and wife, to whom the farm belongs. A son is expected to choose an independent way. Accordingly, a son echoes the parents: "Farming, why I chose it? I had other options, but I chose this life." His choice to farm makes it the son's responsibility to be the business subordinate—not the parents' to transfer the farm to him. Libertyville farms with intergenerational continuity frequently reflect a succession that took place after the death or incapacity of the father motivated a son to give up another career. A son may not see a team position in the picture of "her and me," particularly when the only opening is also the lowest position in the enterprise hierarchy. However, even fathers reluctant to retire seem sad if a son does not somehow overcome barriers and want to succeed him.

Respect for a son's individuality structures the social context for Yankee succession. Parents hesitate to pressure a child to take over the farm, even when they desire it: "We think each person is an individual and you shouldn't force a choice," said a father. Moreover, if a son cannot develop professionally on his own, he may be suspect as lacking achievement motivation. A retired farmer, whose son was not a successor, reflected on his characteristic non-agrarian goals: "Mainly to make a living, pay taxes and debts, and raise the children—that was a full-time job . . . trying to make good citizens out of my children. . . . Neither have been in jail so I suppose I succeeded." His children, he says, have an attachment to the family land, but not as a heritage: "They will want to keep the land, I'm satisfied of that. They won't sell. Both say if you've got a little piece of real estate it makes your credit look good." His comments reveal no disappointment voiced over their leaving farming.

Entrepreneur notions about sufficient land needed to support a family affect how children are socialized. The cultural definition of "adequate" family land controls whether a son is encouraged from an early age to farm. What is sufficient land for a German yeoman family is insufficient for an entrepreneur envisioning a retirement with winters in Florida. Correspondingly, Yankee parents consider the farm a personal possession that assures their independence in old age; becoming dependent on children is a terrible worry for entrepreneurs.[1] Thus, an entrepreneur often sends an ambiguous message to children. With the same amount of land resources, a yeoman family would socialize for farming commitment, making it more likely that at least one child would stay.

Fewer than five farms in Libertyville have sons involved. It is commonly believed that most young people leave because too little farmland is available. "The children can't stay. No way. In the first place they can't get the ground to farm," commented a retired farmer who owned only two hundred acres.

1. I draw heavily, for themes inherent to the Yankee succession process, on the master's thesis of Dwight James Penas, "Always Settling, Never Settled." The thesis was based on a field study carried out in Emerson. Also see Salamon, Gengenbacher, and Penas 1986.

He and his wife are proud of their two professional children: "We didn't discourage them, but we didn't encourage them either. We let them make their own decision," said the father, verbalizing a characteristic entrepreneur attitude. Abandoning the farm is rationalized as the best financial decision. "We're glad our kids didn't go into farming. It's too hard a life and with the cost of farm machinery and everything I'm glad they're out of farming. . . . We hope our kids keep the land as an income," said this couple. So few successors in place or hoping to return suggests weak Yankee parental pressure to adopt farming as a career.

Parents in Libertyville act ambivalent about whether they want a successor. On the one hand, fathers whose sons leave often sound wistful. "I would've liked for my boy to farm. I think I would have enjoyed that, having a working relationship with him. . . . I knew he wouldn't farm by the time he was twelve years old. . . . He did chores because his dad told him to, but his heart wasn't in it," recalled a retired farmer. Yet the same man says leaving was the right choice because farming is a hard and economically unrewarding life. Similarly, another farmer still active said, "I'd like for [my son] to farm with me, but he always had better jobs than farming." On the other hand, even when a son chooses farming, fathers seem unsure about their permanent commitment. A farmer with two sons involved said proudly, "All the kids could make a living [without the farm] if they had to on their own. What they do later depends on them. They can spend [their income from the farm] on land, or use it to make more. . . . It's okay by me."

Libertyville farmers agree: "A young person can't start on his own anymore. He has to have some backing—a parent or other relative." Parents consider, however, that their achievements resulted from personal efforts and that sons therefore should not be given anything outright. In one extended family operation with two sons involved, both boys began to farm twenty acres while still in high school. Explained the father, "I gave them the choice of two financial plans. Either they could finance it by themselves [with a bank loan, for example] and keep all the crops, or I would rent the land to them and furnish seed, fertilizer, and machinery and they would give me one-third of the crop." The boys chose the latter plan. When each began to work full time, he received additional rental acreage. Furthermore, the father formed a partnership in a hauling business, when one son married, in which machinery is jointly bought and expenses and profits are shared equally. Despite the sons' involvement, the father implies uncertainty about whether they will remain farmers. Those Libertyville farmers with successors provided sons similar substantial parental resources early; those not making clear signals with encouragement or resources lack a successor.

The Father and Son Working Arrangement

Sons concur with parental expectations that they should earn the right to farm. "Farming should be just like any other business. It took me six years of off-farm work to get where I could go into farming. I wanted it. But just because I wanted it should it be handed to me on a silver platter?" commented a son involved in an extended family operation. Libertyville families with positive feelings about joint operations have negotiated formal business arrangements to assure an equitable exchange of labor, equipment, and land. "Our oldest son is farming with us," said a full owner of five hundred acres whose son owns sixty acres and farms independently. He "trades his labor for the use of my equipment. I need him and he needs me, so we both can survive. It's the old American system . . . trade something you do have for something you don't have." At another farm, two sons work with a father using a complex, unwritten agreement. To equalize the effects of each man controlling a different amount of land, an elaborate system of dividing the crops and the marketing profits was devised. However, if a son believes the father exploits him by delaying retirement or denying a fair share of resources, the partnership may flounder though succession has begun.

Good working relations prevail if the intergenerational business arrangement allows a son dignity through gradual assumption of decision making, after he proves himself capable. In one family the father as the largest landowner has the final decision, but the sons characterized their decision-making process humorously as "kind of a dog fight," meaning that a hot debate transpires. By going to college and by gaining some off-farm work experiences in agribusiness the sons won their father's respect, and they in turn respect his experience and wisdom. After a few years, this father-son operating agreement is still viewed positively by all members, and a successor is guaranteed.

Without a precise business arrangement entrepreneur families develop rancorous relationships. Entrepreneur sons resist parental demands based on what is best for family welfare because such concerns thwart their individuality and, moreover, are unbusinesslike. A Libertyville father, now retired, attempted to farm jointly with his two sons. According to the son now in control his brother was a lazy ne'er-do-well who took but gave nothing to the farm. Furthermore, the worker-son had an unwritten partnership that abused him "as a slave." A stormy relationship resulted in the capable son leaving and returning several times when the father lured him back with promises of a written operating agreement. Peace came to the extended family only after negotiations forced out the lazy brother and retired the father.

It is difficult for entrepreneur fathers to retire, given their individualistic ownership claims on the farm. Life is justified by hard work and being busy—both equated with making money. If they are not working and making money, Libertyville farmers feel useless and sinful—a sort of death in life. Explained a younger farmer about the older farmers, "People here believe if you're physically active it makes being alive more worthwhile and you live longer. . . . There is a belief that retirement is one step away from the grave." Thus, a son's succession affects a father's ability to control his own life.

Retirement is at the root of many conflicts when the generations labor together. The family embroiled in the succession dispute described above was considered the Libertyville norm by the son's bitter wife: "The sons work hard, but the fathers won't change their ways. You can't teach an old dog new tricks. The fathers insist on doing everything their way and eventually the sons can't hack it anymore, and they leave. It's a matter of control. The fathers control the money." She crystallizes an entrepreneur's perspective by equating power with control over money rather than land and by characterizing farming as a personal choice rather than a family concern. "The fathers they just won't quit. They can't really. It's their whole lives." She went on to identify an entrepreneur's developmental cycle (Goody 1966, 1972): "Anyway it repeats generation after generation. Each set of sons say they won't do it to their boys, but then they do the same exact thing. The sons become fathers and their sons end up feeling the same way."

An articulate man who returned to Libertyville because his father died suddenly at fifty-five years of age sums up the generational hierarchy at the base of family strife among entrepreneurs: "The independent attitude of farmers makes 'em incompatible with their own children, unless a business is so big and complex that a son can take over a part. Otherwise it's a clash as to who is in charge; who makes the decisions. . . . If the son stays working with the father, he is in a very subordinate, dependent position. He can try and fit in, become a hired man and bide his time, but he's under the father."

Generational conflict is inherent to a Yankee family, due to childrearing practices as well as fathers' attitudes about farming. A Libertyville father started a farm-related business to involve his son in the operation and still controls both. His son now jokingly says, "I thought this was supposed to be fifty-fifty, but I don't seem to make any of the decisions around here." But the situation begins to grate once the son proves himself and the father gives up no power. In the words of a middle-aged consummate entrepreneur, "[Sons are] raised to be kicked out of the nest, to take responsibility. . . . It's the young bull trying to root out the old bull. . . . The only way a young male can survive [working with a father] is to be totally subordinate. . . . You can't have two independent people running the same business . . . and the father won't move over." This farmer would prefer that his teenaged son take over, but he feels his son must first develop his unique talents independently. What is eventually guaranteed, he feels, is that the son will share ownership of their centennial family farm with other siblings. However, being successor to this century of heritage did not prevent the farmer from heavily leveraging the farm for production loans. Entrepreneurs believe that a farm belongs to the operator, who can do with it as he sees fit—even lose it. Farms do not belong to the next generation until control is actually transferred (Wilson 1988).[2]

Entry into the entrepreneur family operation is never assumed by sons or fathers. The credential approach to succession means that sons often leave and earn an entry by achievements in the outside world. Even substantive business achievements, however, may not hasten the loosening of control by a father. Yet, the credential system effectively spurs sons with entrepreneurial inclinations to prove themselves, which benefits the farm. However, if a father does not reward accomplishments with concessions that translate into independence or some control, the credential system embitters a son and divides families. Thus the credential system does not assure that there will be a successor, even when both parents desire one and subtly communicate this to a son. The few Libertyville fathers and sons working together point up the family gamble inherent to this succession process.

FREIBURG: THE YEOMAN SUCCESSION PROCESS

Freiburg farmers exude love for farming and the agrarian way of life, and they transmit this love to children (Rogers 1987). According to a farmer with a teenaged son he expects will farm, "The desire to farm is something you

---

2. A similar pattern of reluctance to retire and give up control is reported for modern, Irish Protestant large farmers, the descendants of the cultural ancestors of Yankee farmers, in Wilson 1988.

learn—like you learn religious beliefs." While an agrarian ethic does not preclude yeomen wanting to make a profit, profits are not typically cited as the end desired, but more the means to an end. "The money's immaterial. I want a comfortable living for myself, but the main thing is that it's something I've put together and I want to see it stay together. It's something from the past, and what I really want is to make sure it keeps going. I'd like to come back in five hundred years and see what my great-great-great grandchildren've done with it and see if maybe they've built it up two or three times what it is now," reported a middle-aged Freiburg farmer who has produced a committed successor. Preserving continuity by sponsorship of the next generation is an obligation inherited with the family land.

The socialization process that reproduces committed yeomen is both overt and covert. In the past a Freiburg family was dominated by an autocratic Germanic father. Large Catholic families had many sons; if one could not submit to the father, another wanting to farm would. "They were dictators that's what they were," commented a farmer with an uncle forced to leave and never heard from again. Freiburg families now possess a less rigid hierarchy; but fathers still direct all members, and males predominate over females. "This is a good place to be a teacher because most kids are raised to be obedient, and to treat a teacher with respect. Parents back up the teacher too," said a woman who had returned to the community after teaching elsewhere.

The Father and Son Working Arrangement

According to Freiburg's customary practices, a son should become independent at marriage. Oldest sons in a typical large family married while a father was still young and active and had many other children to provide for. In the past, therefore, fathers bought a farm and sold it at a favorable price to the first married son. This was the son's reward for the full-time labor previously contributed to the family farm. "All those years all my father received was pocket money when he asked—no salary. His father promised to pay-off later. Which he did in the form of the cut-rate price on the farm," related a son. Material support could be expected, children knew, because parents were dedicated to providing them a farming start.

Farmers today feel that they must be more flexible than their fathers to assure succession. A farm woman described their plans for an only son who helps on the farm evenings and weekends: "He's just a junior in high school and it seems like he'll probably stay on the farm. He likes farming. If he does we'll probably expand by trying to get more rental ground. That way he'll have something he's responsible for and can draw a reasonable salary. These days you can't expect a kid to stick around unless he's earning some money on his own. He sees all his friends with regular jobs and money to spend." The message sons receive is unambiguous support for the successor.

If parents only have a single son, he feels particular pressure to preserve the family name with the farm. One high-school-aged only son currently is on salary, and his father works full time off the farm. "I've been hearing since I was little that I was expected to carry on the farm." He dabbles with the idea of attending a technical school but feels he is needed to help with his very old, frail grandparents. "I don't see any point in studying agriculture. I never took those stupid high school votech courses. If you grow up on a farm, you learn most of what you need to know. Maybe you learn how to do things more scientifically, but farming's really guesswork anyhow." His father, an only son, began renting from his father after returning from the service in the late 1950s. The grandparents retired into Freiburg at his marriage five years later but continued a labor involvement, a common retirement pattern. "My grandparents always came out a lot though; my grandfather worked into his nineties. He still comes out for harvest and planting. When I visit them in town the first thing grandpa and grandma ask me is how are things going on the farm."

Yeoman families systematically expand land holdings or the operation to accommodate a successor. A prominent retired couple, parents of many children—six of them sons—exemplifies the Freiburg ideal. They gave a two-hundred-acre farm to each son at marriage; the homeplace was designated for the youngest, who also had the responsibility of caring for the elderly parents. Gradually each son bought the farm at a price well below market value; a portion was an outright gift. Money from a son paying for his farm helped buy acreage for the next. The patriarch proudly related a local joke that "every time another son is born on [our] place old man [family name] is out looking to buy another farm." So famous was this family that in the 1940s someone addressed a letter to "the man who buys land in Freiburg" and it was delivered. Each daughter received only the eighty acres given the sons and a home bought by the parents. One son sponsored in this manner has begun buying land in anticipation of repeating the cycle for his children. "I was thinking if one or both kids wanted to go into farming I would want them to have enough land." Freiburg has around twenty fathers and sons working together and four formal father-son operating agreements, a consequence of unambiguous family support.

Ideally the yeoman pattern of establishing each son (and daughters if possible) on his own farm assures independence, but parents expect children to cooperate. According to the patriarch who set up so many sons, "They all help each other out. That's one thing I always taught them. But, they're basically on their own." Not every family can approach the ideal, particularly those with many children. Parents of large families do not "teach the religion" so fervently to all children and encourage most to seek an education, "to have something to fall back on." A retired farm wife, mother of eight, said, "Every time a son was born my husband said he hoped it was a girl, because a son would expect a farm." It is not surprising that none of their boys decided to farm.

A common Freiburg strategy to involve children despite limited land resources and many offspring is to use family land intensively. As noted previously (chapter 4), Freiburg, unique in a vast region of grain farms, has many dairy and livestock operations. Families anticipating sons wanting to farm have expanded hog operations or added cows to accommodate them. Correspondingly, a family that produced only daughters ended their dairying: "We gradually got out because we had only girls, no sons. You don't do dairy unless you're pretty sure of the farm being continued. Otherwise, the investment doesn't pay off." In this way yeoman families tailor the farm to suit the family. During 1982, when Freiburg was studied, the farm crisis was at its peak. A farmer allowed that most in Freiburg would get by "because they're real tight with their money." He outlined how parents could adjust farm expenditures to meet the ideal of establishing a son under adverse conditions: "Parents will try to see that the farm stays together. There's always a way to cut corners. Don't divide the land is one way, and people have cut back on improvements. . . . Liming is a long-term thing. You can cut back on that, or cut down on buying new machines. . . . After all, farming is a way of life. . . . I'd do better with CDs, but I'd rather not."

The yeoman succession process favors the designated heir, but he as the link to past and future endures parental pressures. Divorce, even in this strongly Catholic community, is a concern. "My parents have talked with my brothers about how they put the farm together, and then with a divorce it's all gone. Especially [the designated heir], because he's inheriting the homeplace. They told him 'You better be sure this is the one,'" related a farm woman. Daughters, not being the conservator of the family patrimony, therefore escape these admonitions.

Nowadays couples must delay retirement longer than their parents did. The lure of the big city is strong, and tending dairy cows is unrelenting hard work. Parents describe a pattern for Freiburg sons in which they reject the farm as a stage of rebellion, only to return after a few years totally committed to farming. Related a farm wife, "Our son has worked with his dad since he got out of high school. We pay him a salary and he works full time. He says he wants to leave, but that's what they all say. . . . But then kids go away for a few years and want to come back when they get to be twenty-five or so. So I don't know what [our son] is going to do, even though he says he wants to leave." A father complained he could have bought a 150-acre farm in a nearby county just before land prices took off; but his sons caused him to deliberate too long, and he lost the opportunity. At that time, "neither boy wanted to farm. Now neither of them wants to do anything else." Anxious to get out of Freiburg after high school, a young father recently returned after army service and work in Chicago, motivated to farm. He recalls telling his parents, "Move over I'm coming back. . . . You discover after you've been out and around awhile, that back home isn't so bad after all. At age nineteen, there's no way you can know that. All you want to do is leave." According to the arrangement, he does all the work on the farm and receives half the income. His father has begun the turning over process and expects to retire within a few years, by the time he is sixty-two. The son's appreciation of the father's sacrifice makes him patient during the transition period.

Parents tolerate sons leaving, expecting them to return. Such indulgence of a son's sowing his wild oats has assured heirs to yeoman family farms. Given the smaller families now in Freiburg (as compared with the families with over ten children a generation ago) a son's leaving for five to ten years resembles the period spanned between the eldest and youngest sons in the traditional larger families. Numerous comments about the ease of finding hired men to assist with livestock or dairy work points up the tendency of young men in Freiburg to stay around and help a father and others, waiting to enter farming as a career.

Honoring a commitment to continuity obliges yeoman parents to make an orderly retirement at least by their early sixties; a timely, independent start permits the expansion necessary for an heir to repeat the succession cycle. In an orderly retirement parents can give some land at marriage, sell some acreage to the heir (keeping enough to support themselves), or retire to a new home in town. Moving off the homeplace symbolizes a real transfer of management in Freiburg. Retired fathers continue to help in the fields, and retired mothers come and milk regularly; but successors do not begrudge this involvement. An understanding seemed to exist that stopping farmwork entirely is terribly difficult. "He gets antsy if he can't be out there every day," commented a wife about her retired husband. If retirement comes before the heir's children are mature enough to provide labor, during the initial transition parental assistance is sorely needed. Perhaps being accustomed to a hierarchical structure mitigates German families' struggles over control; the lack of bitter stories over management transfers indicates it is not the same locus of conflicts as among entrepreneurs. One wife did describe her husband as vowing when he retired never to return unless the sons asked him. The husband remembered his joy when his father finally left him to farm on his own.

Children think the best retirement solution for parents is to move into Freiburg. A middle-aged couple whose parents built a home in the country disapproves because as the parents grow increasingly elderly, "It's too isolated when they can't drive. . . . In Freiburg there's a whole neighborhood of retired farmers and they can get together easily and groan, play cards, or whatever," said the wife. Intergenerational reciprocity is apparent in children's care of retired parents. Until he died in his mid-nineties, a widower lived with his son. "We never put him in a nursing home. He wouldn't of lived long if we'd done that. . . . Oh, we had some bad times with him," recalled the son.

A sponsored succession system entails predictable roles for both fathers and sons: fathers expect to plan retirement as an heir matures and to transfer control when the son marries. Sons expect fathers to retire and to transfer management responsibilities because they represent the farm's future. Relations between parents and the heir to the farm are positive—each helps the other fulfill an obligation to continue the family line. Acrimony, as I will discuss further in chapter 7, occurs horizontally among siblings rather than vertically between generations, as among entrepreneurs. All Freiburg families that produced a son or sons have a willing successor to maintain continuity.

PRAIRIE GEM: THE HYBRID SUCCESSION PROCESS

Prairie Gem, with its mixture of German and Yankee families, produces successions that combine features from each pattern. The most interesting example of this mesh is a German couple (not from the conservative Lutheran church) whose only child, a daughter, married a local Yankee. Because the Yankee son-in-law knew there was not enough land once his older brother began farming, the couple left the community. "I always wanted to farm but never thought it would be possible," said the son-in-law without bitterness. From his German mother-in-law's perspective he "needed a few breaks because he worked really hard as a kid and his family hasn't been very nice to him." Ten years after the couple left Prairie Gem, her parents asked them to return to take over their farm, and they would retire early. To assure the continued viability of the farm, the retired parents purchased an additional one hundred acres to add to their original two hundred. The young couple now occupy the house where her grandparents once lived. The mother helps with a business the daughter started in town.

The Yankee son-in-law recognizes he manages differently than his yeoman father-in-law: "He is not a risk-taker. He does not do anything unless he has the cash to do it. . . . He was even against any improvements on our house. He just couldn't understand why we had to change anything that had been good enough for his parents." The son-in-law has begun to sound more like a yeoman about his successor: "[My son], who already is hauling grain from the fields to the bin, is interested in farming. I plan to try and acquire more rental land if [my younger son] wants to farm too."

•

Effect of the Succession Process on Farm and Family

How succession takes place is pivotal to family farm persistence, for it influences a successor's achievement of expansion, land ownership, or viability of an independent operation. Owned land, unless highly indebted, leads to more profits than rental land. Though many young couples must work off-farm during the establishment years, those with substantial family support can better accumulate surplus capital than those kept on a salary by parents. Although salaried positions range from that of farmhand to that of a generously paid corporate employee, it is more often the former than the latter. In Heartland, early extended family support was decisive for the capital accumulation required for land purchases. Support took the form of access to rental land from relatives, gifts or predeath transfers of family land, or financial assistance for land purchases. Early land purchases are particularly significant in yeoman communities, where ownership is viewed as key to the definition of a good farmer; buying land is symbolic of successful management.

Table 6.2 shows the results of differing pathways into farming with more or less family support. Operators in Heartland were divided according to age

Table 6.2. Source of Land in Operation, by Age of Operator's First Land
Purchase in Heartland (percentage)

	Age at First Land Purchase			
Source of Land[a]	<33 (n=13)	33–45 (n=19)	>45 (n=11)	Never Purchased Land (n=46)
Purchased on open market	25	11	7	0
Purchased from kin	6	14	16	0
Rented from kin and nonkin (potentially could purchase or inherit)	60	59	48	57
Inherited (not purchased from relatives)	9	16	29	43
Total acres	7,005	6,017	2,299	8,130
Mean operation size (acres)	539	317	209	177

Source: Adapted from Salamon and O'Reilly 1979.

[a]A single operation could have acquired land through all four sources, but the first actual
purchase was used for the analysis.

at which they first purchased land: those who bought land before age 33 were
considered early because purchase came close to a decade after they began
farming; those who first bought between the ages of 33 and 45 were considered middle; those who bought after age 45 were considered late because
retirement begins in Heartland within the following decade.

Those Heartland operators who bought land early are the most successful
at meeting yeoman goals. Their farms possess the largest average acreage,
have the highest proportion of purchased land (especially not bought from
relatives), and have the smallest proportion of inherited land. So families that
begin to acquire land early in the development of an enterprise also continue
to buy land throughout the life of the enterprise, often indicating expansion
sufficient to establish more than one child.

The continuum of farms represented by table 6.2 demonstrates that the
yeoman ideal is not replicated by every family. The longer yeoman families
postpone land purchases and are tenants, the more they rely on becoming
owners through inherited land or purchases from kin. That is, some families
simply wait for an inheritance and take no initiative; farm size in this case is

smaller. Purchasing land from relatives is a passive strategy, implemented characteristically at the time of estate settlements, with middle-aged farmers buying land from nonfarming siblings when parents die. The category of those who never purchased land includes 15 percent (n = 7) who as tenants under the age of thirty-three might potentially become land buyers, widowed landlords and pluriactive farmers more dependent on nonfarm jobs, or landlords who lease holdings to other operators. Their farms are candidates for eventual absorption by those families expanding to achieve yeoman goals.

The evidence shown in table 6.2 indicates that extended family support is critical to the growth necessary to remain competitive or to support the eventual division of the farm (Salamon and O'Reilly 1979; Mooney 1988). Family support also suggests an orderly succession, for when parents turn over rental land or make a predeath transfer of owned acreage that they could farm, some management control is yielded. In Heartland this is considered a sacrifice one must make for the future of the family enterprise. Explaining a predeath transfer in the late 1970s when estate taxes were a grave concern (before the enactment of the Economic Tax Recovery Act of 1981), one father commented, "It was time and my father did the same for me. I know it has to be done and if I don't do it now we may lose it."

Evidence from Wheeler (table 6.3) shows that family help among entrepreneurs similarly affects entrepreneur land ownership and tenure status. Those with substantial family support—specifically, access to inherited or family rental acreage to begin farming—own a higher percentage of land and a larger proportion of farm operations. Wheeler operators who received no such kin support have the smallest mean operation size; they independently had to create pathways into farming. That this latter group owns 16 percent of the land in its operations testifies to their entrepreneurial aggressiveness. Although the farm size for rental-dependent operators resembles that of Wheeler operators entering farming with family-owned land, this is deceptive. Rental-dependent families must farm more land than part owners because profits must be split with a landlord. Thus it is understandable why a successor with a start on family-owned land is in a better position to buy more.

Tenure status at retirement reflects achievements of several generations' farming careers. In Wheeler, additional evidence exists for the relationship between a successor's access to land and achievement of land ownership. Sixteen retired landlords and three retired tenant farmers live in the community. Of the landlords 68 percent (n = 11) benefited from entry into farming on family-owned land. None of the retired tenants ever achieved ownership or received kin sponsorship (Sherlock 1992). Without substantial resources

Table 6.3. Operation Characteristics of Active Wheeler Farmers

Type of Kin Sponsorship	N	% of Operation Owned	Mean Operation Size (acres)
None	5	16	506
Start on rental land	11	5	850
Start on owned land	25	45	845
Total	41		

Sources: Community survey and Sherlock 1992.

Note: Active farmers include tenants, part owners, and full owners.

transferred to the younger generation by the older, it is difficult for families to improve their tenure category position.

Timing the shift of management control, measured by the age of the son relative to the father, is also critical to the succession process, as shown in table 6.2. However, evidence from Iowa suggests that premature involvement of the next generation can destroy the family farm (Friedberger 1988). The boom period of the 1970s caused many to use equity financing to involve two and even three generations farming simultaneously. When land values fell and commodity prices dropped in the early 1980s, such precipitous debt-financed expansion had a disastrous sequel. Iowa's yeoman ethnic communities fared better following well-established traditions for gradually incorporating family members into the business without incurring debt (Friedberger 1989).

The control of landed wealth is determined by the dominance of one family dyad over another. The deemphasized dyad is allowed less lengthy control over land (in the context of the lifecourse) and therefore less power over the lives of other family members. Despite some sibling discord, the sponsored-succession system of the yeomen is successful at producing continuity, its goal. The credential system of Yankee entrepreneurs does not produce continuity to the same extent, but then continuity is not of equal priority. Those families that achieved continuity in Libertyville were the larger operators, who according to the entrepreneur's definition of "enough" resources were best able to allow a son access to land. German yeomen try to sponsor sons regardless of their consistently smaller farm size. More people are supported on more farms, which meets yeoman goals for succession but not entrepreneur goals for viability.

Inheritance colors the final outcome of the succession process. Married siblings are torn between the demands of their procreative and natal families, and even so basic a collective goal as the continued viability of the farm may be contested. At the time of parental estate settlements, sibling rivalries culminate over financial support owed the successor to the farm versus pursuit of the nonsuccessors' self-interests. How families deal with the issue of who shall control family land—the successor or other siblings—is the subject of chapter 7.

SEVEN

Siblings and Inheritance
of the Patrimony

Lifecourse imperatives require an intergenerational transmission of family land about every twenty-five to thirty years. How parents transfer family resources to children is strongly influenced by inheritance priorities intrinsic to cultural beliefs about land. Household-level decisions—the inheritance patterns of previous generations and the responses of sibling heirs to the patrimony received—have cumulative effects on farm community land tenure patterns. Loyalty among siblings and to the farm—symbolized by a sense of a shared patrimony—is powerfully shaped by the family environment (Bossard and Boll 1956; Caplow 1968).

Families, aware that sibling strife can potentially destroy a landed patrimony, generally attempt to forge solidarity by socializing children to honor an "axiom of amity." This axiom dictates the masking of personality differences, rivalries, and latent hostility behind a public facade of harmonious relations; family cooperation is made a priority (Fortes 1969). Such kinship practices can make farm viability take higher priority than the psychological tendency toward sibling rivalry (Graham Allen 1977). Siblings are more likely to cooperate if they value group welfare even under circumstances in which no direct personal benefit seems apparent. Because the axiom of amity is most effective for uniting siblings when an external conflict is faced, however, some farm families experience no event that promotes sibling solidarity. Unchecked sibling rivalry is most threatening to the farm at the time of intergenerational land transfers.

How retirement is handled can encourage or discourage sibling struggles by the way parents balance their needs against the needs of their children for resources. Cross-culturally, the elderly in agrarian societies play a sort of game in which personal resources are gradually dealt out to assure continued respect, sociability, and obligation on the part of children. When the elderly lack a future orientation, they tend to give too little or too much early in the aging period. Then children are apparently less willing to socially integrate parents and to honor them, or the children become suspicious about being overburdened (Simmons 1962; Salamon and Lockhart 1980). But it is how parents handle inheritance that is most crucial to sibling relations: what is good for the farm may not appear equitable to nonsuccessors. Sibling behavior becomes particularly crucial if parents transfer land undivided, whether by plan or lack of it. Terminal divisions take place if negotiations cannot accomplish resource exchanges or an internal sale for estate taxes or if one sibling demands cash.

Americans are bound by few legal restrictions on their estate planning. Inheritance patterns are less a consequence of legal codes than of parents exercising a high degree of testamentary freedom (Jeffrey P. Rosenfeld 1979; Sussman, Cates, and Smith 1970). Heirs to the family patrimony like testators are not legally restricted in their disposal of an inheritance but are similarly bound by a cultural schema that channels family responsibilities and obligations. Generally American families want to provide all children with equitable resources to assure each an equal opportunity in the world (Farber 1973; Shammas, Salmon, and Dahlin 1987). This ideal is rooted in a twentieth-century childrearing philosophy that minimizes differential treatment of children according to age, sex, or educational attainment (Jeffrey P. Rosenfeld 1979). These practices of equal treatment diverge from a long history of unequal divisions, from the Colonial period until much later, which discriminated against daughters, who were expected to be provided for through marriage, and which favored oldest sons with larger shares (Shammas, Salmon, and Dahlin 1987; Morris 1927; Bidwell and Falconer 1925; Calhoun 1918; Farber 1973).

Today farm parents face a basic dilemma: whether to treat all children equally or to favor a successor to the farm. This dilemma pits continuity goals against equity goals, particularly when the family's financial and land resources are limited. Furthermore, giving each child an equal portion of farmland can effectively destroy a farm when economies of scale require larger operations (Tweeten 1983). In the past, parents could assure ownership persistence through careful estate planning of equitable but unequal divisions. Daughters or nonsuccessors could receive cash settlements rather than land or inherit smaller portions than the successor. Once farm children began to inherit equally and out-migrate, sibling actions became more critical to farm continuity. A successor as heir only to a portion of family resources has a farm management quandary. Can siblings be depended on for financial and land resources?

It becomes especially difficult for siblings to cooperate for the benefit of the natal family farm after they themselves marry and establish their own families or farms (Salamon 1982). The demands of children, career, and spouse may bring the siblings into conflict later in life following harmonious relations (Netting, Wilk, and Arnould 1984; Laslett 1984). Emerging from farm family sibling sets are three logical classes of individuals combining sex and occupational variables: (1) the successor to the farm business, typically male; (2) nonsuccessor farmers, who can be either male or female; and (3) nonfarmers, who also can be either male or female. Each sibling class is concerned with maximizing resources for its own domestic or economic activities, and these must be balanced against the claims of the parents and the natal farm.

Rivalry, expressed in sibling discord, easily emerges in farm families. One sibling's welfare can conflict with another's at estate settlement time. It is in the best interests of the successor to keep all the family land under his control. For the nonsuccessor siblings who farm, an inheritance represents a means of expansion. For nonfarming siblings, their inheritance is a potential source of cash. How they are raised to think about the family patrimony and sibling solidarity will predispose nonsuccessors' willingness to cooperate or to pursue personal claims against the estate. Resolution of the intergenerational transfer of the farm plays out the final developments of yeoman and entrepreneurial family patterns. The sibling-sibling dyad in conjunction with the inheritance process is delineated in table 7.1.

•

The Process of Transferring Land and Farms

Transmission of farm resources from one generation to the next involves a family equation with two parts, each critical to the outcome of the transfer (table 7.1). On one side, the process is first under the control of the senior generation. Only parents can plan the distribution of their estate and decide whether to give up some resources by making predeath transfers. Whether

Table 7.1. Siblings and Inheritance of the Farming Patrimony

Yeoman	Entrepreneur
Parental Side of Inheritance Equation	
Parents assume responsibility for estate transfer	Parents shift responsibility to heirs for estate settlement
Planning often shared with heirs	Planning not openly shared
Aim to keep all land in family	Will sell land to settle estate
Wish to assure a successor	Not a failure if no successor produced
Most resources invested in farm	Diversified portfolio
Little use of incorporation	Incorporation a business strategy
Sibling Side of Inheritance Equation	
All children value farming	Mainly successor values farming
May be more than one farmer	Typically only a single farmer
Nonfarmers reside in community	Nonfarmers out-migrate
Children feel favoritism according to gender, age, or profession	No favoritism despite gender, age, or profession
Results of Intergenerational Transfer Process	
Persistence of farm and family land ownership	More persistence of land ownership than family farms
Smaller estates divided among many	Larger estates divided fewer ways
Frequent sibling acrimony	Sibling cooperation
Land fragmentation	Tract size stable
Numerous, smaller farms	Fewer, larger farms
Low rates of absentee ownership	High rates of absentee ownership

parents spend lavishly on themselves or plan their estate or muddle it, until both die, children can do little. On the equation's other side heirs must act together. After both parents die, sibling heirs can, united, realize parental goals for the farm, divide resources if parents have abdicated that responsibility, or otherwise settle the estate among themselves in accord with or in rejection of parental plans. An intergenerational transfer of the farm, farmland, and other resources is not finished until both sides of the family equation, parents and siblings, have played out their parts. The communities of Emerson (Yankee entrepreneur) and St. Boniface (German yeoman) are the focus of the discussion (Carroll and Salamon 1988).[1] Prairie Gem, which includes many combined Yankee and German marriages, provides an example of how mixed families deal with intergenerational transfers and satisfy schemas of both cultural systems.

Estate planning becomes biased by the extent to which continuity is a parental priority: what constitutes a successful transfer varies accordingly. Successful intergenerational transfers by yeomen, for whom continuity is a strong motive, involve estate plans begun early and designed to assure the persistence of the farm, to preserve the family name in conjunction with the original homeplace, and to prevent the sale of land outside the family. Only then is continuity actually and symbolically achieved. Yeomen employ business practices in estate planning, but these are always mediated by the continuity goal. Parents typically balance the equation in favor of the successor with gifts, predeath transfers, and early retirement, as seen in chapter 6.

Entrepreneurs, not as committed to continuity, are less concerned with preservation of all land holdings or persistence of the farm. Land is, rather, a resource belonging to the parents that is a means to realize a multitude of goals; farm continuity may rank lower in priority than a well-financed retirement. However, in keeping with the priority for individualism valued by entrepreneurs, parents do not typically handicap heirs with confining estate plans. Entrepreneur families are proud of continuity achieved over several generations, but they can be as proud of a new direction an heir chooses, if the endeavor meets with substantial financial rewards. Intergenerational transfers are deemed successful by entrepreneurs when embodying such good financial practices as little tax loss or the least land sold to cover the estate settlement.

1. The tables and the inheritance argument are adapted from Carroll and Salamon 1988.

•

Yeoman and Entrepreneur Inheritance Patterns

SIDE I: PARENTS AND PLANNING
INTERGENERATIONAL TRANSFERS

Probate archives record how estates were transferred from the settlement period to the present and reflect the customary practices families passed along
with land and other resources. To find out how past yeomen and entrepreneurs acted on their beliefs, I examined the probate archives of Emerson and
St. Boniface, located in neighboring counties. The wills filed by testators
revealed how yeoman and entrepreneur priorities for family and farm influence testamentary behavior. Successive generations choosing similar testamentary solutions influenced how land tenure in a rural community evolved.
This causal chain emerges because individuals plan for their property to be
divided or distributed after their deaths in accordance with personal beliefs
acquired from cultural systems.

Typically four to five intergenerational transmissions of farm and land have
taken place since original settlement in Illinois. The usable samples of 101 St.
Boniface cases and 91 Emerson cases represent the settlers and their persisting
descendants whose estates were probated. These samples were obtained by
randomly selecting 17 sections (47 percent of the total surveyed) in St. Boniface and 25 sections (48 percent of the total surveyed) in Emerson. An approximate 50 percent sample of landowners' names from the selected sections
on earliest available plat maps was drawn and sought in the probate records.
Due to county variations for plat maps issued, the plat maps examined for
Emerson were 1875, 1907, and 1915, and those for St. Boniface were 1893, 1913,
and 1929. From a list of 138 Yankee landowners compiled from the Emerson
plat maps, 56 were found connected with estates recorded in county probate
records. A list of 100 German landowners was compiled for St. Boniface, of
which 46 were connected to estates in county probate records. The 46 St.
Boniface families had 59 heirs whose estates were also recorded, making a
total of 105 cases. The 56 Emerson families had 38 heirs whose estates were
also recorded, a total of 94 cases. In both counties some records (4 in Emerson and 3 in St. Boniface) were lost to genealogists and land title companies.

Inheritance studies necessarily involve those individuals who live long
enough in a community and acquire property so that when they die their
estates reach probate court and thus the public record. Urban probate case
studies have found proportions of estates reaching probate from 15 to 47

percent, with some indications of a higher incidence for rural areas (Dunham 1962; Ward and Beuscher 1950). Table 7.2 illustrates the proportion of cases filed testate (with a will) and those filed intestate (without a will) in time periods roughly corresponding to thirty-year intervals, beginning with the 1870s when Emerson was settled and St. Boniface was receiving the bulk of its German immigration. One of the most striking differences between the two communities is that while over three-fourths (78 percent) of the St. Boniface yeomen filed testate, fewer than half of the Emerson entrepreneurs (44 percent) did so. St. Boniface Germans maintained fairly stable percentages, while Emerson Yankees showed a steady rise in people leaving wills. Before 1930, in fact, most Yankees died intestate. Thus from the outset yeoman farmers in St. Boniface took writing a will as an obligation to the next generation, while Emerson entrepreneurs allowed the law to take its course or shifted the estate settlement responsibility to children.

Planning for continuity is a parental duty according to the yeoman notions about intergenerational transfers. In contrast to the nine Germans who wrote wills and the one who died intestate during the period before 1900 (table 7.2), only four Yankees bothered to write wills, while fifteen died intestate. A St. Boniface yeoman spoke about present views of parental responsibilities to assure continuity: "Keeping the land you inherit and land your family has worked hard for is very important." The intestate transfer pattern implies a lack of concern about what happens to property; it suggests that a farm belongs to the current owners, who carry no specific obligation to arrange its

Table 7.2. Manner of Estate Planning,
by Ethnic Community (percentages)

Community	Before 1901	1901–30	1931–60	After 1960	Total for All Periods
Emerson Yankees	(n=19)	(n=39)	(n=24)	(n=9)	(n=91)
Testate	21	44	54	67	44
Intestate	79	56	45	33	56
St. Boniface Germans	(n=10)	(n=36)	(n=34)	(n=21)	(n=101)
Testate	90	75	79	76	78
Intestate	10	25	21	24	22
Chi-square value (1 df)	12.59	7.61	4.19	0.29	23.84
Significance	p<.001	p<.01	p<.05	p>.58	p<.001

Source: Adapted from Carroll and Salamon 1988.

transfer to the next generation. Commented a present Emerson farmer about his conception of farm ownership, "Everyone should work for what they have—money shouldn't be accumulated and then just passed on to the heirs—money should be seen as a reward for working hard and using one's brains or ingenuity or whatever it takes to do well." In this view parents feel less obligation to plan transfers of the estate that assure continuity.

Today, estate planning in Emerson is referred to as a desire to avoid unnecessary taxes more than as a duty to the next generation (Salamon and Markan 1984). A new strategy to meet this tax-saving goal recently emerged—incorporation of the farm. When Yankee parents reflect on their decision to incorporate, they commonly say, "We'd rather give it to the kids than let Uncle Sam have it." Rather than ease of property transfers or continuity being the foremost reasons for incorporating, tax benefits to the parents are of high priority. A farmer in his early forties commented that incorporation provided him and his children with maximum autonomy: "I was thinking about estate planning too; mainly, that my estate would not be burdensome to get rid of. I know it's important to plan early. You can't wait until you're 60 and then wonder how to get rid of what you acquired." Additionally, three Emerson couples who had incorporated and two more actively investigating the possibility of incorporation saw the structure as a means to transfer wealth tailored to parental intentions. Changing a corporation requires complex and potentially expensive legal procedures that lock heirs into a business format chosen by parents, however unintended.

Entrepreneurs value privacy greatly, and because transfer plans concern their personal possessions, they feel no compunction to keep other family members informed. Elderly brothers, although both Emerson residents, tell each other nothing about their wills. One heard indirectly that the other was incorporating his farm: "Maybe [he] is planning for the future. I don't know who the land will go to. I don't feel I should ask, in case he doesn't think it's my business." Likewise, Emerson children are not informed regarding details about the corporation structure parents adopt. Commented a farm woman about the perpetuation of parental control a corporation implies, "None of the children know too much about it. . . . I don't think they need to know, and I don't think they should be given everything. They need to work for something too. We wanted to set things up so that the kids could not live off what the corporation made for them."

Some farmers in Emerson delay making estate plans until so late in life that they, like previous generations, may die intestate. A farmer in his late sixties, owner of over one thousand acres, was still only considering what his transfer plans should be: "I'm worried about the future, I don't mind telling you. I've got to start making some decisions about how to do it. I sure don't envy [my children] having to come up with the kind of tax they'll get hit with. . . . Nothin' much you can do except sell off some in order to pay off what you want to keep." Another farmer, in his fifties and owner of five hundred acres, also expressed feelings that responsibility for handling taxes connected with inheritance lies with the heirs. At the peak of high land values (around 1980) he ruled out predeath gift transfers: "The gift tax [on a large transfer] would eat me up. I'm limited to giving $3000 [tax free]. Well, that amounts to about one acre. I figure that if I wait, I don't have to worry. The gift tax would be my responsibility, but I won't be around to worry about the inheritance tax. . . . I do have life insurance to soften the blow."

A local explanation for why Emerson farmers were loath to transfer any land before they died focused on parental fears of losing the independence land ownership guaranteed. A woman recalled that her grandfather held on to his land until he was in his nineties, preventing children from reaping any early ownership benefits from an inheritance: "He was afraid to turn over too much. Somehow it's as if once the second generation takes control, they're going to put the older generation out. My grandfather always talked about being afraid of being put in a nursing home and abandoned there. I don't know where the idea arose, but it's general in the community." Entrepreneurs identify with the business they built and resist turning over control of this prized possession. They feel less obligation to pave the way for heirs to enter farming. Perhaps entrepreneurs fear the next generation will act as they did and will treat the matter of placing their elders in a nursing home as unsentimentally as the elders decide what is good for the business. By not obligating children with indications of clear transfer intentions, however, entrepreneurs are more likely to risk a lonely old age if children become alienated and provide little reciprocity (Salamon and Lockhart 1980).

Most yeoman parents outline estate plans for heirs, particularly those assuming full financial responsibility for the intergenerational transfer. The quality of intergenerational relations experienced by retired parents is directly connected to their handling of the prerogatives accrued from control of land (Salamon and Lockhart 1980). One retired St. Boniface farmer has already transferred some land to all his children and leases the remainder to the successor. He indicated by these arrangements willingness to keep not as much personally in order to assure continuity. In some sense it may be easier for a yeoman to carry out a predeath transfer of land control than for an entrepreneur. An entrepreneur sees land as a possession symbolic of self; yeomen view themselves as temporary stewards of a patrimony—land is symbolic of family. According to a St. Boniface yeoman farmer, "We don't really own the land. We're just taking care of it while we're here and then it will get passed on to our children."

Historically, yeomen and entrepreneurs not only went about estate planning differently, but they also gave heirs differing resources, which had important implications for farms. Contrasts in the amount of fluid capital available to heirs are evident. St. Boniface Germans had less capital and smaller estates (mean 155 acres) compared with Emerson Yankees, who inherited more capital and transferred larger estates (mean 198 acres). Not only did Yankee testators avoid handicapping farmland heirs with financial obligations to others, their estates contained stocks and bonds. Most common among the stocks held by Emerson entrepreneurs were investments in grain elevator companies, railroads, and utilities. Yankees also held war bonds and, later, savings bonds in fairly large amounts ($500 to $15,000). Germans did not own stocks, nor did they buy bonds until the 1940s, and then in only smaller values of $100 to $1,000. Yankees often purchased life insurance policies; many held three or four policies. Prior to 1931 Germans seldom held life insurance and usually held not more than two policies (Carroll and Salamon 1988).

The stock and bond ownership of past generations of Emerson Yankees underscores their entrepreneurial management style. Yankees did not plow all their profits back into the farm. They tended to diversify their investments; 65 percent of all Yankee estates after 1900 had some stocks and bonds. The desire not to put all financial eggs in one basket and the patriotic purchase of war and savings bonds indicate a willingness to engage in nonfarm investments to achieve profit maximization. Alternatively, varied investments are a manifestation of a willingness to take on financial risk and reflect approaching farming as a business.

A retired Emerson entrepreneur, wealthy owner of one thousand acres of land purchased through shrewd investment and because "I worked my ass off," casts some light on the motives behind the historical Yankees estate diversification. He freely gave advice to the interviewer about his approach to postretirement investments. "I've started to put my money into stock. Wish I'd started a long time ago. . . . You've got to look to the future . . . make what you've got work for you . . . be sure to spread out into a variety of things. That's what I've done, and while it hasn't made me rich yet, I keep trying. . . . I kinda decided a long time ago, that it would be easier to walk out to the mailbox and collect dividend checks than to farm. . . . I got started late, but I'm on the right track now." Diversifying out of land, which this entrepreneur stopped buying when values reached $500 an acre, attests to a profit rather than a long-term farming goal. "Now I'm kinda into making money," he said. Coming of age during the Depression, which "makes you kinda careful," this large landowner represents an entrepreneurial type who does not "live too high," and a modest home belies his wealth. However, younger Emerson entrepreneurs are not as averse to spending money on impressive homes, boats, or vacations (Barlett 1991).

The investment diversification pattern found in the probate record contributed to the higher-valued estates that Emerson farmers historically passed on to their children. Differences in capitalization was one of a cumulative set of factors with profound consequences for the greater amount of real estate controlled by entrepreneur heirs over time.

Division of the resources among heirs differed historically between the yeoman and entrepreneur communities of St. Boniface and Emerson. Despite the phrase "share and share alike" recurring in the German wills of every period (table 7.3), providing land to sons and equivalent sums of cash to daughters was common. Equal division among all heirs usually meant that the estate was divided into shares with each heir given both cash and an undivided interest in family land or that the estate was divided into equal parcels with each heir receiving a land parcel, equivalent cash, or a parcel plus cash. The periods 1901–30 and 1931–60 saw German wills including an elaborate division of the land and cash as well as specifying a balanced distribution of household items, personal effects, and even pigs or cows. No aspect of the transfer was left to chance. Before 1901, in the two cases of inequality, land went to sons and cash to daughters. The unequal division was meant to concentrate the land in the paternal family line and to ensure yeoman family farm continuity, a value which took priority over equality in these cases.

Division of estates was definitely compounded by the large Catholic families typical of St. Boniface. Recent cases of inequality cited by St. Boniface families were, in effect, parental attempts to even the distribution of resources by taking into account what was transferred to children during the parents' lifetime. In one family each sibling received eighty acres except for two who got only forty acres because their religious vocations were financed by the parents. In another family it is considered fair that two sons will receive equal amounts of land and the daughter considerably less. "Dad paid for her college education and the boys didn't go to college. . . . Her education is part of her settlement, though there'll probably be some cash settlement in the future." The father is said to be concerned with equity because of his unfair treatment:

Table 7.3. Probate Cases According to Testamentary Behavior in German St. Boniface and Yankee Emerson (percentages)

	Before 1901		1901–30		1931–60		After 1960	
	Yankee	German	Yankee	German	Yankee	German	Yankee	German
Planned equality	11	70	22	43	25	40	38	58
Planned inequality	5	20	17	27	29	37	25	16
Equal by default (intestate)	84	10	61	30	46	23	37	26
N[a]=	19	10	36	30	24	30	8	19

Source: Adapted from Carroll and Salamon 1988.

[a]Total Yankees (n=87) and Germans (n=89) for all periods. Excludes some cases with missing or conflicting documents.

"My Dad's aunts were treated very specially and he got a bad deal in his family . . . so now it's real important to him to be real fair." Unlike the secrecy maintained by Emerson entrepreneurs, these yeoman heirs already know the terms of their parents' will.

Yeoman parents carefully specify a division of resources motivated by the desire to "avoid a squabble" among children. One St. Boniface mother has put together an album of old family photos for each of her eight children. "This way it's all decided ahead of time who gets which photos. The kids won't have to figure out how to divide them up." Similarly a farmer outlined his plan to transfer land to his sons: "I'll give each one their own acreage. If you all start operating out of the same pot, you can really run into some problems. . . . One wife will complain because her husband works harder than the other two. I've always thought it was better for each to have his own ground."

Lacking a firm commitment to continuity weakens the motivation for estate planning. In contrast to the German historic and current preoccupation with achieving equality, previous generations of Emerson Yankees (table 7.3) accomplished an equal division without writing wills. Intestacy prior to 1931 among Yankees permitted a default equal division of estates to take place as a result of actions by probate judges, appointed administrators, and heirs. This default choice meant in all likelihood that the farm, as the principal asset, was sold to provide an equitable solution. Under these circumstances the farm remains in the family only if one child can buy out the others and the widowed mother, who is a one-third heir, when the law takes its course (Friedberger 1983, 1984). When wills were made in Emerson in the past, the estates were divided equally among heirs, with fewer distinctions made between male and female children than in St. Boniface. Smaller families among Emerson Protestants and few, if any, heirs remaining in farming at the time estates were probated perhaps contributed to the even treatment of women and men.

Today, Emerson entrepreneurs are firmly committed to inheritance according to an idealized, dispassionate division in which no child is considered special, even the successor. Fairness is the paramount priority for arranging intergenerational transfers; fairness entails equal treatment of all heirs. A farmer with two children farming and two not explained his perception of Emerson's inheritance pattern: "Well, I can't speak for the community. That's an individual thing, and kind of private, really. . . . It comes down to there being no standard, no general rule, and it's pretty much at the whim of the donor. But it's usually pretty much equal. Oh, that's not to say that everyone gets the same. A father might give this heir life insurance and this heir the land and let them hassle it out later among themselves. But usually it works out pretty fair." Others echoed this farmer's view of intergenerational transfers: "Oh we just divide what there is. There's no sale, or anything like that. Everybody gets an equal share, and there's no complaining. That's the best and fair way, I guess." Equal treatment is the expectation of both parents and children.

The historic equal treatment of heirs, evident in both St. Boniface and Emerson estates, was not the manifestation of underlying shared family goals. The results, while similar, were produced by differing processes and had markedly different effects on both heirs and, ultimately, land tenure. Among the early generations of Yankees, the state laws governing intestacy determined the division of shares between the widow and the heirs; among the Germans, the testator made decisions about the allocation of resources. Key differences also existed for how past estate settlements were implemented and in what resources were available to heirs. For example, in several instances unequal divisions among St. Boniface yeomen actually were schemes that achieved equity by obligating land-inheriting heirs to meet a cash payment schedule to those not receiving land. While this pattern favored farming sons, it prevented their concentration of capital and created potential liquidity problems. This pattern was not found among Emerson's Yankees.

SIDE 2: SIBLINGS AS HEIRS IN THE
INTERGENERATIONAL TRANSFER EQUATION

Three factors contribute to potentially problematic negotiations among siblings over estate settlements. First, family size—that is, the number of heirs—influences the type of estate plans made and therefore whether settlement responsibility is shouldered by heirs. Second, the extent of heirs' outmigration affects whether heirs have a commitment to a priority of farm financial needs over nonfarm demands for resources. Third, the persistence in agriculture of more than the family farm successor affects pressures to divide land holdings.

Family size contributed to the historical divergence in inheritance patterns between St. Boniface and Emerson. As a Catholic community St. Boniface maintained a large mean family size of around 5.2 children before 1900 (determined from heirs in probate records), declining to 4.8 in 1931–60 and further to a still large 3.3 in the families surveyed and for whom genealogies were collected. Before 1901 Yankee mean family size equaled that of Germans in the probate records, but it showed a rapid decline to 2.6 mean size in the families surveyed in the 1970s. The association of a larger family size with planned inequality and small family size with intestacy was significant for both communities over the 100-year period and generally was significant for each of the shorter periods (Carroll and Salamon 1988). German families today still have more heirs competing for smaller estates in contrast to the fewer Yankee heirs potentially dividing estates in which families own 30 percent more land on the average than do Germans.

Family practices inform heirs of the probable outcome of parental wills and retirement plans. This information tailors the heirs' life choices. Emerson's and St. Boniface's heirs were all faced with resource fragmentation during intergenerational transfers in the past and present, as a function of the equal division of estates. However, nearly half the Emerson heirs from 1931 to 1960 left the community (table 7.4), compared with less than one-quarter leaving St. Boniface, despite the smaller family size in the Yankee community. The geographical out-migration of Yankee heirs in the past appears linked to occupational shifts, since many heirs took up residence in large Midwestern cities where, presumably, they did not farm. Emerson's historical out-migration of heirs therefore led to an increase in absentee ownership, and for those who stayed, changes to nonfarm occupations were reflected in estate inventories. In Emerson today the entrepreneur priorities for personal independence and personal profit maximization lead parents to encourage children's

Table 7.4. Heir Residence Location (percentages)

	Before 1901	1901–30	1931–60[a]	After 1960
Emerson (Yankee)	(n=80)	(n=121)	(n=106)	(n=21)
Remained[b]	96	86	58	67
Out-migrated	4	14	42	33
St. Boniface (German)	(n=53)	(n=208)	(n=175)	(n=104)
Remained	93	78	77	76
Out-migrated	7	22	23	24

Source: Adapted from Carroll and Salamon 1988.

[a]Chi-square=11.249, 1df, p<.001, all others not significant.
[b]Within the county.

occupational out-migration despite an expected inheritance of farmland, aiding and abetting an increase of absentee heir landlords.

The persistence of yeoman heirs within the community boundaries of St. Boniface and the increasing density of German names per section in successive plat maps coupled with the decreasing density of Yankee names in Emerson point up the contrasting effects of intergenerational transfers (Carroll and Salamon 1988). Unlike Emerson heirs who left farming and/or the area, St. Boniface heirs stayed and attempted to farm despite the smaller proportions of land and less inherited liquid capital. Farmland fragmentation was increasingly a greater problem for the German yeomen who successfully encouraged more children to stay and farm, thereby making less land available to successors.

Between 1870 and 1960, Emerson entrepreneurs produced fewer heirs, slightly more land, more capital, and higher out-migration rates than St. Boniface yeomen. The result was larger estate proportions received by each Yankee heir. In the earliest period, heirs in both communities seemed to inherit roughly similar portions, but Emerson Yankees possessed more capital, making the same estate worth considerably more. From 1901 to 1960, Yankee estates were divided into significantly larger portions than were the German. After 1960, the inherited Yankee proportion jumped to one-third, a change related to the decline in numbers of Yankee heirs and, ultimately, to the decline in family size (Carroll and Salamon 1988).

In Emerson today an entrepreneur son does not expect favored treatment by virtue of being the successor. The requirement of proving himself assures siblings the successor qualifies for the job according to an objective criterion of worthiness. Parents strongly insist, "I don't think it's fair to leave one more than the other," and this message is clearly communicated to all children. An Emerson successor foresaw an equal division of the estate, just as his father had received: "I haven't had a chance to see my Dad's will. . . . You kind of want to see that everything is kept equal. I don't expect to get any special share, even though I've been running the place. That's [father's] decision and he'll have to make it. That goes with owning the place."

Emerson children, though not privy to the actual will, in every case firmly believe that parents would handle the intergenerational transfer fairly. A son salaried by the family corporation said, "I think it would be fair to leave us equal amounts of [corporation] shares. One of us could always sell out to the others. But, as I say my father hasn't said much about it." Almost every statement about equality, by Emerson parents or children, was connected with the belief that siblings could and would sell their inheritance to the successor. Out-migrating siblings rarely envision farming and thus are apt to part with their share. A farmer with a son working in the enterprise gave his view of the process: "I think every child should get an equal amount. Even in a large family of four or five children, the chances of all the kids entering farming are slim. And if one or two were to farm they could always farm the land for the other kids." The fairness inherent to succession and transfer processes gives entrepreneurs assurance that siblings will get along. A farmer looked with disdain on heirs squabbling; such heirs only got what they deserved: "I know of a few cases around here in which the heirs were unable to agree on how the land should be farmed. Then they ended up selling the farm completely. But as far as I'm concerned if the people in a family can't get along with one another then they're not worth much."

The predictability of a fair inheritance, the probability that only one sibling will undergo the rigorous proving process required of successors, and the tenuous vested interest of heirs in holding on to inheritance provide little basis for a sibling struggle over estates. The absence of feuds reported over the family patrimony suggests satisfaction with equity achieved among Emerson entrepreneurs.

The yeoman preference for family ownership continuity signified to St. Boniface heirs in the past that some land would eventually come their way. Today small estates are divided equally, with each heir in a large family expecting to inherit an undivided interest in the whole. Among St. Boniface siblings, the challenge is to keep heirs in agreement regarding inherited farmland until one or more farming heirs can purchase the others' shares or can work out some long-term leasing arrangement. "You can lose land real quick when brothers and sisters start bickering," commented a farmer. Parents expect that children share their commitment to continuity of the family name in conjunction with the homeplace. According to a retired St. Boniface farmer shared values were the rationale for a predeath land transfer: "All the kids that inherit land need to stick together so that all can keep the land. . . . We knew our kids would stick together when we gave them the land."

Inevitably, yeoman parents treat the designated farmer differently; he is first among equals. This can create jealousy among siblings. Though all know the land will be divided evenly, it is the successor's opportunity to enter farming with the way paved on the homeplace, which raises hackles. When a St. Boniface farmer died unexpectedly without designating a successor, the mother described what she did: "I sat all three boys down right here at this table, their sisters and grandma were here too. We talked about who . . . wanted to take over the farm. [One son] said that he did, and the others agreed. His dad always kind of thought [he] would be the farmer in the family: he was always the hardest worker. . . . I think the other boys are a bit jealous of [him] 'cause he always had the things he wanted: a pick-up and a car—but he worked hard for those things."

Continuity achieved by the father and the successor together emphasizes that bond at the expense of sibling bonds (Hsu 1971). Until a father dies, successors tend to have an easier time working with him than with a brother. Difficulties working with a brother, who subsequently left farming, caused a successor to comment, "Having a partnership is just like having a marriage. There has to be honesty and trust. [My brother] and I never had that. Dad and I worked pretty well together. Right from the time I joined him, he let me make my own decisions and my own mistakes. Maybe more than he should've, but he was always there to give advice."

A family settlement that favors the successor can provoke trouble for him after both parents are gone. An eldest son, now farming his retired father and mother's operation full time, is conscious that some of his eight siblings envy him: "There's a couple of them who would really like to farm, but there's not enough land. . . . Of course, no one says much. Just once in a while 'I wish I was in your shoes,' or something like that. I guess it will all come out when my folks die and the land gets passed on. I've seen that happen so many times; a lot of hidden feelings really come out when that will is read."

A standoff over what to do with the land is avoided when yeoman parents dictate a specific division in their will. St. Boniface families tell many tales about sibling disputes, grudges, and alienation over settlement of undivided estates. Disagreements over land sometimes force the selling of land; the loss of continuity becomes a family tragedy. Not only might nonfarm heirs have uses for the money, but those farming elsewhere in St. Boniface need cash to finance land purchases for their farms. The successor, who has a vested interest in avoiding fragmentation of the farm, is in a good position if he has the resources to buy out siblings.

Yeoman parents are confident about a bond forged between children and the family land. According to an elderly farm wife, "Even for the children and grandchildren who have moved away, this is home. This is where their roots are, where their parents and grandparents are buried. This is where their land is." As a consequence of the yeoman fixation on land ownership, successors face a complex attachment to the homeplace among out-migrant siblings. This bonding causes problems with sibling landlords if major management changes are required. The attachment sometimes becomes symbolized by family heirlooms or the homeplace. "At the homeplace, it's never yours. It's always the whole family's. Everybody comes home. If you've moved something they get all sentimental," complained a successor ambivalent about eventual residence in the homeplace now occupied by his parents.

Suppressed sibling problems emerge with estate settlements. In St. Boniface there is some evidence that latent rivalry is compounded by larger families, smaller estates, and the societal ideal of equal treatment of all heirs. Entrepreneur parents close the door early to more than one successor by saying there is not enough land. Yeoman parents like to think that somehow, someway, it may be possible for all the children who wish to, to farm. This ambiguity combined with covert or overt privileges accorded the successor sets the stage for sibling jealousy that can threaten the realization of the yeoman continuity goal.

HYBRID TRANSFERS: PRAIRIE GEM, THE MIXED YANKEE/GERMAN COMMUNITY

A few Prairie Gem families (12 percent) combine yeoman and entrepreneur traits because each spouse feels strongly devoted to a different set of cultural priorities. One of the largest landowning families is headed by a German patriarch and a Yankee woman who entered the community as a schoolteacher. Fully committed to a farm the couple built from nothing, the wife takes pride in her New England Yankee heritage. The elderly couple worked closely with the husband's brother their entire farming career. So close were the two households that neighbors commented the couple lacked privacy. "But I saw it was in our best interests so I made do," the wife said.

Their enterprise transfer plans incorporate elements of both farming patterns. A son's early succession of the father, now in his seventies, indicates a yeoman perspective. The German father accepts the priority of the successor while recognizing the potential for bad feelings among the other children any favoritism causes: "Heirs should sit down and talk quietly among themselves about how to handle the estate. People should keep their anger to themselves and work together. If every heir gets a lawyer think how much the lawyers will get of the estate. . . . An inheritance is really a gift. It isn't something you earned yourself so you should be happy with whatever you get. . . . But, perhaps the guy who stays at home should get a little more. Maybe that's fair. . . . My brother got a little more than I did. He got the homeplace, but I didn't let that make me angry." However, his Yankee wife feels strongly about equal treatment. "The fair way is for the kids to draw straws for their share and we've discussed this with the children. I think the land should be divided in forty acre plots and [the successor] should get first choice. They'll have to mortgage the land to pay off the inheritance taxes, but they each have other income so they ought to be able to do that. If . . . the children had borrowed from the parents, well that amount should come out of their share. . . . I do hope they'll cooperate so they don't get lawyers involved." Though they have planned equal treatment, some preference for the successor worries the parents that jealousy may eventually threaten continuity.

EFFECTS OF THE CONTRASTING TRANSFER PROCESSES

Inheritance is pointed to elsewhere in American society as a mechanism for concentrating wealth (Chester 1982). That is, inheriting substantial wealth aids in further accumulation. Translated to the rural community, this means that early landowners have an advantage in their ability to add to family holdings—growing larger at the expense of smaller owners (Lancelle and Rodefeld 1980; Friedberger 1988). In this way each generation increases the base received from parents through inheritance. Differences that emerged between yeoman and entrepreneur farms are outcomes of how succession and inheritance were handled in the transfer between generations (table 7.1). In the past, entrepreneurs in Emerson transferred larger estates and more liquid capital to fewer heirs less likely to squabble over the settlement. Nonfarming siblings tended to out-migrate; eventually they or their heirs, with less sentimental attachment to the land, were likely to sell inheritances. These processes have favored land consolidation in Yankee communities, reflected in the larger operation size (chapter 4, table 4.2) and larger tract size (chapter 1, table 1.1).

In St. Boniface the historic process that transferred small holdings and little liquid capital led to present-day farmers seeking full-time and off-farm employment as a means of maintaining the farm and an agrarian way of life. Of course, the persistently large Catholic families have exacerbated the fragmentation in each generation. Though St. Boniface yeomen have expanded ethnically controlled acreage over time (chapter 1, table 1.1, and chapter 9), it was not to the same territorial extent as Heartland Lutherans, who reported controlling family size after the pioneering generation (Corner 1928).

Success in socializing all children to value farming as a way of life can endanger achievement of yeoman goals. High fertility and inequitable treatment of children are points of yeoman family farm vulnerability for preserving continuity of a viable homeplace farm. Siblings feel exceedingly bitter about being exploited in favor of the eventual successor. To one in Heartland, "Land is the whip" that patriarchs use to control children. Sibling rivalry is heightened in such a context. Entrepreneur families make it easier for nonfarmers to let go of an inheritance. A willingness of nonfarmers to give up ownership is associated with less fragmentation—the pressures on land use are therefore weaker. Family farm vulnerability among entrepreneurs occurs in producing a successor, but since continuity is not such a concern to them, when a farm does not persist through an intergenerational transfer, it is not considered a family failure. Among yeomen, in contrast, those who lose land are remembered through oral history as having failed to maintain the family patrimony. A Heartland widow, when relating her mother's sibling rift over land, spoke as if it were her own: "Well, it stays with you." Entrepreneurs do not dwell on the past and move on to new endeavors with a clear conscience. Their family patrimony is, after all, a resource that provides an opportunity for any entrepreneurial activity.

In the inheritance process as in farm management and succession, families are involved in choosing alternatives and making trade-offs in a context shaped by cultural beliefs that weigh personal rewards against group welfare demands (Kantor and Lehr 1975). Family members trust that they will not be exploited in the course of these trade-offs (Barber 1983). The basis for this trust is a belief that all family members want the best for one another, bear responsibility for this, and have a moral obligation toward each other. The down side of farming is that exploitation does occur. With the emphasis on a single dominant family dyad comes particular potentials for trust violations.

Thus, family exploitation differs between yeomen or entrepreneurs. Families avoiding alienation among various members are those more likely to preserve the family farm through intergenerational transfers.

Families successful at achieving land and family goals produce the distinctive land ownership and farming patterns that identify a yeoman- or an entrepreneur-dominated community. No farm family lives in isolation but as a unit embedded in a larger social structure, the rural community. How the farm family is joined to the community, primarily through links formed by the marital couple, is the subject of the next chapter.

EIGHT

Social Networks:
The Links to Community

Family members interact with members of other households via networks based on bonds of kinship, friendship, religion, and service or political activities. Network links are the connectors where family members intersect with the community. Neighboring has long been cited as one of the hallmarks of rural society; that networks deliver social and emotional support is assumed for farm families. Neighboring, however, is filtered through a network that also serves families as a mechanism for attaining farming goals. Networks thus are instrumental as well as socially supportive, and families must actively cultivate and nurture the relationships. Yeomen and entrepreneurs construct different sorts of networks, and therefore their social lives take distinctive forms. In both groups women more than men organize and tend the family's social networks. After children are launched from the natal home, wives and husbands are more dependent on one another's company, and the character of the couple's social network becomes more salient to everyday life.

How a farm couple is linked to extended kin and to other men and women in the community is related to the gender hierarchy integral to the conjugal roles described in chapter 5 (Bott 1971). The segregated conjugal roles of German yeomen are associated with a close-knit network in contrast to the joint conjugal roles associated with a loose-knit social network of Yankee entrepreneurs. The network also takes its character from the family's social status in the community: the size and type of farm a family operates and the status of previous generations of kin favor cultivating links with specific people.

Ownership of a homeplace provides families a nexus of social relationships: through inheritance with a link to the past; through residence with a stable neighborhood; and through kinship with farming helpmates. How many relatives live in close proximity, however, varies as a consequence of pursuing particular land and farming goals. For example, yeomen who emphasize an agrarian way of life are more likely to keep nonfarming children nearby than are entrepreneurs who socialize children to value alternative, independent social pathways. Furthermore, whether children are encouraged to succeed parents in farming influences the makeup of the farming couple's daily work and kinship contacts. The rural church offers a farm couple the next most accessible network of relationships in the community. These ties are structured by religious practices that underscore family and community gender and generational hierarchies.

A close-knit network peopled by kin and friends of the same gender provides rural men and women with a solidarity group. Female solidarity groups, another term for a personal network, cross-culturally assure a better status for women by providing social support where other female contacts are restricted (Friedl 1975; Moore 1988; Rogers 1975; Rogers and Salamon 1983). When no land the couple farms is derived from the woman's relatives and when the woman has little contact with her kin, her network is limited. The availability of solidarity groups through the church is thus particularly important when a woman is prevented from regularly socializing with women other than her husband's kin. Farm men, in contrast, typically have many opportunities to bond with other men, having greater freedom to circulate than do wives, who are more bound to the domestic setting.

Table 8.1. Family Links to the Community

Yeoman	Entrepreneur
Social Network	
Tightly knit	Loosely knit
Sexually segregated but parallel	Social network joint, business and church networks sexually segregated
Kin oriented	Individualized household networks
Mediates outside world	Not a filter for other societal institutions
Readily mobilized for social support	Less available for social support, and this is preferred
Church Affiliation	
Reinforces gender hierarchy	Reinforces gender and social hierarchies
Overlaps with community	Reflects community hierarchy
Integrates community	Echoes community social structure divisions
Kin network all in church	Kin network potentially split among different churches
Women and men participate similarly	Women more religious
Social and religious functions equally important	Primarily serves a religious function

Table 8.1 synthesizes the connections between the yeoman and the entrepreneur conjugal relationship, the organization of the farm, and the links channeling social interaction in the community. Relations between a couple are shaped by their land acquisition goals and how their children fit into that plan. The social structure of the community and the church reflects that of the family; each serves to reinforce the other. Heartland's church is hierarchically organized just as is the yeoman family, and the close-knit networks filtered through the church are sexually segregated. Like Wheeler's entrepreneur conception of a jointly owned farm, network participation is also a joint matter, albeit loosely knit. The exception is women who are from farms that have recently grown large through consolidation and whose contribution is superfluous due to employment of hired laborers. Such women have become more religious, independently of their husbands. The network provided by the church represents an alternative arena in which women can find solidarity, although an arena also regulated by men.

•
Contrasting Social Networks

Heartland couples are deeply embedded in social networks that are tight-knit. Network members are relatives and neighbors, and de facto gender segregation occurs because women and men, even when socializing jointly, drift into separate circles. Visiting patterns illustrate these practices. Women, even retired women, tend to be homebound, by habit or custom, while Heartland men circulate among kin and in wider networks, ostensibly for the benefit of the farm. Men stop by one another's farms, for example, during harvest to ask about the moisture of beans or in less busy seasons just to have a beer or to gossip. Many retired men make a daily round of stops at the homes of married children and siblings to chat. Married children not farming still visit parents, most frequently when children are small and on a weekly basis as children reach maturity. If children do not visit, mothers and daughters in particular talk on the phone almost daily.

In the recent past women baked on Saturdays, and relatives visited on Sundays; this Sunday visit was the most formal and institutionalized kin network gathering. A retired Heartland woman said her husband's parents had a livelier social life than families do today: "They were very social. They used to have people in every evening or go to someone else's place. They liked to play cards, drink, and talk about the goings on." After her husband's parents retired to a nearby village, the pattern changed. His widowed mother came out often, and they had to visit her every week. "I had to get all those little kids together. We'd drive over in the car. . . . She gave me lots of advice too; she knew the right way to do things," she recalled with a laugh.

Neighbors from the same threshing ring also socialized in the past, mixing business with pleasure. A yeoman farmer fondly reminisced that for ten years shortly after World War II the neighbors congregated each summer for male-only beer parties under a tent pitched in a small grove of trees. His wife commented on how this reinforced male solidarity and female isolation. "We women were not invited; we were supposed to be at home with the kids." Today other events provide the context for socializing that maintain the asymmetry of gendered behavior. A blizzard produced a communitywide party, with the Heartland countryside spotted with men riding about on tractors. As part of plowing people out, the rescuer sat and drank some wine or beer afterward while young wives remained cooped up at home with the children.

Sons move quickly into the male world. A Heartland woman described this process for her eldest son, now a farmer. "[My husband] wanted a son. . . . We had our boy [first] and . . . from the time [he] could he was with [my husband]." For women, social interaction is most often with relatives. Mothers, daughters, and sisters are extremely close. A retired farm woman explained how relationships develop: "I wanted a girl and really spoiled [my daughter]. We've always been close. [She] was home with me most of the time. She worked on the farm, but mostly in the house and with the animals."

Pressure on yeoman women, in particular, is strong to marry German, for endogamy maintains the homogeneity of kinship networks and assures parents that a mate shares the right beliefs about land. Examples are often cited of women marrying outsiders and then experiencing a struggle when the mate urges inherited land be signed over to him. In one case, after a woman refused, the man eventually divorced her; this action reinforced Heartland beliefs about the real motives of nonyeomen. Two cousins with identical, traditional fathers shared a background in which they were pressed to marry German farmers. They formed a sisterly bond. When one married a non-German and moved out of Heartland, the relationship was maintained, although "all the time I was dating she was held up to me as an example of what I should not get involved with." In similar ways women single out a sister, or perhaps a cousin, as a special confidant and create a personal network that is a solidarity source.

Women lacking sisters or a mother are more dependent on neighbors for intimacy because custom circumscribes a narrow social circle. One middle-aged farm woman butchers and cans with a neighbor, and she and her husband go out to dinner with other neighbors. But such relationships are more fragile than are kin ties. "I had another good friend, but my husband had a falling out with her husband and now they don't speak at all," commented a farm woman sadly. When a husband breaks a network link, it is broken for the wife.

After children mature, women often broaden their regular contacts to church networks, an acceptable outlet. Women do weekly stewardship, and many participate in a twice-weekly Bible study group. However, patriarchal husbands even complain about church activities. "He'd say, 'I'm away all day long and I want you here in the evening if I'm home.' . . . Well, sometimes I'd stay at home and other times I'd go, especially after he's fallen asleep," explained a retired woman. When younger wives join church groups or other activities while children are small, this may meet with disapproval. "My place is in the home," said a woman criticized for taking aerobics and a Bible study class. Social controls act to keep the kinship network of highest priority for a woman.

Men's networks are usually wider than are women's in Heartland. This contrast is expected because a man's circulation in the community and among non-Germans is considered vital to the farm. Crucial information such as tips on available land or a better elevator price on corn come through such contacts. One retired farmer heard about land outside Heartland through the "grapevine" at the coffee shop he visited daily at dawn. According to his wife, "[My husband] always says, 'It's not who [*sic*] you know, but whom you know.'" That is, she explained, "You can be acquainted with all sorts of people, but that doesn't help. You need to know the right people; ones who can help you out, do you favors." A successor commented about his retired father's infallible sources for bits of information he drops by "letting it slip" in conversation. "I'd like to know where he goes. . . . I've learned not to ask. . . . I have contacts too, but not like Dad's group."

Younger Heartland men start to cultivate social networks that include non-Germans when they are ready to begin farm expansion. For instance, the young president of the church congregation is involved in tractor-pull competitions; another man participates in a service club; yet another plays cards regularly at a nearby village pool hall. Afternoon visits to local bars, filled only with men, are common. A farmer, married about fifteen years, suddenly enlarged his network, to his wife's surprise: "He's been nominated for church offices before and always turned them down. Then he came home a few months ago and said, 'I joined the volunteer fire department. I think it's about time that people in [a nearby village] know who [I am].' . . . Actually what it means is he goes over there and drinks coffee with a bunch of men and shoots the breeze."

Each spouse has social responsibilities, through his or her respective network, that are vital to the success of the farm. Heartland women are responsible for maintaining good extended family relations. To further family farming goals women seek to garner all the potential aid, information, and support available in their network. It was considered impudent of a son-in-law to complain that his wife's parents were favoring a son over her—parents felt such complaints were only acceptable from their daughter. The wife's father contemplated withdrawing some planned support as a result. Correspondingly, men are responsible for developing business contacts providing access to land, whether for rental or purchase. Male kin (not limited to those working together) with a special affinity are considered a farmer's closest network links. One brother-in-law was favored over another by a retired farmer. "He and I are real close. If I'm doing some investing he's the first to know and he lets me know too." Plans for land purchases and other major farm transactions are discussed with these chosen relatives.

Next to kinship, proximity operates as an important derivation of yeoman network links. Most Heartlanders can trace some distant kinship with everyone else, but because yeoman ethics, religion, and experiences are shared, neighbors can be readily incorporated in a network. However, a principle of selectivity according to affinity operates; not every neighbor is a friend. In one neighborhood each spouse of a couple obviously headed for a divorce leaned heavily on a different neighbor for support.

The close-knit character of the networks in Heartland has many social benefits. Those undergoing trauma can count on neighbors as well as kin for support. Seldom, except for wives with small children isolated during blizzards and busy farming seasons, does anyone complain about loneliness. Quite the opposite—people have too many visitors, too many social obligations. If an individual in crisis lacks a wide network, the minister tries to create support or social outlets. An elderly unmarried woman, for example, hospitalized with surgery, received flowers and hundreds of cards from the community. The teenaged son of a newly widowed woman was virtually adopted by neighbors and employed on their farm to assure his receiving the usual Heartland apprenticeship. An elderly widow said, "I don't know of a single elderly person who needs outside help. The families take care of them." Network loyalties extend to all relatives even in business situations. A farmer said he did not bid on land being auctioned because "my cousin wants it."

Close-knit networks, incorporating daily contacts and constant monitoring of behavior, carry social costs. People in Heartland lack much privacy, and the constant gossip and criticism by relatives aim at maintaining the required conformity such intimacy entails. "Someone's always stopping by for a cup of coffee. Sometimes that's bad, especially when it's someone you don't care for," explained a farm woman. "You can get more done without people in your kitchen all the time." Every detail of one's life is scrutinized. For example, a target for criticism was the purchase of a Toyota by a young farmer. "No one [in Heartland] drives anything but a Ford or Chevy," said a scandalized relative. Daily visits by retired fathers who moved to town were accepted by previous generations without rancor but are more troublesome today, particularly if the wife is not German. Certain divorces were attributed to a father who "after telling those kids they could take over . . . wouldn't leave them alone. That poor girl, she had no privacy." Young mothers expect babysitting. "I'd go loony if I never got away from the kids," said one. But assistance comes with gratuitous advice. "We don't agree on how to raise kids, but that's typical for mothers-in-law," said one young mother.

Language formerly reinforced the distinction between Heartland network insiders and outsiders. "I can remember when I was a boy listening to the farmers from Heartland talking in German in public so no one else could understand. We don't do that so much anymore," said a farmer in his fifties. Although some younger couples make an effort to teach their children German, this community boundary marker is no longer strong. Yet yeomen still prefer to conduct extrafamilial social and economic transactions through either the kinship or community network. Bankers, insurance agents, travel agents, hardware sellers, machinery dealers, seed corn representatives, and grain elevator operators are chosen according to whether they are a relative, are related to a community member, or have a history of community business. If kin or community links are not available, families turn to the church as an intermediary with the outer world. For example, families have adopted children through the Lutheran church and have used schools for the handicapped run by the church.

The tight-knit networks and the effectiveness of social control in Heartland and other yeoman groups have kept the communities relatively homogeneous and highly cohesive. Individuals at odds with local cultural notions about land are the object of substantial social pressure and might even feel forced to leave to experience freedom and privacy. However, the extreme solution may not be as necessary in the future since endogamy and the social isolation of yeoman communities have been broken down a bit more in each successive generation as children have sought more education and school districts have consolidated.

ENTREPRENEUR COUPLES' SOCIAL NETWORKS

Social networks in Wheeler reflect the individualistic stance couples take toward their farming operations. Despite a joint network among relatives being maintained, couples preserve considerable independence and privacy. Families farming together may not actually have close social relations, particularly when the enterprise involves relatives other than father and son. Joining forces for efficiency and profitability does not require, according to entrepreneur practices, that related households share more than labor. Because the wives are not involved or work off-farm, they may not have the daily kin interactions. Thus, work bonds are easily segregated from those network links utilized by families especially for sociability.

Beyond the enterprise boundaries other kin, though part of the loose-knit network, are potential business competitors, and relations are guarded. Couples expect relatives to operate with the same rule: primacy of the nuclear family. Explained a Wheeler woman about the segregation of business from kinship, "If [my husband] and I hear of a piece of land which is available we might go to see the landlord and put in our bid. Probably [my husband's] cousins would go too, but we don't tell each other that we went. We would never tell relatives that we were going to see someone over land." When retiring, relatives, except for a parent or a grandparent, are rarely expected to pass on rental land or to recommend as tenants to a landlord those who are not direct descendants. For example, when asked if her husband's uncle would refer him as a tenant to a landlord, the wife exclaimed, "No, that wouldn't have happened. We heard he was one of the one's trying to take [land] away from [the current tenant]."

Being in competition with relatives does not preclude having some kinship allegiance, but relations are more social and less instrumental in character. "We care about [my husband's cousin and his wife] but that doesn't prevent us from having to sometimes compete with them. In a way you are competing with them, but they are also family so they offer you support also. . . . It gets competitive because all the relatives are trying to do the same thing." Wheeler families with several branches farming allude to those sharing a family name or kinship as possessing group traits, as in "the Smiths are all good farmers." Shared characteristics recognized, however, do not denote intimacy. "There's one thing our family has never had, is a sense of closeness. . . . There are a lot of [us] in the area, but [everyone] seem[s] to go their own way. Each was busy with their own kids and we never did get too close," reported a middle-aged farm woman a bit envious of other families she views as more close-knit than hers.

After children marry and set up independent households, entrepreneur families get together weekly. A Wheeler woman, whose husband farms with a son and whose other married children live nearby, insists the extended family attend church and eat together on Sundays. As the wife of one of Wheeler's largest operators with little involvement in the operation, she also does not work off-farm, and her hostess activities bring the family together: "Usually Sunday is a day of rest, but I'm so busy on that day. After church everybody wants to eat right away, especially if we're going out on the boat. . . . Before [my father-in-law] remarried I'd have him over for Sunday dinner every week. . . . That's when we see our kids, on the weekend." Relations with kin are connected with land; ties are negotiated more easily when children do not farm or farm independently. When a daughter and her husband, for example, farm with his parents, they become potential competitors with her parents for rental land, and this precludes great intimacy. One such daughter feels torn by what she considers preferential treatment of a sibling farming with her parents—"I can't even get Mom and Dad to watch my kids." She worries that the sibling will inherit rights to her parents' rental land, acreage that she and her husband sorely need. "One reason I don't say anything . . . I enjoy getting together [on holidays] and I'm afraid we'll lose that. . . . I wonder what my mother thinks. She doesn't say much." Thus, when relatives are potential land competitors, women are cut off from the female kin who otherwise are their natural solidarity group.

Work is frequently cited by entrepreneurs to explain their lack of a close-knit kin network. "My parents say we never go to visit them, but we never visit anybody. We're too busy," said the wife of a large Wheeler tenant operator, mother to several children and with a job outside the home. Those who do socialize with relatives choose kin with whom interests are shared and who are unlikely to be competitors for land. In general, friends are not business contacts. For example, a farmer in his late fifties tries to play golf several times a week. Several in his group are cousins by blood or marriage and another is a businessman—none farm. Because he actively farms with his sons, "I have to skip more days than the others because they're all retired, and I'm not." Friendships among women also develop when land is not likely to bring their families into contention. Two women, neighbors on large, fully owned family farms not in an expansion phase, maintained a warm and close relationship. Business competition seems to preclude social closeness and channels a family's social life according to their operation type.

Women in Wheeler, particularly those from large farms, form friendships with women with whom they feel comfortable, rather than for business reasons. Among the Old Guard group, women choose those of the same age who are conservative and wealthy but who do not flaunt their money. They distinguish themselves from another group of more aggressively entrepreneurial couples considered more flamboyant "movers and shakers" or "free-spending swingers" given to planes, boats, motor homes, and travel. The latter group also includes local businessmen and professionals, spans several neighboring communities, and is involved more in school district than in church affairs. Women from middle- and smaller-sized farms participate in numerous weekly or monthly card groups with friends of a similar age or neighborhood proximity.

Families most involved in nonkin, community-level Wheeler networks have farms more dependent on rental land. As larger landowners construct a social network based on people they are not likely to compete with, so tenant operators cultivate a wide network to maximize contacts useful for access to land. A woman from one of the larger enterprises in Wheeler commented how the quest for land dominates lives of tenants in particular. "[My husband] and I are sort of alienated. We don't need to be involved in town. . . . I think it's harder for the others to separate family and business. . . . We don't have to go into town and talk to people for the business."

Each Wheeler village meeting spot is associated with a distinctive group of men sharing an operator category and a similarly sized farm. Patrons of the coffee shop are a network operating smaller and middle-sized farms—those who rent all or most of their land. Explained a regular member: "I go to the coffee shop most every morning . . . more in the fall and winter. . . . We go to compare our farming over coffee—then go out and farm. . . . I think it's good we discuss our farming together. . . . We talk about government programs and the Cubs and the Cards. . . . Mostly the same people go—it doesn't vary much. We have some ninety-year-olds all the way down to young ones." Because it is a group with similar farming concerns, the group cuts across the community and mixes ages. Another group meets regularly at the grain elevator; the larger operators are more likely to stop here, though they might eat at the coffee shop. Some men meet at the tavern in the evening. The church is less central to business than it might have been a generation ago, said the Methodist minister, "By the time I hear [gossip] at church it's been around town a week already."

Male network links are in reality potential business connections for obtaining land. Aggressive farmers dependent on rental land develop a variety of community contacts. Along with their regular coffee shop attendance, they may stop in at the elevator and the tavern. An operator described the actions of three family members farming together. One is a morning coffee person while another likes to have an evening beer at the tavern. In addition, "We've got the churches covered. Dad goes to the Baptist and we go to the Methodist. There are farmers in the Baptist church and rich farmers in the Methodist." A farmer, acknowledged as a community mover and shaker, explained: "If you just sit back, nobody's going to come to you." He is active in Wheeler's men's service club and in other activities. "I was president . . .

and that shows I care. . . . It makes you more visible, more respectable. . . . It helps."

Farmers with larger Wheeler operations disdain the "coffee shop group." They feel information gathered in this manner does little to increase competitiveness; they prefer "to keep to themselves." An older farmer, owner of a large amount of acreage, commented on the coffee shop network: "There's a group that goes into the coffee shop and they talk. . . . If one finds out that somebody else is going to start plowing today, then . . . you could go driving around and see that whole group doing the same thing in their fields. . . . They lack confidence, don't have any business savvy. Farming is a business and these people don't understand that, and don't know how it works." However, men just beginning to build an independent operation (that is, before they inherit any family holdings) are more apt to be in the coffee shop network than are their fathers. To establish themselves, entrepreneurs must obtain rental land unless a father is ready to retire. Wheeler parents seldom think their land holdings are sufficient to support two families. Explained one young farmer, "I hang around people I don't like, but it's because they are farmers just like me, and I need to know what's going on." Entrepreneur sons must cultivate their own contacts, unlike yeoman sons in Heartland. However, retired fathers of the larger operators participate in an elite network consisting of the Wheeler bank board, the Farmers Home Administration Board, and the Township Board. These powerful contacts have proved instrumental in gaining access to land for wealthier farmers and thereby reinforced the hierarchical social structure.

Each Wheeler male network is centripetal, revolving internally, rather than centrifugal. "It segregates according to cash [sic] structure," explained a retired tenant. Relatively little interaction bridges the male networks associated with each farm tenure category; similarly women seek friends having a comparable farm size and tenure type. "People are really involved with those in their own group. Interaction in certain groups is pretty strong. For those not too intimate with these groups it can be pretty lonely," said a farm woman who often commented on the social distance among Wheeler households. Men not seeking community contacts are either those content to remain small, marginal operators or those who control the most land resources.

Once Wheeler couples are not in the land market, they begin to disengage from the community, maintaining contacts with only a few friends and relatives. "We don't visit with neighbors anymore. . . . I don't know why we don't go over," explained a farm woman who considered her neighbor a close friend. Another woman attributed the lack of network contacts to business. Older couples—not elderly retired ones but those with grown children—speak of a distance that develops in their lives as they withdraw from previously established networks. Said one woman, "[My husband] and I don't get too involved in town. We just sit out here and watch what's going on." Another woman's comment underscores that aggressive land competition sours social relations: "Out here [neighbors] are all doing the same thing. They are taking care of things in their family, trying to protect their boundaries, like we are. So we don't see much of them, because we're all doing the same thing."

Entrepreneurial goals of stable big farms, owned acreage, and much wealth are goals that can also isolate people. For example, commenting on why people want to expand or own land in Wheeler, said an Old Guard member, "It's not really having freedom from having to look for landlords, because everyone rents so much land, anyhow. It means more that you can be independent and successful and nobody can touch you. The goal is to have a successful operation and owned land helps you. Other people might not agree with the way you made it . . . but they have to respect you, because in the end you are successful."

A woman who by any measure is from a successful Wheeler farm speaks poignantly about the lack of closeness even among her family members: "There isn't much visiting back and forth. Everybody's too busy to take the time. . . . In a crisis they help, but we're too busy to get involved otherwise."

Although people say an entrepreneur-dominated community rallies for a crisis, the evidence indicates that people respond for a ritual like a funeral but not for personal turmoil. A Wheeler woman dropped out of church after a falling-out with the minister. She felt she could not return to the congregation because her former friends "didn't reach out . . . didn't try hard." She considered them sympathetic but not willing to become involved personally. Many reflected on the self-imposed distance people maintain between one another in the community: "[My husband] and I have sat up here on our porch and asked why we are sitting here alone. We're all trying to preserve our boundaries." This isolation is particularly evident as people reach their late fifties and sixties and have no strong economic imperatives toward continuity to motivate interaction. A Prairie Gem Yankee widow with children farming reflected, "Sometimes when I'm feeling lonely or low I think my kids don't love me. Then I remember how I taught them to be independent. . . . What can I expect?"

The loose-knit character of networks in Wheeler is manifest in social behavior. Families care deeply about preserving their privacy and respect the desire of other families to erect the same barriers. Scarce unannounced dropping in of friends occurs as a result. People know so little about the family life of those belonging to a different social strata that they relate highly inaccurate statements about them. Gossip is an ineffective social control mechanism because of misinformation, and the isolation by social strata means that the community can exert relatively less control over individual lives. The loose-knit community also means that a considerable latitude in unconventional behavior is tolerated. A woman was a bit critical of an elderly relative redecorating a new house, but she reserved judgment: "I guess if you've got the money go ahead and do it." An extended family with many branches farming only owned land was considered particularly eccentric. "They always had money . . . but they were so tight. [The oldest] used to [in high school] loan money to his siblings and charge them interest. . . . You have to respect them because they march to the beat of a different drummer." When a woman found herself on opposite sides of a political argument with a neighbor of equally wealthy status, she recalled, "I went up to him at church and told him that I didn't agree with him, but I admired him for taking a stand." Individualism is condoned, especially if backed up by considerable wealth.

•

Church Participation and the Social Network

Rural churches have always served an important integrative function for communities. A church, aside from the grain elevator, is the largest physical structure and serves the community as the focal point for religious as well as social affairs. Particularly relevant to cultural schemas motivating social practices is the balance maintained between gender divisions of labor on the farm and church involvement. Religion can be pursued primarily to develop spiritual fulfillment, social life, or, as we saw previously, network links useful to achieving economic goals (Granovetter 1973, 1983).

YEOMEN AND THE CHURCH

Heartland, St. Boniface, and Freiburg farmers point to their single church as "what keeps us together." People in Heartland are religious; they pray before meals, attend church regularly, observe Lutheran rites of passage, and counsel with the minister. Parents involve children regularly in church activities from summer Bible school to youth groups. "We always insisted they go to church, and they still do. That was our responsibility," said a mother about her family. However, church participation is equated with community involvement—church life is also social life.

While the church undergirds the solidarity of Heartland, religion has a well-defined place in lives dominated by family and farm. Religiosity pursued for its own sake is not evident. For example, the minister pointed out that during the golden period of the mid-1970s when commodity prices were highest, stewardship funds for the church stayed absolutely level. The farm comes first in family economics. Elderly church members criticize their peers as spending too lavishly when they purchased an expensive organ in the 1920s to furnish the newly built church. After retirement, church involvement remains consistent; it does not replace, for example, the prominence of quilting groups for elderly women. The centennial celebration of the church combined religious ceremony with a lusty weekend of beer drinking, just as the annual mission festival does. People see no conflict between drinking heavily and supporting church goals.

Organization of the Heartland church reflects the gender hierarchy in German families, for the ministers and the elected board are all male. Women, as in the home, provide the equivalent of domestic labor to make the church function. Female employees run the church office, and female volunteers staff the Sunday school as well as donate labor to the Circle groups that support families facing crises. Men rarely cross the segregated boundaries of the networks that result from the division of labor. If the women want a new stove for the Circle groups, they must convince the men on the church council to buy it. A troubled young father in the midst of divorce was encouraged by the minister to teach Sunday school as therapy, but he was the only male involved. Across the lifecourse, religious involvement is similar for men and women. The church for most yeomen is consistently the major pivot of networks that integrate the entire community.

ENTREPRENEURS AND THE CHURCH

Because Wheeler has a variety of churches, affiliation can be chosen according to either religious or social criteria. According to perceptions of the past, social position rather than religious belief dictated church membership in Wheeler, but this has recently changed. "It used to be that belonging to the

Methodist church meant prestige. Only certain people went there. Now it's different. They'll take anybody; so belonging to that church doesn't mean the same thing anymore." A change began when a more fundamentalist Methodist minister took over the church several years ago. This minister counts the number of souls saved rather than the size of the congregation as the measure of success. After a Methodist church in a neighboring community closed, a member of an Old Guard family who had attended turned to Wheeler's church. Because of her social standing, she assumed easy acceptance. However, she was astonished to be told by the dogmatic minister to participate for a six-month trial before her application would be reviewed. This shift to fundamentalism coincided with the consolidation of farms into fewer, larger operations in which entrepreneur women were less involved. Typical of the new religious focus are the popular weekly discipleship groups for men and women started by the minister and copied by the Baptist church. "Each week we do things for people [in the community] like call them or take them a little something," explained a female member about the social by-products of the basically religious groups.

Evidence of Wheeler church membership for purely religious reasons is supplied by branches of the same extended family attending different community churches; it may be because of a spouse's preference, but religious doctrine seems pivotal. A wife and one or more of the children may be very religious while the husband is not even a church member. In part, this is connected with the tolerance for variant behavior characteristic of the loose-knit social organization of Wheeler. More important to the diversity of religious behavior within a single family is that church membership entails religious commitment and thus involves more obligation than does the more socially based church membership in Heartland.

The most religious people in Wheeler come from either the top economic strata or the bottom. Some hired farm laborers living in the village belong to the strict Pentecostal church and have no television, and the women do not cut their hair or wear makeup. Retired farmers, but more commonly middle-aged farm women from the largest operations, uninvolved in production or bookkeeping, immerse themselves in the church. These women describe a lack of closeness in their families and almost an alienation from community. A somewhat isolated farm woman claimed, "People are friends with who they go to church with." Husbands of such women are deeply immersed in running the farm and have a strong network of male buddies. Furthermore, they are drawn into community life due to the prominence of their operation.

Wives with empty time and lacking purpose in their daily lives, not surprisingly, "get religion." Church provides women uninvolved in the family farm (as well as retirees) with a close-knit social network otherwise unavailable.

COMMUNITY NETWORKS AND CHURCH INVOLVEMENT

For yeoman farmers, embedded in tight-knit networks of relatives, friends, and neighbors, the church serves as one of many arenas for social interaction. Families possess overlapping networks for work, friendship, and church life. Access to land is typically through members of a kin-based network; kinship holds highest priority in yeoman tenant selection. A community reputation as a hard worker with good farming practices such as clean fields, along with devoted church service, can improve a young farmer's reputation. But the relatively small amount of land controlled by absentee owners (chapter 3) assures that yeoman farmers are more likely to find land through personal, face-to-face contact with kin or neighbors inside and outside the church. Sometimes a retired farmer lacks any kin farming, and the church's network then figures importantly as a tenant source.

For entrepreneur farmers, the church-based network functions differently for rental-land access than it does among yeomen. Networks do not integrate entrepreneurs into a cohesive community but rather reinforce pronounced social strata. People interact primarily with relatives and a small circle of friends who are noncompetitors for farmland. Community networks are loose-knit beyond this small set and are segregated according to those with comparable size and land owned in farming operations. Much rental land comes from absentee owners, some of whom maintain a stable relationship over three generations with the same family. As tenant farmers having a high proportion of absentee landlords, entrepreneurs deal with bankers or professional farm managers rather than with local residents. Thus, the local network is not as key to the outcome of rental decisions. Farming patterns therefore have favored the evolution of entrepreneur church participation as specifically religious; church economic and social functions diminished with land access becoming more professionalized.

Despite the contrasts between yeoman and entrepreneur networks, both buttress similar gendered relations and community social strata. Each type has a church hierarchy based on male dominance and a fatherly god, with women domestic servants to both. Large-scale landowners among both ethnic groups have their influence enhanced by positions of high status in the church or via preferential opportunities that stratified social networks assure. Though similar gender and social hierarchies are reproduced following a yeoman or an entrepreneur pathway, the family dyad that dominates in management, succession, and inheritance determines dramatically contrasting farming and group characteristics. I now turn from the nexus of the farm to the wider implications of family choices. Family processes writ large by ethnic communities bring to light how microlevel actions produce macrolevel trends that shape the patterns of local land tenure and community life.

PART THREE

Implications of
Family Practices beyond
the Farm Bounds

NINE

Land Tenure

How a group values, transfers, buys, or sells land constitutes its land tenure system. Without access to land, whether through ownership or rental, a family cannot farm. This means that landowners control a farm community's most valued commodity and that a land tenure system underlies the social divisions in rural society (Newby 1980). What happens to family land as a consequence of farmers working through the processes of management, succession, and inheritance causes yeoman and entrepreneur communities to evolve distinctive land tenure patterns. Specifically the national trend toward consolidation of farms is retarded or accelerated by these processes. I do not mean that farm families are solely responsible for the rate at which farms or land are consolidated in their communities; they are not. Other forces in the economy—markets, oil prices, world grain supplies—influence the rate of consolidation, but families do make choices critical to shaping their particular community and farming situation.

A land tenure system develops from the interaction of forces external to the community with responses by farmers (shaped by cultural beliefs and specific environmental constraints). European farmers deal with a tenure system matured over one thousand years of land use. By contrast, the Midwestern land tenure system is very young. Whether, as in Freiburg and Heartland, ancestors were the original homesteaders or, as in Prairie Gem, Wheeler, Emerson, Libertyville, and St. Boniface, ancestors bought land from the initial investors, the communities share an agriculturally based economy that has assured social dominance by farmers rather than villagers (Hatch 1975). Despite initial differences, by the 1890s the baseline of ownership in all the communities was fairly similar (table 1.1, chapter 1). The average tract size for both ethnic groups began at the same point, and this correspondence generally prevailed until the Great Depression. Favorable commodity markets during wartime coupled with stability in technological advances forestalled continued consolidation in any of the communities until the 1950s.

Starting in the 1950s profound changes occurred in Midwestern agriculture. Land became an increasingly scarce and precious resource. Many smaller operators left farming as new equipment spurred land acquisitions because more acreage could be handled by a single family and because the investment involved required larger farms for efficiency (Strange 1988). Once farmers could plow, cultivate, and harvest more rapidly, elderly farmers witnessed the doubling of the amount of acreage in farms during their lifetime. For example, in Heartland during early mechanization 160 acres supported a yeoman family, whereas by the 1970s, farms of 320 to 400 fully owned acres became common. Among entrepreneur families 500 owned acres (double that in rental acres) came to be considered necessary to support a family. The numbers of farm families in debt accelerated as the capital investment requirements for hybrid seed, chemicals, equipment, and land drove up costs for those pursuing the ideal that "bigger is better," while driving down production returns (Barlett 1989; Reinhardt and Barlett 1989). A retired yeoman commented on management changes during his lifetime: "You know the actual farming of the land is much easier nowadays, but the business stuff is a full-time job."

Two major views predict contrasting developments for United States land tenure under these conditions. According to one, family farmers are assumed to act uniformly solely from entrepreneurial motives. This view predicts that the laws of capitalism produce an inevitable land tenure scenario: the demise of the classic mid-sized family farm in which the family owns the majority of the assets, provides most of the labor, and obtains the bulk of its income from the farm (Buttel 1983; Goss, Rodefeld, and Buttel 1980; Schertz 1979; Office of Technology Assessment 1986). The high end of the expected bimodal distribution is foreshadowed by a new breed of Midwestern entrepreneurial farmers. In central Ohio a family consisting of a father and two sons farms a large and specialized farm of 8,500 acres, only one-third of it owned. When land prices peaked in the late 1970s, some family land was sold to outside investors. From the business perspective of the entrepreneurial father, too much equity was tied up in land, and selling off some would be more profitable in the long run. Other community farmers, operating from a yeoman cultural system that regards family land as sacred, were appalled at the sale of local tracts to outsiders, which they saw as a violation of norms (Wall 1984). Differing cultural meanings attached to land can thus exist in the same community.

The opposing view predicts more pluralistic structural developments related to varied commodity, regional, and historical circumstances (Gilbert and Akor 1988; Pfeffer 1983). Without disputing the obvious national trend of farm consolidations, one need not see a single land tenure outcome as necessarily inevitable. This view of land tenure takes into account the Midwest's cultural mosaic. It assumes that differing agricultural and social structural outcomes result from a variety of cultural systems that value land, ownership continuity, and community commitment differently. Culturally driven behavior, these proponents argue, can significantly impede or foster consolidations of farmland and farms by setting the conditions of the local land market.

•

The Evolution of Land Tenure

Intergenerational transfers of land processes are the engine of the evolution of land tenure. As a consequence of the lifecourse, a normal intergenerational transfer of farmland occurs about once every twenty-five years, amounting to approximately a 4 percent annual turnover. Because some of this land is transferred within families through inheritance, gifts, or preferential sales, only a small percentage reaches the open market each year. Over a generation, however, this 4 percent can amount to a considerable proportion of the land in a rural community (Reiss 1976). Census of agriculture figures from 1978 showed that two-thirds of agricultural owner-operators had purchased land from nonrelatives in the public market. In Illinois, the ratio was more striking: the great majority (82 percent) had purchased half their land from non-kin (U.S. Bureau of the Census 1982a).[1] Clearly, the ratio of farmland moving out of family hands to that transferred within has the potential to transform within a generation the land tenure system and thus the class structure in a small community.

Nationally aggregated statistics mask variation in local land markets. Factors such as the timing of the owner's death, family size, and gender of heirs are realities of human existence that affect whether the intergenerational transfer process keeps land in family hands. Larger families make the presence of at least one successor more probable and land sales outside the family less likely. If an owner dies suddenly or early or rejects estate planning, wills or other arrangements may not be in place. An untimely death makes the intergenerational transfer more problematic for heirs, often forcing the sale of some or all holdings because a parent delayed planning for taxes. Male heirs appear to keep a farmland inheritance in contrast to women, who appear to sell. Despite the shift to equality in national inheritance patterns, the amount of land controlled nationally by women has not increased (Geisler, Waters, and Eadie 1985). In Pike County in western Illinois, for example, over half the land transactions of women over a five-year period were sales out of the family (Wright 1969). (Lacking comparative data, we do not know if male sales would reflect the same trend.) A high turnover among female landowners, if they control ownership as widows, could represent a considerable proportion of land, since in western Illinois women owned approximately 42 percent of rented land (Reiss 1967). Cumulatively these factors can affect community ownership patterns over several generations (Salter 1943).

The cultural context for the social act of land transfer compounds the outcome of natural family factors by affecting the amount of land available in the local land market. Inheritance customs (chapter 7), support for successors (chapter 6), and the meaning families attach to land (chapters 2 and 4) constitute this context. When continuity is paramount, as among yeomen, land is a sacred family trust not easily parted with. Little family land reaches the public market, therefore. In contrast, when land is treated as a commodity,

1. I am grateful to Franklin J. Reiss for pointing out this relationship.

as among entrepreneurs, its symbolic value is inherently financial. Accumulation of land in this latter context is a means of elevating families in a power hierarchy or a mechanism for generating profits to be converted into nonagricultural endeavors. Decisions to buy or sell in the entrepreneur social environment are based more firmly on business strategies for financial goals than on family concerns.

Inherent risks exist in farming, from the weather, markets, and land values. Farmers call themselves gamblers because they take financial chances compounded by these unpredictable factors. Willingness to take on debt-risk and the priority placed on land ownership influence land market behavior, particularly when prices fluctuate wildly, as during the past decade. For example, entrepreneurs might invest when they think prices will rise and sell when they think values will drop. Such investors will be shorter-term farmland owners than an owner-operator dedicated to preserving family continuity. While yeomen do not discount the financial worth of the land, little benefit is obtained from market upswings when sales are not intended. In fact, since much of Illinois local financing is tied to property taxes, those who own land and do not borrow on the equity suffer from higher values. Yeomen are particularly reluctant to place family holdings in any jeopardy with debt, and they are also exceedingly frugal. Entrepreneurs do not have the same perception of risk and are apt to spend more freely (Salamon and Davis-Brown 1986).

When farms are concentrated and distribution bimodal, a few wealthy families control most of the community's resources, and other families are forced to operate small farms. This system is inherently hierarchical, and economic differences are expressed through striking contrasts in management and living styles. When land resources are distributed more homogeneously and most farms approximate the average in size, a community's social structure more nearly approaches a democratic, egalitarian system (Rogers 1985). In this context less sharply differentiated strata prevail since families control relatively equivalent resources and other qualities can underlie the community's social hierarchy. For example, producing many children with religious vocations conferred respect in Catholic communities, at least until recently (Beale 1989a). Success, according to community standards for land owned and farm size, automatically confers higher status among both entrepreneurs and yeomen.

First, I show how land tenure systems evolved among Germans and Yankees over a century of land transfers. Then, Heartland and Wheeler are used as examples of a land tenure system in process.

•

Factors Affecting the
Evolution of the Local Land Tenure System

The Midwest is typified by a high proportion of those who own or rent land actually farming it; the ratio of self-employed family farmers to hired workers is more than two to one (Beale 1983; Pfeffer 1983). In contrast to the past goal of owning most or all they farm, families today expect to own only some land—minimally that which includes their farmstead. Despite this shift in operation goals, land still symbolizes more than the tangible acreage controlled, and its ownership is still highly valued.

CULTURAL SYSTEMS AND AVAILABILITY OF LAND

Because all land is already owned in Midwestern farming communities, expansion, whether for yeoman or for entrepreneur family imperatives, is possible only when acreage surfaces in the local land market. Although two land markets exist, it is the sale market rather than the rental market that illuminates the connection between culture and land tenure. Availability of acreage for purchase is a consequence of a willingness of locals to sell family land or of absentee owners to dispose of holdings. The availability of rental land also relates to the extent of tenancy in communities and whether landlords are typically relatives or nonresident investor-owners with land handled by farm managers. The two markets are linked when, for example, a tenant receives first option to buy land rented.

To fulfill yeoman goals, a family producing more than one child must expand the farm with land purchases. In Freiburg, where large families put extra demands on a tight land market, people say, "Land is so expensive because everyone's German Catholic here, and they keep the land in the family. If some land comes up for sale, you know it won't come up again. It'll get into a family and stay there. . . . Most people around here have some money put away so when some land comes up for sale, they just snap it up." Thus community land obtainable for purchase is exceedingly rare. Freiburg's soils are less productive than those farmed by Heartland and St. Boniface Germans, but local pressures have driven land values to a similar price. Explained a Freiburg farmer, "Around here people are willing to pay a lot for land. Maybe it's ego, or wanting to go in with sons before a farmer is ready to retire. Big tracts would never sell here for the $3,000 or more it's going at.

What people are interested in is an extra 40 lying next to their ground. If you could just open up the ground and add in 40-acre slices, you'd be all set."

In all three yeoman communities, land located in the community center has the highest value. Yeomen have a saying that land within sight of the church steeple has the highest value (Ostergren 1981b). For example, in Freiburg, "The old grandfathers around here used to say as long as that church steeple was in sight, the land was too expensive." A common yeoman strategy is to buy cheaper acreage elsewhere to farm or for "speculation," which can be traded when land becomes available within the community. Yeoman-owned land is more likely sold by being offered to neighbors, for sealed bids, or at auction. For this reason, yeoman expanders must seek non-German land outside the community social system.

If young yeoman families delayed getting started until community land was obtainable, few would enter farming. Freiburg farmers procure land outside the community rather than postpone beginning until the right, rare parcel becomes available. Farmers recently have had to jump over the sections adjacent to Freiburg, controlled by German Lutherans and other German Catholics, to fifteen miles south, where demand has not driven up land prices so steeply. Young farmers prefer to haul equipment the long distance rather than reside outside of Freiburg. "I wouldn't want to live there because [Freiburg] is home. A lot of people own land [in the Yankee area], but most commute," commented a commuter farmer hoping to eventually find land in Freiburg.

In 1930 no Germans from Freiburg owned land in the county immediately to the south (Freiburg Centennial Committee 1939).[2] The earliest purchase in the few Yankee townships nearest to Freiburg was a 60-acre tract in 1953. By 1979, six more tracts for a total area of 611 acres were bought by Freiburg yeomen. A threefold increase of territory, 2,074 acres, had occurred by 1982 with the addition of seven more tract purchases, all by different families. The likelihood that this invasion and succession will continue is high, due to the exceedingly tight Freiburg land market. After watching the young farmer quoted above work his newly purchased acreage, the Yankee landlord of the adjacent farm asked him to take on his acreage. "They're Yankee farmers down there . . . , they don't wear themselves out much. They don't even farm all the land they've got," remarked the young German farmer, with an aware-

2. Owner names on plat maps were compared with the names of the original Freiburg founding fathers, of participants in the 1939 community centennial celebration, and of current owners.

ness of ethnic differences. This yeoman critically observed that since he began to farm five years ago in the Yankee county, all the farms bordering his have come on the market. He attributes the turnover to profit rather than agrarian motives. "There's a lot more rentals compared with [Freiburg]. A lot of the land is owned by people for investment—they've got nothing to do with farming." A Freiburg farm woman concurred by referring to the Yankee farmers disparagingly as "Yahoos."

More flexible land markets exist where Yankees dominate. In Libertyville some are proud centennial farm owners, but others expressed little distress about selling family holdings. For example, although farmers claim most are "holding onto land," when a public utility claimed a large block of county land, a displaced farmer had little difficulty in buying five hundred acres near Libertyville. Furthermore, because Yankees encourage children to leave farming and the community, the children consequently become absentee heirs to family farms. In Emerson, an elderly retired woman reported without any perceptible regret the probable sale of her farm: "Well, eventually the land will probably break up. My nephew and his son are farming it now. But after they're gone it doesn't look like any of the grandchildren will farm unless one of my granddaughters should marry a farmer. I guess once it's passed to the grandchildren they'd sell it. There's not enough acreage to go around." Several Emerson entrepreneur families sold portions of inherited land to finance tax payments prior to the late-1970s change in the federal tax law that relieved many estate tax pressures. When some heirs wanted to retain land bearing the family name and other siblings wanted to sell in one Emerson family, concerns for farm viability took priority, and the land was sold.

The logical outcome of Yankee operators treating land unsentimentally, as a commodity, is pride in profits made from land sales. When yeomen buy a tract of land, it is permanently withdrawn from the community market because families are loath to sell. Only as a last resort would yeomen adopt the inheritance tax solution proposed by an Emerson owner of large holdings: "Nothin' much you can do except sell off some in order to pay off what you want to keep."

THE LAND MARKET

Farmland values rise and fall with commodity market fluctuations and credit availability. Changes in Illinois land values, according to U.S. Department of Agriculture market data over a century, are displayed in figure 9.1. The values,

Figure 9.1. Illinois Farmland (Land and Buildings) Values per Acre in 1990 Constant Dollars (calculated using the Consumer Price Index)

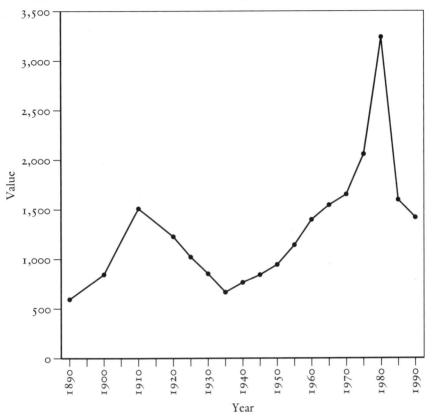

Sources: 1850–1950 values, Pressly and Scofield 1965; 1955–85 values, Jones and Barnard 1986; 1990 value, Illinois Department of Agriculture and U.S. Department of Agriculture 1990. Consumer Price Index 1890–1945, U.S. Bureau of the Census 1975; Consumer Price Index 1950–90, U.S. Bureau of the Census 1991. Necessary calculations for this figure provided by Linda M. Ghelfi.

aggregated at the state level, are approximately one-third lower than land values for the better soils in the Black Prairie counties in which Emerson, Heartland, St. Boniface, and Prairie Gem are located. Long-term trends are similar, however, for Illinois as a whole and its more prosperous counties (Wunderlich 1989).

Since wide-scale settlement after the 1850s, the agricultural economy of the Midwest has varied greatly, indicated by land value fluctuations shown in figure 9.1. (Because figure 9.1 is depicted in constant dollars, the Great Depression is reflected in the drop in land values earlier than in other parts of the economy.) Corn Belt depressions all were marked by farm foreclosures of those who borrowed on equity gained from inflated land values and were vulnerable when values rapidly dropped. During the 1870s Illinois farmers experienced a depression with land foreclosures. The 1890s are acknowledged as a period of low commodity prices that made survival in farming difficult (Allan G. Bogue 1963a). Midwestern farmers enjoyed prosperity during the two decades before the 1920s. Fueled by wartime demands, the value of farmland and buildings increased almost 75 percent in Illinois and more than doubled in Iowa (Kirschner 1970; Friedberger 1989). The 1920s were also marked by high mortgage indebtedness associated with the rise in crop values and land prices. By around 1925, however, land values had dropped by almost half, and the sales of implements and machinery plummeted.

Starting in 1934 commodity prices began to improve with new corn price programs, and a slow rise in Illinois land values began. Land prices did not reach 1920s levels until the 1950s. Farmers then had a twenty-year period of gradual but steady value gains. Finally, in the early 1970s, dating from the Russian grain deal, land prices rose sharply, fueled by high commodity prices, rising exports, and equity financing. This ended with a peak reached in 1981 followed by a sharp downturn to the present. From 1977 until 1980 actual Illinois land values were at times flat (Scott 1985). The conditions described previously that preceded and followed each market shift are indicative of circumstances during the farm crisis of the early 1980s (Strange 1988; Friedberger 1988).

Whether a community was dominated by yeomen or entrepreneurs figures importantly in local land market participation. Local land market activities are evidenced by fluctuations in the amount of ethnic land controlled within a community's boundaries, according to the historical plat map record. Beginning in 1893, when Yankee owners controlled 39 percent of Heartland acreage and Germans 55 percent (6 percent was Irish and Swedish owned), the two ethnic ownership paths quickly diverged (fig. 9.2). Yankee ownership plunged as Germans bought out Yankees until a relatively fixed level emerged at around 1,000 acres. Note that until the Germans reached a stable level of almost 6,500 community acres, land purchases were made at a fairly steady rate despite rising land values prior to the 1920s and in the midst and after the depression in land values between the 1920s and mid-1930s.

St. Boniface (fig. 9.3) presents a modification of the yeoman pattern represented by Heartland. Germans initially owned only about one-quarter of the community land and over the century increased that only by around 1,000 acres. As a consequence, although Germans are overwhelmingly St. Boni-

Figure 9.2. Heartland (German Yeoman), Acres Owned by Ethnic Group

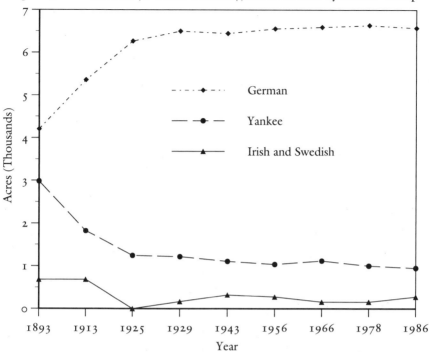

face's farmers, they never dominated as landowners. German settlement after the area's drainage was completed perhaps made expansion prohibitively expensive. The consistency of Germans buying land during the Depression when Yankees sold is, however, apparent. St. Boniface's ethnic ownership picture is confounded by an interstate highway put through the community in the 1960s. Due to the placement of the highway, German owners lost the most land, and their territory controlled declined relative to that of Yankees.

Wheeler (fig. 9.4) had Yankees predominant from the beginning, though ownership rose and fell in response to market fluctuations. Wheeler gives clear evidence of a drop in Yankee ownership after the Depression period, rising again to peak in the late 1960s and then dramatically falling again in the late 1970s and early 1980s. The few larger German owners are absentee investors and have behaved in an opposite manner, buying when Yankees were selling and selling when they were buying.

Prairie Gem (fig. 9.5), the mixed ethnic community, has mirror-image ethnic ownership trends. Throughout a century marked by land value fluctuations, Prairie Gem Germans consistently expanded control over community land beyond their original 24 percent, compared with the vastly greater 65

Figure 9.3. St. Boniface (German Yeoman),
Acres Owned by Ethnic Group

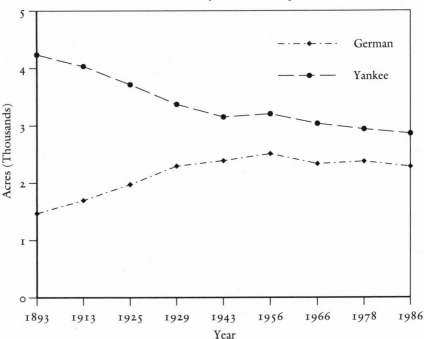

percent controlled by Yankees. German owners lost a little ground during the Depression, but after World War II they resumed their inexorable upward climb toward majority land ownership. The slight decrease shown in 1986 might be explained more by a German landowner incorporating (making ethnic identification difficult) than as a consequence of the farm crisis. Or, alternatively, Yankee investors might have responded to rising land values in the late 1970s and bought German land reaching the open market.

The mirror-image figure of ethnic area controlled over three or four generations shows that the yeoman Germans and the entrepreneur Yankees in all communities tended to make complementary transaction choices. Clearly, over the century, the yeomen bought land sold by the entrepreneurs. Yeomen purchased land throughout the years of falling land values (1920s–30s), but less so when land values rose steeply. It looks as if the yeomen and entrepreneurs in each community coexist in an ecological balance. It is possible that entrepreneurs speculate and help drive up the price of local land in a rising market. When land values drop, the land is sold to yeomen who have deferred land needs, unwilling to take financial risks. Yeoman Germans tend to be consistent in their farming and, by implication, land purchase decisions, while entrepreneur Yankees buy and sell cyclically.

Communities of farmers motivated by yeoman goals for farm and family are persistent landowners, as seen in chapter 1, and gradually increased their control of local areas over the long term. Correspondingly, landowners in entrepreneur-dominated communities bought and sold land more readily, and the extent of land controlled fluctuated over time. Yeoman Germans acted consistently to fulfill continuity goals despite hard times. Entrepreneurs tended to lose ground as a result of financial downturns, while yeomen gradually gained and expanded.

•

Evolution of Land Tenure at the Family Level

The goals embodied in a cultural system are best understood in the context of family land histories. Yeomen and entrepreneurs manage farms, expansion, and intergenerational transfers according to motives handed down with the family patrimony. As past generations strove to achieve shared goals, their choices developed a particular community's land tenure system.

Figure 9.4. Wheeler (Yankee Entrepreneur),
Acres Owned by Ethnic Group

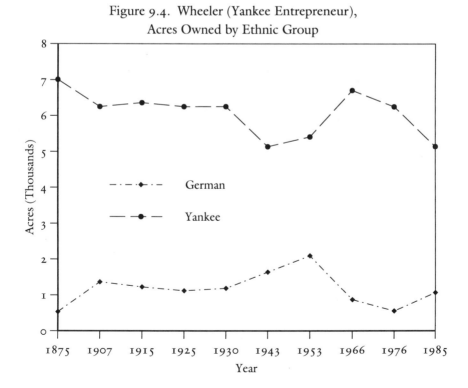

Figure 9.5. Prairie Gem (German/Yankee Mixed),
Acres Owned by Ethnic Group

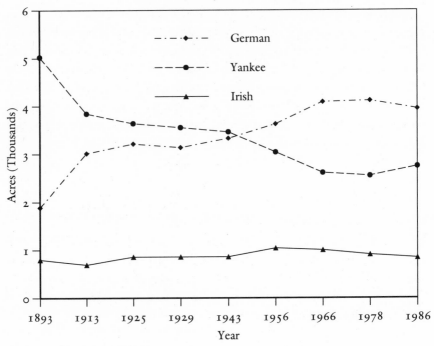

A WHEELER ENTREPRENEUR FAMILY LAND HISTORY

The original pioneering member came to Illinois from Ohio in 1870. He had to clear and drain land, eventually accumulating 800 acres. "We've always been landowners in the area," said a descendant. Of the twelve children the founder and his wife had, only a middle son went into farming, and most of the others left Wheeler. The successor eventually ended up with 600 acres, having purchased many of his siblings' shares. He farmed and, with a non-farming sibling as his financial partner, ran a grain elevator.

His three sons, the second generation, all became farmers with varying success. One did little with his inheritance of 180 acres. The other two successors were as entrepreneurial as their father. Each aggressively bought land and simultaneously ran other businesses. One brother owns 800 acres and once also ran a hatchery business. The other brother benefited from marriage to a woman from a wealthy family, and her land combined with his substantial expansion meant that at his retirement they owned 1,300 acres. Both brothers formed corporations with their children, and each now has an only son farming the land.

The third generation is middle-aged, and their fathers still head the corporations. A son of the least entrepreneurial brother would like to farm, but his father rented everything to a brother. "Probably it's because I don't have the big equipment to do the job right," said the son unhappily. He must work at a Wheeler agribusiness firm while his wife commutes to a job in a nearby city. The second successor has bought 100 acres and rents another 1,000 with his father. The son of the third and wealthiest farmer, starting with a small farm rented from his father, has bought more than 100 acres and rents another 700 acres independently. A sibling expects to receive half the father's 1,300 acres but, having married and left the community, will continue to rent to her brother. His son, representing the fourth generation, works on salary for the family corporation, but the parents expect him to gradually buy his way into the corporation, from his two siblings who will also inherit equal shares. After the son marries, the parents are considering retiring at age sixty and extending their annual winter stay in Florida.

Four generations of the family were entrepreneurial, adding substantial amounts of acreage to an inherited base. The fourth generation has merged operations, and the combined acreage of the two corporations made the joint operation one of Wheeler's three commonly acknowledged large farms—the local definition of an operation of over 3,000 acres. Merger of the two farms suggests a pattern of farm consolidations in Wheeler. The present generation has expanded more with rental land rather than with the land-purchase strategy of their fathers; inheritance of a substantial stake provided the financial base for expansion. Small family size after the pioneer generation with all but the successor leaving Wheeler has also fostered the consolidation of farms and the continued expansion to achieve Yankee ideals for success.

A HEARTLAND YEOMAN FAMILY LAND HISTORY

The first generation as German immigrants were among the original Heartland settlers who bought land directly from the railroad in the late 1860s. They sloped and drained the land by hand and paid it off, according to a descendant, with money generated by the wife's endeavors: "Egg routes paid for that land." Together they had twelve children and labored to accumulate

600 acres: "[The wife] worked all day in the fields and came home and baked bread," related a great-grandchild successor.

In the second generation, the youngest son as successor bought out the shares of his three brothers, who used the money to buy land elsewhere; the daughters received cash settlements or land at marriage. The successor's wife came from the adjacent farm and brought 100 acres to the marriage, which allowed them to expand the farm nearby. Together they built up a farm of almost 800 acres, which was divided among their three children. Each daughter was given a 200-acre farm at marriage, and of course their son as successor inherited the homeplace. His marriage motivated the parents' retirement move to town.

In the third generation, the siblings diverged in their land acquisition strategies. One sister and her husband, who inherited land from his family, accumulated over 800 acres, ranking them among the largest yeoman landowners in Heartland. With only a single child, this farm will not be fragmented when transferred. Another sister merged her inherited 200 acres with 150 acres inherited by her husband, and the couple were content to farm that acreage their entire career. The male successor had as his goal to "do for my kids what my dad did for us," a goal achieved without marrying land. His soon-widowed mother arranged a deal whereby she and the successor jointly bought her sibling's 100 acres next to the homeplace; later she gave it to the son. According to the son, his mother was frugal. At her death, twenty years after her husband's, the mother's estate paid the inheritance taxes on the 80 acres that had supported her. Through an elaborate series of purchases and trades the successor accumulated 300 additional acres while involved with his wife in diverse on-farm activities. He ran a seed corn business for thirty-five years. They kept chickens and hogs and also milked twenty head of cattle until the 1950s when new federal regulations caused him to tell the inspector "to shove it." He is self-described as eager to "make a buck any way I can."

In the fourth generation, a daughter was set up at marriage on a 200-acre farm; the son took over the 260-acre homeplace when he married; and the parents retired to a house they built in town. A third child was also designated to receive 200 acres and remained unmarried at home with the parents. Each fourth-generation heir received predeath land transfers of 60 acres (the spouse's name was not put on the land) when the parents used the onetime, $30,000 tax-free gift eliminated by the 1977 federal bill.

The fourth generation continued to buy land with substantial parental financial support. After the parents retired to town, father and son worked together for another decade with a favorable arrangement under which two-thirds of profits went to the son and one-third to the father. The father found a bargain 60 acres and helped the son purchase it. "I had money in the bank and nothin' to use it on. . . . My folks have always said land is the best investment," said the son. As the successor he also farms the acreage desig-nated for his unmarried sibling. The daughter and her husband have added 80 acres in two purchases, helped by her father's $10,000 gift each time. In addition, the couple farm 200 acres owned by various relatives. This successor generation, because they rent some land, differs from the previous genera-tions, who were full owners. However, their landlords are relatives, making the tenant relationship a personal one. The daughter and son-in-law have 500 pigs, and the son feeds beef cattle and some hogs. His father commented on the son's diversified operation: "He keeps hogs because of the way he was brought up." After her husband's death the widowed mother bought land alone and in conjunction with the successor, who farms it all. "What else is there to do with my money?" she asked.

This family, descendants of original settlers, represents the yeoman ideal in size of holdings, in having all children in farming, and in achieving "land in the community and a house in town" when successive generations retired. Siblings always farmed autonomously, though some labor exchanges oc-curred. Because all children farmed, each generation had to expand their di-vided share just to reproduce the same sized farm for their heirs.

ENTREPRENEUR LAND TENURE IN PROCESS

Wheeler's social structure, by channeling access to information and financial resources, affects how a family competes for land. Rental opportunities must be responded to quickly, and obtaining a parcel from an absentee owner may supply a first-purchase option. An 850-acre parcel of institutionally owned Wheeler land recently was leased through a bidding competition when the longtime tenants retired. Two families, each of a different tenure category, were among those involved, and their rivalry crystallizes the ongoing com-munity farm consolidation process. The lease competition was publicly an-nounced at the Methodist church, where both families are members. Farmers were asked to make a cash-rental bid; later it was announced the bid should include purchase of fifty acres. How each family went about their network mobilization, operation adjustment, and financial planning illuminates the social strata and networks in which each was embedded.

The family farming history brought each to the leasing competition with vastly differing resources. The part owner, successor to a large landowner, is established on the family land. In contrast, the other, like his father before him, is a successful, large tenant operator, but he never expects to become a landowner. His father's reputation and well-established network enabled the son to enter farming on his own rental land. Due to his aggressive business tactics the son ranks among the larger Wheeler operators.

The expansion potential represented by the large tract accelerated development of a strategy viewed as "better business." The part owner decided to combine operations with a landowning relative to become more competitive. "The way farming is it's better to work together," remarked his wife. Their joint bid hinged on the three years they calculated as necessary to pay off purchase of the fifty-acre parcel (split between the two families). "That way we'd have our 50 acres, and if the lease wasn't renewed we wouldn't be out anything." A substantial owned land base assured that the purchased land could be paid off quickly. Community pundits said the shorter rental term the partners bid is always more attractive to a landlord. For this family, victors in the lease competition, "It's all business who gets land."

The tenant farmer felt confident of an inside track on the lease: "We thought we had it, because the men farming it recommended us to take it over before they retired." Unlike the large, landowning family, he was prevented from merging operations with a relative who also is a tenant farmer because "he's my biggest competitor." His bid, for four years, was made in conjunction with some trusted tenant neighbors. Their longer-term bid and the capital required to buy acreage worked against them. According to this tenant operator, however, "It's all politics" that the other bid won. From each social stratum the event was judged accurately. It is business for those able to consolidate, or a conspiracy of "haves" against the "have-nots," who also aim to consolidate.

Over time this rivalry has been enacted repeatedly and, particularly since the 1980s, the tenant operator, despite having far-flung contacts and a large rental base, lost a series of tracts to the same family. Prior to this period the network cultivated by the tenant, his father, and a brother was effective. Almost every parcel they rented came through a contact made in voluntary and service organizations or in church. He is a past president of a local service group, his father served on the school board, and his wife participates in many activities. "It's who you know," he remarks. After three direct confrontations the part owner, together with kin, bought over 400 acres previously farmed by the tenant farmer and kin and gained the 850-acre rental tract. The tenant farmer had the direct loss of over 400 rented acres plus the potential to expand with 850 acres "to one of the local land-barons."

The part owner operator disdains land-hustling. Rather than learn about land from the tenant, he talks with other landowners or farm managers. For example, an estate executor called several adjacent landowners about a tract an absentee heir wished to sell. "In three phone calls all that land was sold," commented the part owner's wife. Acreage consolidation is occurring throughout Wheeler. The tenant described a competition in which a good friend made a purchase bid against the part owner operator family, who got the land. Somehow his friend's loan was held up at a critical time by the Wheeler bank, where the latter family wields a great deal of power.

In the future the equation will be tipped in favor of the new, two-family corporation farming 3,400 acres (much of it owned) versus the tenant extended family group farming 1,500 acres, all rented. The tenant operator recognizes his vulnerability. "I'd like to farm two to three hundred more acres than I need. Because the way things go, there's always a rollover from the landlords. It's better to have some extra." The two incorporated families invested in larger equipment after winning the 850-acre lease. Such equipment is preferred by farm managers, according to many in Wheeler, because the operators are perceived as easily able to absorb additional acreage. Farm managers choose the large operators over the small, and absentee owners or their agents seeking a quick sale follow the same logic. Being bigger not only causes rental land to gravitate toward the operation, but size attracts land purchase opportunities as well. Thus, the land market has favored further consolidation in entrepreneurial Wheeler as large part owner operators grow bigger at the expense of tenants and smaller owners.

YEOMAN LAND TENURE IN PROCESS

Land purchases are the hallmark of families successfully meeting yeoman goals. The extent of kin backing provided for land purchases, and the timing of that support, has been critical to who can or cannot expand and thereby gain land for the reproduction of the cycle. Young Heartland families purchasing land in the public market do so with substantial family support: a father retired at age fifty-five to allow a son to take over the farm; relatives gave rental land enabling early independent farming; or parents supplied financial assistance. Clearly, such actions are restricted to prosperous families.

If by the time the male head of a household reaches later middle age a family has not bought land, the likelihood of much expansion is small due to both lack of resources and age. It is families in this group, in particular, who provide what flexibility exists in the Heartland land market. At retirement or death their holdings tend to be sold or leased by heirs who by then have left farming. For example, when land prices were rising, a couple ready to retire sold their 160 acres at auction. The farm was too small for even one of their sons to make a living farming, though both sons continue to live in Heartland but commute to jobs nearby. Three expander families "looking ahead to the future" jointly bought the acreage to add to existing farms. However, expansion is done cautiously, and substantial risk is avoided. One of the three (the fourth-generation family described above) considered the acquisition feasible only because they were close to paying off a 40-acre tract purchased five years previously.

The small amount of Heartland land reaching the public market came, as seen above, from holdings too small to support a family even within the community's modest standards or from estate settlements. Two estate cases, for example, generated bitter comments about inappropriate behavior in the community. Each was the estate of a bachelor who died intestate, "too stubborn" to leave a will. "Even if you only own a dog, you should make a will," cautioned a woman critical of the trustees of sacred farmland who do not adequately plan the intergenerational transfer. Because over ten heirs existed in each intestate case, auction sales were the solution to divide resources evenly. A retired Heartland farm wife commented on the results of one auction: "People . . . just hate to see any of the land get out of the family. . . . Eighty acres were sold to a seed company, and it just made people sick. The family that sold should never have let that land go."

Three relatives arranged to buy one of these auctioned parcels jointly for later division. A relative commented on the cooperative effort: "People just don't have the capital to go higher on their own. . . . Area farmers can bid on land and keep it in the community that way . . . to make sure we have good neighbors and increase our land. If we hadn't done that . . . an outsider with a lot of cash could have outbid us." Although the newly purchased tracts were used for expansion, the auction exemplifies how intergenerational transfers can fragment tracts as smaller farms are absorbed by families striving to accomplish yeoman goals.

Auctions appear to be a recent phenomenon in Heartland, perhaps an effect of the high land values in the 1970s. "For years you never saw land going to public auction. Now you see it everyday, and these are whole farms. . . . I don't understand how people let it happen," said an elderly retired Heartland farmer. He had accomplished the expansion to set up two sons by buying land from Yankee absentee owners; however, this pathway to expansion is now closed with the saturation of yeoman owners within Heartland's bounds (fig. 9.2).

The tight land market in yeoman communities is a consequence of meeting family goals and the priority of preserving ethnic control of community land. Observed a middle-aged farmer, "In Freiburg, land that sells is sold about half the time by sealed bid and half by public auction. Public auction is better [for the buyer], because if someone really wants the land they might be willing to up the bid to just a little higher. . . . But you don't get a chance to up your bid if it's by sealed bid. On the other hand, a sealed bid gives you the option to sell to who you want, you don't have to sell to the highest bidder. That lets you keep out outsiders like corporations." As in Heartland, Freiburg yeomen pay higher prices for community acreage than do entrepreneurs buying comparable land. Similarly, yeomen buy small tracts and use savings or borrow a relatively small amount to make land purchases. A Freiburg farmer gave several reasons for why yeomen are willing to pay high land prices: "One is if you've got a boy coming into the operation so you need the extra ground. . . . The other one is you know if you don't get it . . . it won't be sold again in a hurry. It's a once-in-a-lifetime chance for that piece of ground. . . . You'd rather see yourself get bigger than see your neighbor do it. There's lots of competition for land around here." While cynics in Freiburg consider sealed bids a mechanism to bring higher prices, it gives the seller control over the buyer. In Freiburg the process has operated to keep out German Lutherans, and the neighboring Lutheran community has prevented Freiburg penetrations by the same method (Rogers 1987). Ethnic integrity of the community is thus preserved at the expense of smaller, more marginal yeomen who cannot afford to play the game.

•
Community Implications of Land Tenure Processes

Consolidation is ongoing in both yeoman and entrepreneur communities; all attest to fewer farms now than a generation ago. The proportion of farm loss in Illinois, as an indicator of the consolidation process for the Midwest, saw farms drop from 206,000 in 1945 to just 43 percent of that number (88,786) by 1987 (U.S. Department of Agriculture 1962; U.S. Bureau of the Census 1988). The plat map evidence for ethnic ownership patterns suggests, however, that land consolidation has not proceeded uniformly. Consolidation can progress more easily in entrepreneur communities as a consequence of how management, succession, and inheritance take place in the context of their farming goals. Yeoman communities are not apt to have wide divergence in operator size because farming goals do not spur aggressive expansion nor condone much financial risk.

A competitive land market and farm consolidation, not unexpectedly, are perceived differently by yeomen and entrepreneurs. Yeomen are troubled that the future of the family farm and the preservation of their ethnic enclave are threatened. High land prices (prior to the farm crisis) and the ensuing problems for intergenerational land transfers worried a retired Heartland farmer: "Sons can't buy out their fathers anymore. At $4000 an acre, who can? . . . So, the land is sold at auction and the family name is lost. Then someone else comes in, and no one knows what will happen, what they'll do with the land." A smaller Heartland operator expressed a yeoman view of the economy: "If all we have is large farms, you lose competition, and when you lose competition you lose incentive," he said emphatically.

Entrepreneurs view the competitive land market as energizing for those who are able to benefit by growing bigger and hence richer. "One thing the competition has done is make the farming better. Everyone really keeps their fields clean because that's how you keep your landlords. . . . The higher the tenancy rate, the more competitive it is. Everyone in [Wheeler] farms the same and needs the land so everybody is out for the same thing; everyone competes harder for it," said a farmer approvingly. Entrepreneurs, in contrast to yeomen, look with favor on farm consolidations. According to an Emerson operator, "On the whole, I'd say we have a pretty good group of farmers around here. . . . What we'd say are poorer farmers have been weeded out. . . . In the sixties, farms were smaller. But then as it became necessary to obtain more farm land to pay the expenses, some farmers didn't make it. . . . Those farmers who are still here had seen it coming and had made some decisions to expand. Farming is not just putting seeds in the ground and watching them grow. It takes management skills too, but some poorer farmers didn't have those skills." This same farmer offered some comments on the progressive consolidation that was taking place in Emerson and drew an imaginary map as he talked. "You know, when dad moved here, there was a house here, one here, another here. And now I farm all of that. . . . Those people all moved into town," he explained. Large fields unbroken by the more numerous farmsteads of previous generations now typify entrepreneur communities.

A Wheeler farmer, raised by German grandparents and farming land inherited from his Yankee father, reflected on his ethnic ancestors and their management practices with implications for land tenure: "It's been part of the [Yankee family] tradition that they were ambitious about getting land. The [German] side was more concerned with good farming and keeping the land looking nice. The [Yankees] weren't bad farmers, they just wanted to expand. They were shrewd businessmen. That's the difference between the Germans and English. Now though, all the [Yankee relatives] in the area are pretty good farmers. They are still ambitious and want to expand, but they're better farmers."

Entrepreneurs, unlike yeomen, welcome the infusion of capital that outside investors bring to the local economy. When community health is measured by growth, investment, and efficiency of farms rather than by intangible, nonfinancial factors such as continuity of a family name or ethnic integrity, farm consolidation (as long as your farm is growing) is the yardstick of progress. A brash young entrepreneur from Wheeler commented on the transformation of the community's land tenure: "It's better to have an outside investment of capital. . . . Sometimes we need outside investors to shore up what is already there. . . . A blend of landowners who live in the area and absentee landowners is better. The ideal way to do [farming] is to own a small acreage with a house and buildings and rent the rest. . . . Only bad thing is, absentee landlords don't care about conservation. So they don't take care of the land like they should."

As some entrepreneur farms grow through consolidation, size is wielded to gain a management advantage over competitors. For example, in Wheeler one such family insists the fertilizer service do spraying on demand, so their planting proceeds without interruption. They refuse to take their rightful turn, and as a major operation, they get away with it. According to a relative, "That's the way it is around here, everybody's out for what they can get." A consequence of tradesmen being forced to comply with such pressures is more downtime for other farmers. Farm managers are impressed with the quick planting and harvesting managed by clout and large equipment and are likely to remember when they have land to award in the future. Power correlated with farm size is apparent even to nonfarmers in Wheeler. "Groups are perpetuated in Wheeler. . . . People who have been here a long time are still called outsiders. . . . If they farm they are tenant farmers. This makes the locals angry because they feel cheated out of community land [lost to 'outsiders']. . . . Landowners control it, control growth," explained a minister relatively new to Wheeler.

Landowners exclusively focused on profits can undermine community welfare. Such a group opposed to higher taxes in Wheeler wrote to absentee landlords informing them their tenants were urging passage of a school bond issue. According to a big tenant farmer, "That letter hurt a lot of smaller tenants. It didn't bother me too much. My landlords knew they'd have to pay for it one way or another." Possibly the motives of the large operators were twofold: to defeat the school bond issue, which would save taxes; and to cause landlords' failure to renew leases, making new land available for their expansion. The school bond issue passed with the support of nonfarming village residents. Commenting on one of the important landowning families involved in the antibond group, a school board member said, "They tend to push people around because of their land. . . . Owning land has prestige. They think what's ever good for them is good for everybody else. It's not that way anymore." Although the school board member perceives social strata narrowing, those involved in land competitions think divergence has increased.

Yeoman- and entrepreneur-distinctive land tenure patterns can be expected to evolve beyond the distribution of operation types now typifying each type of community (table 4.2, chapter 4). Entrepreneur communities are likely to develop with fewer, larger part owner farms and correspondingly to increase tract size as a consequence of ownership consolidation. Operators of five-hundred-acre or smaller farms now tell children to look elsewhere for careers. As farms become larger, families should become increasingly dependent on hired labor, a category of rural residents already evident in entrepreneur communities. Correspondingly, among yeomen the part owner category should grow with a gradual increase in farm size, but tract size is likely to decrease only slightly because family size (dictating estate fragmentation), except among the Catholics, is already small. Entrepreneur communities should continue to differentiate toward a bimodal distribution, but yeoman communities may inch only slowly in that direction. Yeomen have a number of factors (succession, continuity, and smaller farms) that actually favor the persistence of the middle range of owner-operated farms.

Yeoman and entrepreneur land tenure and social structures effectively regulate farm and land consolidation opportunities (Schulman, Garrett, and Newman 1989). Among both groups those landed families with the longest legacy and owning a sizable proportion of the operation's base are in the best position to accumulate capital for consolidation purposes. Some clear effects of consolidation on the communities are evident. In Wheeler a member of one of the big farm families commented that since the 1960s, when consolidation accelerated, "people seem to be more spread out, less neighborly. When everyone owned land it was more of a closed society. When more people started renting it made different relations, but not necessarily bad. A bitter Heartlander made a similar observation about Germans: "All [the wealthier families] want to do is sit at home and think about their land and money."

As farms have consolidated, local populations have declined, and rural communities have had to respond to these shifts. Whether yeoman or entrepreneur families dominate affects how households relate to the community as a whole. Community persistence during this period of rapid change in rural society is the issue I deal with in the next chapter.

TEN

Community Personality

Rural society has undergone a fundamental restructuring, due to diminishing numbers of rural residents between 1950 and 1980, from 15.3 percent to being only 2 percent of the total United States population. As farms consolidated, fewer workers were needed to produce the same or more agricultural products, and rural residents were lured by nonfarm opportunities in urban America. A decline in farm family size (always larger than urban family size) also contributed to shrinking rural populations (Beale 1989d). These trends meant fewer families with children to fill country schools or customers to patronize rural businesses. When school systems consolidated, churches merged, or village businesses closed, rural communities lost crucial integrating institutions. Under these same economic and social circumstances some Midwestern rural communities maintained vitality while others deteriorated. Illinois villages only a few miles apart, such as Yankee Libertyville and German Freiburg or entrepreneur Emerson and yeoman St. Boniface, visibly differ in the numbers of businesses still open on main street, the makeup of village residents, and the involvement of people in community affairs. Such divergence suggests that farming-dependent communities are fundamentally different. In this chapter I focus on how reproducing family relationships with land creates fundamental differences among rural communities. I am particularly concerned with the core village as symbolic of community social relations: vigor of central institutions is a barometer of a group's cohesiveness, attachment, and commitment to maintenance of a collective identity.

Families recognize a cohesive community, as does the anthropologist, because cohesion can be measured according to certain benchmarks. In a cohesive community gossip and scandal, in the form of ritual discourse, are effectively employed by those having a vested interest in maintaining the established order (Bloch 1985). Thus, an indicator of cohesion is whether people conduct their lives attending to community expectations. Another measure of cohesiveness is whether people mobilize ("pull together") readily to achieve group goals. Actual acts of mobilization, evidence of people disposed to do things for others, are the source of critical "social capital" (Coleman 1988). In contrast to the human capital that is produced by investments in individuals, social capital is produced through interpersonal relationships and is productive itself. Social capital generates strong networks, social support, and reciprocal trust among community members (Coleman 1988). Intangibles such as integration, attachment, and social capital identify people living in close proximity as an actual community (Wilkinson 1990).

People can live as neighbors without sharing a sense of identity in which the community answers certain questions about self-characterization and belonging (Hummon 1986). Some argue that rural communities now, in contrast to the pre–World War II past, are less inclined to function in this manner due to farm families becoming more focused on private concerns and economic achievement (Hatch 1979). Recent Midwestern ethnographic evidence suggests, however, that multiple "cultures" or ways to organize communities exist in both rural and urban contexts (Schwartz 1987). Whether a community has dense social networks, effective channels of gossip, or a rich set of activities that crosscut social strata is indicative of its underlying cultural concerns about solidarity and cohesion. People can be tolerant of diversity and yet act as a community with a shared world view, or, alternatively, they can focus on individualism to such an extent that communalism is lacking. Rural community interaction can exist without the cohesion, support, and loyalty often assumed to be "natural" for small town life.

The rural community, some argue, provides cultural continuity amid the "flux of change" (Faragher 1986). The cultural system of land and kinship relations that farm families seek to reproduce molds their responses to change. A community social structure therefore evolves according to outcomes resulting from the internal family processes of management, succession, and inheritance that tailor connections of households to the wider community. When continuity is a paramount farming goal, by extension it is important to families that community continuity be maintained. Similarly, farm discontinuity as an outcome of kinship priorities breeds less concern for community preservation. These contrasting links between farmers and their communities have been considered evidence of an evolutionary shift in the conduct of rural life: the yeoman attitude is viewed as more traditional and the entrepreneur attitude as arising as the nation as a whole became focused more on the individual (Hatch 1979; Bellah et al. 1985). I argue that, rather than a single route of community evolution, multiple pathways exist in the distinctive links families forge between household and community in the rural Midwest.

Due to the historic Midwestern settlement during the nineteenth century by northern and western European peoples, rural communities were developed using a limited set of organizing principles. Domination of the ethnic mosaic by Germanic and British peoples (chapter 1) means their cultural conceptions shape a family's community attachment and involvement just as culture shapes how they handle land. Patterns of community affiliation produce differing potentialities and limitations to the context of daily life. In this chapter I discuss how the amount of social capital generated by the actions of community members ultimately affects the viability of village life. Rural villages now are particularly vulnerable, for in order to endure the strong competition from regional malls and cities, Main Street is dependent on family loyalty.

•

Culture and Community Characteristics

Farming according to differing cultural systems has direct implications for community life. Yeomen consistently prefer communities that derive their economic vitality from a single enterprise, agriculture. These communities are surrounded by relatively small, conservatively managed farms. Landowners typically are community residents, and the villages are heavily populated by farm retirees. By contrast, entrepreneur communities have fewer farmers and farm retirees living in the village, and the surplus housing produced by the farm population decline has lured renters who earn their living in a more diversified economy. Entrepreneurs are more dynamic, risk-taking individuals. They are less likely to regard community continuity as important and prefer change to replicating the past. A higher absentee landowner rate means more outside capital, but many absentee landlords have little vested interest in local issues. Entrepreneurs tend to regard community well-being as best served by a strong, diversified local economy.

Cultural systems, in particular, shape family practices that produce priorities ranking family welfare versus group welfare. For yeomen, the practice that defines the relationship of family to community is a commitment to continuity. Yeomen act in ways that assure the village near their farms persists so that future generations of successors can benefit from support of people with like agrarian values living in close proximity with strong group cohesion. For entrepreneurs, the practice that defines the relationship of the family to the community is a commitment to maximizing individual financial returns. Entrepreneurs act in ways that make business goals consistently of higher priority than community involvement. Neither community cohesion nor viability is a prerequisite to personal advancement.

To a considerable extent these contrasting practices account for community responses to social and economic changes. Each organizational style fosters a different manner of community functioning. Yeomen are community oriented, a trait highly suited to mobilizing cooperative efforts. They are willing to work together because yeomen believe that what benefits the community over the long term benefits them. Strong agreement about what a community should be facilitates group mobilization but also emphasizes preservation of what exists rather than economic development for its own sake. An innate insularity and conservatism makes yeoman communities more likely to take risks or develop initiatives for institutional maintenance than for breaching historical forms and concerns. Entrepreneur communities typically lack a unifying institution. Fundamental divisions according to distinct social strata and a variety of churches make community mobilization difficult. However, the greater diversity generates a variety of perspectives and experiences, a situation with potential for innovation. Entrepreneur communities bubble with ideas and energy for economic and social activities but lack the yeoman consistency and leadership required to sustain initiatives. Projects that promise growth and rapid payback best capture entrepreneurial energies.

Table 10.1 summarizes how a yeoman- or entrepreneur-dominated community is characterized by traits clustered according to the dimensions outlined in chapter 3. Each cluster of traits produces a distinct community culture that organizes the quality of everyday life. The following sections provide examples to illustrate the divergent yeoman and entrepreneur communities and village ambience.

ENTREPRENEUR-DOMINATED COMMUNITIES

Wheeler's settlement exemplifies the character of the entrepreneur communities. It namesake-founder, of English ancestry, began as a meager carpenter but eventually amassed seven thousand acres. When disease decimated his cattle, the entrepreneur then platted Wheeler, obtained a railroad right-of-way, and sold half his acreage to small farmers. Wheeler developed cumulatively as individual Yankee families bought tracts. Kinship links and a shared common past were therefore initially absent among households. Wheeler was divided early into well-defined social strata with the hierarchy dominated by those landowners who, having arrived earlier, came to control large land holdings and eventually diversified into businesses. Biographies featured in county histories illustrate that privileged position was maintained through intermarriage and political power (Wheeler Centennial Committee 1984; Wheeler County Historical Society 1879, 1911).

Farm consolidation is further along in entrepreneur communities than in yeoman communities, and Wheeler, perhaps because it was studied most recently, has the most consolidation. A retired farm wife, having left Wheeler at marriage, returned recently as a widow. She described the rental land market in the 1940s much as farmers do today: "It was hard to get land in those days. . . . Everyone fought for what they got. . . . Then when you got some land, there was always someone trying to undercut you; trying to take it over. It was a real dog eat dog world." A small-scale Libertyville operator described similar community relations in conjunction with competition for land: "They say rural life is neighborly, but it's not. It's dog eat dog. . . . The bigger guys are all paid up, and so they want more land, want to expand, want to get mine. . . . The little guys get gobbled up by the big guys."

Farmers in entrepreneur communities recognize that the population is ag-

Table 10.1. Dimensions of Rural Community Variation

Trait	Yeoman	Entrepreneur
	BACKGROUND	
Manner of settlement	Group or chain migration	Individual choice
Premise of community founding	Agrarian covenant	Cumulative, business orientation
Ethnicity	Common origin, self-consciously ethnic	Irrelevant to identity
Religious structure	One dominant church	Variety of competitive churches
	LAND TENURE	
Ownership	Fragmented	Concentrated
Absentee ownership	Relatively low	High
Farm size	Smaller than average, cluster about mean	Larger than average, bimodal distribution
	DEMOGRAPHIC FACTORS	
Population	Stable	Declining
Retired residents	Concentrated in village	Scattered throughout countryside or elsewhere
Social classes	Homogeneous, farm oriented	Diverse, distinct class differences
Age patterns	Young remain	Young leave
Village population	Farmers or farm related	Many nonfarming newcomers
Housing	Filled by locals	Surplus available
	INSTITUTIONS	
School	Everyone involved	Involvement when children attend
Businesses	Locally supported	Local loyalty tenuous
Voluntary groups	Few, long-lived	Diverse, short-lived
Communitywide social events	Varied, strongly supported	Limited, support casual
	SOCIAL STRUCTURE	
Boundaries	Tight, closed to outsiders	Open, highly permeable
Diversity tolerance	Low	High
Gossip	Effective as social control	Social control effect weak
Household networks	Close-knit, all overlapping	Loose-knit, segregated by class

ing and much of the land is controlled by absentee owners. An elderly retired Wheeler farmer considers the out-migration of young people and farm consolidation as related: "The reason farms got bigger here is that young people left to do something different. When their parents died, they inherited land, but they didn't want to come back here and farm. So they rented it out to the farmers who'd stayed." Thus, an awareness exits that family actions influence the pace of farm consolidation. Libertyville small-scale operators, in particular, encourage out-migration of potential successors, making eventual absorption by larger operators almost inevitable. "Men don't care about their boys being farmers. They think there isn't enough money in it. So they influence them into other businesses," explained a Libertyville farm wife. Welcoming outside capital investment also contributes to increased absentee ownership, a factor that may also spur consolidation. In Emerson a farmer said, "I would not mind if a stranger bought some land as long as he was a good person and a competent farmer. . . . I don't think Emerson closed people out like Heartland does." Financial or individualistic goals justify such entrepreneurial business means, even if community unity diminishes as a consequence.

Divided religious allegiances characterize entrepreneur communities. At one time five churches separated people in Wheeler and Libertyville. Today each community has three churches, but families also belong to congregations elsewhere. Religious ideology is a higher priority for entrepreneurs than allegiance to a particular local church. Each church has a cohesive congregation, but competitive relations prevail among them. A Wheeler minister commented that divided loyalties reduce community integration: "The only things that bring people together are the churches and schools. . . . Some big names in town don't even go to any church." An awareness exists that the churches reinforce community divisions. "Each church is composed of people with common interests," said one Wheeler minister. Another minister suggested, "You tend to socialize with people who belong to your church."

People are highly conscious of clear social divisions in entrepreneur communities, and although the numbers of farmers have declined, the amount of land a family controls remains the measure of status. "There are a lot of cliques in Wheeler, and there always have been," said a retired farm wife. "The first thing people ask you is how much you farm. Then, if they know you well enough they'll ask how much of it you own, like 'You own your homeplace?' Then, they subtract to figure how much you rent," explained a large landowner. A big operation with a substantial proportion of rental land also warrants respect. "Well, really the size is the main thing people talk about. . . . It signifies success, prestige, shows you've grown," said the same farmer. Those at the top of the land hierarchy expect to wield power. "Being a landowner has some advantages. . . . I can walk in somewhere and even though people might not want to talk to us they know they have to . . . and treat us with respect. We have some clout," explained a farm woman from a large Wheeler operation. Repeatedly, remarks were made about whether a person "deserved" to act snobbish—as if wealth justified particular behavior. For example, an old farmer related how his neighbor neglected to wave when he drove by. "He's getting too much money to wave to us," was the comment.

Entrepreneurs, who adhere to a booster mentality, consider dormant a community that does not grow. Libertyville families deem their community dead. A businessman's wife living in Wheeler reflected on the village's decline: "The younger generation doesn't stay. . . . There's not much farmland. . . . This town is made up of widows; every other house is up for sale." A middle-aged farmer agreed: "The town has changed. Used to be businessmen lived there, they and the landowners. Now it's just hired help. It's like a bedroom community." In Wheeler and Emerson the cessation of farmers' retirement in the village brought new families: professionals attracted to period architecture and others lured by cheap housing available for purchase or rental. Streets in these villages are lined by artistically decorated homes standing next to properties that are rented by transients and need paint, lack landscaping, or have junk-littered yards. Farmers in Emerson and Wheeler speak disdainfully about the influx of new residents. "Emerson just can't seem to attract a better type of people," one said. Both categories of newcomers tend to remain uninvolved; the village is just an address. Similarly, the farmers speak of sitting on their porches and observing their village decline.

Farmers are now a distinct minority in Wheeler and Emerson. According to the Wheeler mayor (and local records) over half (53 percent) of the 236 village households are blue-collar, including active and retired farm laborers, active and retired factory workers, clerks, and salespeople. Only about 14 percent of the village residents are retired or active farmers; 15 percent are professionals using Wheeler as a bedroom community; and 18 percent are widows or disabled people whose former occupations or that of their spouse are unknown (Heyman and Salamon 1987). Farmers of the Emerson community could only point to three farm households in the village of 540.

Entrepreneurs do not show particular attachment to their communities. The farm generation now in its fifties and their children do not intend to spend retirement in the village; this foreshadows loss of a critical village-countryside link. A middle-aged farmer, despite involvement in civic activities, has limited community commitment: "I'm not going to retire in Wheeler, Illinois, on the seat of a tractor. . . . We like Hawaii, or the Northwest. It won't be around here." A Wheeler farm wife expresses alienation from the village: "My mom draws me to town. There are a lot of aged people in town. People go to see relatives and pick up some things from the store, but that's about it. The day my mother dies will be the last day I'll set foot in town. We'll sell the house, and then that will be that." A lack of loyalty to town businesses is also evident. Farmers often bypass the local Wheeler grain elevator "because we can make more money" elsewhere. Emerson farm families say their village "has little to offer," and, consequently, they do their shopping elsewhere. For entrepreneurs, business matters take priority over any larger community good when financial choices are at issue.

Boosterism is still advocated by entrepreneurs, especially as a solution for community decline. For example, creative people constantly propose development projects such as festivals or business recruitment, only to have them flourish a short time and then wither away. The Wheeler Lions Club started an annual barbecue years ago that was widely imitated by nearby towns. After a decade the event is dying because so few people are willing to work at it. Wheeler could only muster people to produce a thin community history for its centennial celebration. "After the centennial everyone was up about potlucks. . . . The Village Board would hire somebody to sing or play music and everybody was invited," explained the newspaper editor. At first potlucks were held once a month, but they faded within a year. A historical society started up recently but is not expected to last long. Even 4H groups dissolve with the graduation of key members and have to be started again. People participate initially with great energy and innovation, but they quickly lose interest if an immediate payoff on time invested does not result. A Wheeler businessman recalled never missing a Lions Club meeting for years and served as president several times. Once his store became well established, his commitment waned: "It's not that important anymore. I don't have to go."

Hustlers are the most consistent participants in entrepreneur community affairs. In need of rental acreage or intent on establishing a reputation, hustlers exploit civic activities for contacts potentially useful for access to land. They brag about the impact their involvement made in an organization or voice pride about community accomplishments. However, because tenants in particular are financially vulnerable, their commitment is subject to economic pressures. Well-established families with a considerable owned land base can afford to be more selective about their civic involvement. Their social focus is outward, and the elite, especially, tend to look down their noses at local matters as petty.

A sense of community is visible among entrepreneurs for the school district. Yet, strong identification with the schools is transient and depends on receiving direct benefits through children. A school board member commented on the firm opposition of the larger landowners to the bond issue that divided Wheeler several years ago. A wealthy farmer called and complained that his taxes would go up if the bond issue passed. "That guy's got six kids who all went through the high school. He figures he's done his duty; that he doesn't have to pay anymore. . . . The ones that complain the most have put all their kids through already," commented a farmer on the school board. Once children have graduated and leave, the firmest link to the wider community weakens for most entrepreneurs.

Because individualism and financial success are so prized by entrepreneurs, their communities tolerate eccentricities among the wealthy. "Other people might not agree with the way you made it . . . but they have to respect you because in the end you are successful. . . . It all comes down to land," commented a farmer. Land control equals status, making the social system open to new, successful entrepreneurs. "There's a money clique [in Wheeler]," said a member of an Old Guard family, unhappy that longevity no longer guarantees community status. "Used to be more important twenty years ago because that was how people got started in farming. Now outsiders are accepted more easily."

Entrepreneur families practice a farming pattern that allows maximum independence, privacy, and flexibility and that gives their children latitude in career choice. Autonomy has social costs but is preferred by Yankee families to having behavior narrowly restricted by rigid standards. Though social mobility is feasible when substantial wealth is achieved, entrepreneur families often speak of having unsatisfying lives. A middle-aged Wheeler farm wife from a respected family commented, "It's very lonely. There's a lot of loneliness in people's homes. . . . I go over to someone's house and they will talk of being lonely. Connections that might bring people together just aren't made." In Emerson a farm wife, mother of a young child, complained that the women's club was her sole social outlet: "But there's no one near my age in it. I think the youngest is probably thirty-five. It's hard for me to meet people on my own." Without any relatives in the community and because so few young families now enter farming, a woman can feel quite unconnected. In general, individualism in entrepreneurial communities is asserted at the expense of cohesive relations that support families.

YEOMAN-DOMINATED COMMUNITIES

Each yeoman community was settled through chain migration from a single area of Germany, so at the outset families shared language, kinship, and origins. Germans have used ethnicity (it was also used against them) to clarify their exclusiveness from the surrounding society, populated by entrepreneurs. They viewed their villages and farms as neater, cleaner, and more orderly than those of "Angles." An elderly Heartland woman spoke of being proud of being German: "Even when times were hard the pride was there." Another widow reflected on changes in their self-contained community since she was a young bride: "Heartland was much tighter, more isolated than it is now." Perhaps as a consequence of their agrarian covenant and homogeneous "stranger" identity, German yeoman communities early were wary of outsiders, and World Wars I and II increased this suspicion. The non-German nonagrarian world could be shut out when communities opted out of the political system. For example, a neighboring yeoman community where many from Heartland retire did not formally incorporate until the 1960s, exceedingly rare for a village of 650 persons but indicative of a nonbooster attitude or dislike of governmental interference (Beale 1989b).

Attributes of land tenure in yeoman communities suggest a high value placed on farming as a way of life. Commitment to an agrarian ethic spurs the more aggressive families to expand the farm sufficiently so that each child who wants to farm has that opportunity. "I want to get my family involved. I'd like some or all of my children to be associated with the farm. . . . I want to get enough together so they can get the kind of start I got," explained one of the largest operators in Heartland. With the yeoman commitment to farming and strong attachment to the community, it is not surprising to find a lower rate of absentee ownership of farmland and more fragmentation of ethnic-owned land (chapter 1, table 1.1). These factors contribute to more numerous, smaller farms in Heartland, Freiburg, and St. Boniface, which foster as a by-product villages with a stable, farm-related population (chapter 4, fig. 4.1).

Yeomen prefer ethnic control of land within the community and relate negative outcomes when land goes to outsiders. For example, a large tract in St. Boniface was bought for investment by a national corporation in the early 1980s. People were extremely unhappy that the absentee owner had no connection with the ethnic community. "No one likes to see a big company coming in. They dictate their own terms, which are usually better than the going rate in the community. Around here it's 50/50 [crop share between landlord and tenant], and they want 60/40. They got a new farmer in there this year. He's a big farmer, lives about eight miles away. He lost some ground, and he's got all that big equipment, so he rented it," lamented a young St. Boniface operator about the loss of control over the community's land.

A spire visible from most farmsteads symbolizes the dominance of a single church unifying yeoman communities. Heartland is a tightly knit, vibrant community despite the absence of a village core. A small grocery store once functioned, but now only the church, an elementary school, and a few retirement homes physically mark the community's center. It has only been since World War II that most Heartlanders received even a high school education, excepting the half-dozen ministers the small community produced. An elderly farm wife, a longtime teacher in the Sunday school, remarked, "The big operators had parents who pushed farming and didn't care much for education. . . . I guess they just knew what they wanted. . . . The farm is their whole world." Perhaps little advanced education among families explains why, according to several ministers, the Heartland congregation still places the minister on a pedestal. In the past, yeoman marriages were arranged, businesses set up, and the community largely directed by their religious leader. He heads the community just as a father heads the family hierarchy.

Freiburg lies close to a large town, and St. Boniface is near a major highway and a metropolitan area. Yet these villages, unlike those of entrepreneur Emerson and Wheeler, have not become bedroom towns. Furthermore, locals vigorously repel newcomer invasions. St. Boniface, in response to a small subdivision built on the edge of town, enacted a strict zoning ordinance that effectively preserves an exclusively German community. Yeoman villages benefit from continuing the practice that parents retire and move from the homeplace when a successor marries. "A farmer moves into town when there is someone to take over farming for him," said a retired farmer. Heartlanders, lacking a village, retire to several small towns nearby, where Germans also dominate. Because parents retire as early as their mid-fifties, daily visits of the old by the young may extend over several decades. Village businesses benefit from the traffic generated by this yeoman retirement practice.

Young people remain in yeoman communities even when not successors to the family farm. Despite some farm consolidation, with nonfarming kin occupying farmhouses, the yeoman landscapes seem unchanged. Such families also fill the village housing that, in entrepreneur communities, due to greater farm consolidation and little farmer retirement into the village, becomes surplus. Many nonsuccessors live in Freiburg, for example, commuting to jobs and hoping some means to farm will arise. One operator said, "It's easy to find hired men because there's no room on the home farm, and boys want to stay around here." In Heartland and St. Boniface, nonfarming families are able to reside locally because work opportunities are available within a close commuting distance. Nonfarmers provide a source of labor for farming relatives during busy seasons and for local craftspeople who build and repair homes, farm buildings, cars, and equipment—often in the informal economy. Furthermore, because young families sustain stable populations in St. Boniface, in Freiburg, and in Heartland's nearby ethnic counterparts, main street cafes, grocery stores, and bars survive. Though Emerson and Wheeler have comparable populations, businesses in these villages have disappeared.

School consolidations caused loss of cohesion among the three entrepreneur communities but had a less dramatic impact for yeomen. From settlement, yeomen were not as dependent on public schools to define community identity, due to dominance by a single church. For example, by historical accident the Heartland church was built at the juncture of four townships. As a consequence, children attended different primary schools and two separate high schools—and still do. The church's German school that prepared the Heartland children for confirmation reinforced a high degree of ethnic endogamy until it was abandoned in the 1940s. Catholic St. Boniface had a parochial school until relatively recently, and Freiburg and the neighboring German Lutheran communities gerrymandered their school districts to keep them exclusively local and one-denominational. As yeoman children began attending consolidated schools, however, they increasingly chose mates from outside the community. Yeomen enthusiastically attend consolidated high school basketball and football games, and their support does not waver even after children graduate, unlike that of entrepreneurs.

Except for church-sponsored activities, Heartlanders are not joiners. A Cooperative Extension Homemakers' group was founded by a few in-marrying women and still exists, but young mothers from prominent landowning families meet with kin disapproval even in church group participation. However, when the church calls for mobilization, the community responds. From settlement Heartland carried out various anonymous welfare programs directed either by the minister or the male church elders involving financial support and loans, fieldwork, housekeeping, and jobs for indigent or handicapped households (Corner 1928). Such support continues. According to an elderly farm woman—who ethnocentrically views Heartland as a typical farm community—rural areas require no public social services: "The families make sure relatives are taken care of. . . . The minister also keeps an eye on people. If the family is tied up, someone else, friend or neighbor, takes over." Recently, the Heartland minister decided the congregation should support a county nursing home, envisioning that church families might need the facility and would want it nearby. The small community raised over $200,000 to finance it, and church elders backed bonds for the construction. The women's group provides weekly services, such as pie making, and regularly visits residents. The Heartland church's involvement has made the nursing home one of the best in the county, according to local social workers. Such initiatives point up how yeoman communities unite to maintain continuity with the past and, by doing so, generate social capital.

So effective is the yeoman church at reinforcing ethnicity and integrating families that community boundaries are considered tight, both internally and by non-Germans from neighboring communities. Germans in all the communities are suspicious of newcomers. A non-German middle-aged woman who married into Heartland recalled, "For three years I went to church and not one person came up to talk to me. Well, I just came home and cried and cried." A young Freiburg woman moved back to the community with her husband and family recently. She came back because "first, family and next because everyone knows everyone and you can feel part of something—like you belong. It's okay if you are from here, but even my husband had a hard time at first."

Internally, yeoman community gossip (ritual discourse) effectively controls social life, apparent in the frequent references made to criticism experienced. People are watchful about personal behavior, being aware that others monitor every act. "When I was a little girl it seemed like we could hear for miles. At night especially, if we had company we didn't say anything outside the house we didn't want our neighbors to hear," recalled an elderly Heartland woman. The party-line telephone system of Freiburg until the 1950s exemplified the lack of privacy and tight social controls among yeomen. According to an older farm woman, "The ol' party line used to be best for getting news. It rang in everybody's house so you'd pick it up and hear everything. Sometimes so many people were listening if you had a long distance call you'd have to ask the neighbors to hang up so you could hear. When the men came home they'd ask 'What's the news on the phone?' instead of what's the news on the radio."

Group control is not as strong as in the past, but it remains effective in yeoman communities. Pressure to conform to a humble and frugal demeanor shapes behavior. When a young Heartland family purchased a recreation vehicle, they kept it under wraps rather than be criticized as ostentatious or wasteful. People constantly stop in unannounced for a cup of coffee. A farmer in Freiburg commented on the social control present: "Germans may be good farmers, but not always good neighbors." A younger farmer reported that a relative of a man being buried dropped by to ask that he observe the Heartland custom of not harvesting during the funeral service while the bell tolled the traditional number of times corresponding to the age of the deceased. "My land is not near the church or the graveyard, but I did what he asked," he said begrudgingly.

Social restrictions reinforce status and gender hierarchies among yeomen. A Freiburg woman from a family having a marginal farm complained about the rigidity of status there: "Certain people can get away with anything. . . . You're really defined by the status of your family. For example, my father was never one of the big guns so he couldn't ever really take a leading role and he'd get judged more harshly for certain behavior."

Tightly knit yeoman communities are maintained by members' firm belief that their farms and social life are superior in comparison to neighboring entrepreneurs'. Driving outside Heartland a farm wife pointed out a farmstead with an old car in the yard. "We don't know the people over here. . . . It doesn't look like our area." She warned me not to leave my purse in the truck while we walked in their newly purchased field, though no one was in sight for miles. On reflection, however, a Heartland farm woman said that "the Flats don't shine the way they used to. . . . People have bigger farms and they let houses they don't need fall apart; so they don't look so good." Having the community shine is an important component of Heartland's proud identity. Heartlanders are also united by the pervasive suspicion that outsiders are after their land, assuming everyone values it as they do. Explained a retired farm woman, "Family and community are tight. They distrust people who are out to get their land. People have to be suspicious to survive and hold on to land." The uniformity of this world view has served to maintain both Heartland's farms and the yeoman community. "Between the farm, my family, friends, and the church I've always been busy," said a retired farmer about the completeness of his world.

A MIXTURE OF YEOMAN AND ENTREPRENEUR TRAITS IN PRAIRIE GEM

Prairie Gem is split into the tightly knit German yeoman group, focused on its church, and the Yankee entrepreneur group. The cultural contrast is evidenced by the active German Lutheran congregation, which has kept its young families firmly attached, and the forced merger of the other three community churches into a congregation only half as large. A retired farmer deeply involved in organizing the Lutheran church's centennial celebration exemplifies the yeoman commitment to continuity. He spoke of purposefully including younger congregation members: "I saw to it there were younger men on the committee of 27 to 30 years old so that when the 125th anniversary came there would be men who had experience . . . and would remember what was done before."

Prairie Gem has some of the cohesion of yeoman communities, though revolving in two segregated circuits. The Germans, aside from a few crossovers, interact among themselves, though persistence in agriculture has kept them a force in community life. Their farm elderly have consistently retired into town and own several key businesses, such as the grocery store. Said a non-German farmer, "The German people living here have money. They save it and they come to town to spend it. That's to their credit. There will always be young German farmers here in this area because they will take over from their fathers. They don't go away; don't go to school." The Yankees, some married to non-Lutheran Germans, and the descendants of Germans who broke away from the Lutheran church in the 1890s comprise the other circuit. It is also a tightly organized and community-committed group. A Community Club (about 50 male members, 20 of whom are active) in existence for over 30 years underwrites many local improvements and sponsors a successful homecoming each year that attracts about 2,000 people. It functions much as the single church does in yeoman communities—to support the community. Farmers give the most time, being "more flexible" than other townsfolk.

Prairie Gem's unifying institution is its school system. People in Prairie Gem are knowledgeable about school affairs, and involvement persists even after their children graduate. A retired schoolteacher (also a retired farm wife) described a seasonal Veteran's Day program for which "the place was packed. Of course, it wasn't a busy season so that's why so many came." Though consolidated with two other school systems in the 1950s, the Prairie Gem district—led by its unique advisory committee—resisted further consolidation by paying higher school taxes. Education enjoys broad-based community support: both Germans and Yankees serve on the school board, and many women actively volunteer in the classrooms and reading lab.

A measure of the integration of Prairie Gem is the effectiveness of gossip. A younger farmer commented, "The community is very conservative. Everyone else knows what you are doing even before you do. Everyone talks about each other . . . but not really in a malicious way." The German church exercises tight control over its members' activities, and the remainder of the community is highly aware of being excluded. Commented a retired farmer, "I've lived all my life among these German people and they are okay and hard working. They'll tell you just what they want to, and no more."

•

Comparison of Ethnic Communities

An examination of the seven communities as a group reveals German/Yankee contrasts and, within the same ethnic category, similarities. Table 10.2 compares the populations of the communities at regular intervals during this century. Note that these are village populations; a community population would include the farmers who, because they live in the countryside, are not combined by the census. (The community population appearing in table 4.2, chapter 4, is an estimated combined village and countryside population.) Though a group shares common origins and culture and has frequent social interaction, community size does not necessarily correlate with cohesion.

Table 10.2 indicates a distinctive population trend for each community type. Though all the communities have experienced farm consolidations, which logically would create population loss, a decline in size was not inevitable. The yeoman communities of St. Boniface and Freiburg doubled in population during the seventy years, and the Heartland area also grew; but the Yankee communities of Wheeler and Libertyville and the mixed community of Prairie Gem all lost population. Only Emerson gained population, but like the Wheeler population maintenance, this resulted from new people

Table 10.2. Village Populations of Selected Years

Village	Ethnicity	1910	1940	1980
Emerson	Yankee	385	420	540
St. Boniface	German	375	365	650
Wheeler	Yankee	740	650	625
Heartland[a]	German	—	605	770
Libertyville	Yankee	415	345	280
Freiburg	German	590	805	1,400
Prairie Gem	Mixed	480	360	346

Source: U.S. Census 1930, 1950, 1980.

Note: Totals rounded to disguise community identities.

[a]Heartland is an unincorporated community; figures reflect a nearby German Lutheran village that did not incorporate until the 1950s despite its relatively large size.

moving into surplus, cheap housing rather than retention of young, native families. In Wheeler, farmers in the village are outnumbered by newcomers five to one. Newcomers tend to live in the village but resist social integration. St. Boniface, Heartland, and Freiburg kept young families who commute to nearby metropolitan areas for jobs. Consequently, the countryside in the German communities is more densely populated with nonfarming households. Yankees all speak of a loss of young people.

Community viability is based on a combination of factors: the ability to provide amenities for homes and farms, and whether families feel attachment to and receive social support from a cohesive structure. Figure 10.1 represents a village viability continuum. Starting from the left with the village that has the least potential to persist as a self-sufficient support to its members, villages are placed along a continuum with the right end having the village with the most potential for this support. At the least viable extreme, families in Emerson can sustain the farm by patronizing existing local businesses, but little else. Although farmers may gather at the grain elevator in Emerson, as they do in many of the communities, nonfarmers are not likely to frequent it. Furthermore, most village residents are not present during the day because they commute elsewhere for work. Emerson supports no public gathering spot such as a restaurant, and thus has no communication channel that cuts across the community. Libertyville, while very small, supports an informal meeting place where a cross section of people meet regularly and drink coffee together and buy some groceries. Until 1988 Prairie Gem had a cafe, but perhaps the population loss shown in 1980 (table 10.2) was instrumental in the recent decline. However, the village still supports a tavern where people can meet and a grocery store. The consolidated high school in Prairie Gem is a constant source of activity and traffic. Wheeler has all of these amenities as well as a newspaper and a library, yet it lacks a school in the village. Although Heartland does not have a village, its members patronize two other German villages, each about five miles away. Germans from one of these communities attend the Heartland church; the other has its own Lutheran church. Each of the yeoman villages has stores, a tavern, a restaurant, a grain elevator, a video outlet, and other businesses. St. Boniface has a full set of core businesses supported by the community, as does Freiburg. Half again as large as St. Boniface, Freiburg also has medical and legal professionals resident in the community.

Religion is often considered pivotal to rural community life, but this centrality differs according to ethnicity. The three Yankee villages all have at least two churches. Size does not dictate religious diversity; Libertyville, though

Figure 10.1. Scale of Community Viability According to
Amenities and Social Integration

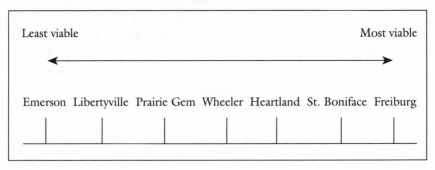

the smallest, has three churches. The expansion of this institution among Yankees appears to be purposeful, for people find a sense of belonging and community there. Among the German communities people experience an overlap between community and church. A member of the ethnic group is also a member of the church; this is more a social fact than a theological decision. Prairie Gem Germans easily sustain their church, while Yankees cannot depend on the same loyalty to sustain their now-merged church.

Yeoman-dominated communities manifest cohesion—everyone is well acquainted, people fraternize actively, and most speak positively about their social lives. The streets have life. St. Boniface, Heartland, and Freiburg are all lively, vital communities with distinct identities; residents think their community is the best place in the world to live. People are gregarious in groups, whether of relatives, school chums, or card players. They take vacations and go out to dinner together. Entrepreneur-dominated communities manifest division—people often know little about their neighbors or are inaccurately informed about them. Though entrepreneur families like rural life, they are critical of the village. Streets are more silent in entrepreneur communities. Emerson, Wheeler, and Libertyville are in various stages of decline at least in part due to the detachment of their farm families. Wheeler is the liveliest of the towns, but many of the businesses that give life to Main Street are run by outsiders. Because people do not retire to town and many leave, Emerson and Wheeler contain surplus housing that is occupied by commuters. Explained one retired farmer, "They do their shopping in [a nearby metropolitan community] and only come to sleep here. They're not really a part of the community." Libertyville simply disappeared as a functioning community once the railroad departed. People in these entrepreneur communities do some things with close friends, but many people speak of being lonely or alienated and trace their feelings partly to the competitiveness of the agricul-

tural environment. According to a farm wife, people in Wheeler are concerned with "fencing themselves in, protecting what they have," and this
tends to separate them from one another along class lines. School closings,
loss of a railroad, and church consolidations all tend to be catastrophic events
for entrepreneur communities. Their residents are held together mainly by
such institutions and, aside from these connections, share only occupation
and geographic proximity.

Prairie Gem has profited by having non-Lutherans produce activities to
replicate the cohesion enjoyed by the Germans in their church. Responding
to the tightly knit Germans has galvanized community unity. Each group is
aware of the activities of the other through crossover personnel: a few German farmers meet daily at the cafe with other farmers; some German couples
have joined card groups; and key people, such as a Yankee widow, have married into the Lutheran church. Innovative entrepreneurs come up with ideas
for the community, and there are sufficient yeoman soldiers present to sustain
the initiative. The interplay of the potentialities of yeoman and entrepreneur
has helped Prairie Gem maintain its vitality, population, and village.

Entrepreneur-dominated communities are split by social strata based on
economic criteria. Pervasive competitiveness makes consistent community-
level cooperation problematic. Entrepreneur-dominated communities are
also more diverse because they tolerate more deviance. Contrastingly, yeoman
communities have less clear social strata distinctions, due to a more egalitarian land tenure system. Yeomen are also more willing to comply with social controls imposed by a religious leader or the community. Pressure to
conform to group standards is so strong that deviant personalities are forced
out. Those who conform to community practices are rewarded by the security of social support, integration, and acceptance. Community welfare issues
are considered an important and valid demand on yeoman households,
though not to the extent that such demands endanger sacred family continuity goals.

The social costs coupled with the emotional support available to members
in each type of community are apparent in observations made by two farmers. A young Emerson farmer commented on his entrepreneur community:
"I'm friendly with the farmer next over, and we share things some. Same with
the farmer that direction. But that's unusual. Oh, people are friendly, but
they're not friends. They don't help each other out." A retired yeoman
farmer replied to an inquiry about why he only wanted to own land in Heartland: "They're our type of people. We all hate each other, but we give each
other help."

RESPONSES TO CHANGE

Yeoman and entrepreneur community personalities, as outlined in table 10.1, have differing potentialities to respond to change. Historically, we know that no farming area in the United States has ever been able to absorb all of the young it produced. High rural fertility, combined with the constant push to expand farms due to increased mechanization, and the lure of the big city have pressured youngsters to seek their fortunes outside the community. Yet, without young families a community does not persist. Yeoman families and communities have successfully pulled their young in—even those not farming—while entrepreneur families and communities have tended to push theirs out. Kin choosing to live in Heartland and to commute for work and those who live elsewhere and attend its church cite the church and family as their anchors. "I thought of transferring my membership to another church, but that's the only time I see people, and I enjoy seeing them," explained a woman who married a nonfarmer and non-Heartlander. The pull of yeoman communities is so strong that young families "filter back" and attempt to make a living by combining jobs with a small farm. In Libertyville a few retirees who left after high school graduation returned at retirement age to enjoy the slow pace of the countryside. They have little commitment to the community's future.

Yeoman communities cooperate to preserve valued institutions (businesses or support services) by organizing through the single, hierarchically structured church that dominates their lives. Under church leadership such communities have formed corporations to buy and reestablish defunct stores and restaurants, remodeled empty storerooms as community centers, and financed missionary activities to start churches in nearby villages. The cooperative activities themselves have helped maintain the centrality of the church. Strong agreement about what a community should be, based on shared ethnicity, religion, and an agrarian covenant, facilitates the mobilization of yeomen to implement social initiatives. Once the community is committed to an initiative, people work together with sustained actions, building social capital that is available for other initiatives. Changes are made with the fewest possible alterations in the community, but the acts reinforce cohesion and identity.

Entrepreneur communities mobilize populations for purposes of boosterism—to attract business they hope will promote economic and population growth—according to the plan for progress of those who energetically sell it (Boorstin 1965; Hatch 1979). Involvement has a commercial motive rather than the social capital motive of yeoman communities. When compared with families in a yeoman community, entrepreneur families belong to a greater variety of clubs and organizations, but their loyalty is more fragile. A few very interested individuals keep an organization going, but the sustained commitment to a group cause, present among yeomen, is absent. When improvement does not come from the individual efforts of the committed, they give up. Profits translated in the form of "progress" make community investments worthwhile for entrepreneurs.

These Illinois cases do not exhaust the ways that rural communities work. However, Germans living elsewhere in rural America have developed similarly cohesive communities despite growing different crops in very different environments (Brown 1990). In Washington state, for example, to avoid direct competition with the village drugstore, a German grocery store owner does not sell toothpaste. This community in a wheat-growing region shares many traits with Midwestern yeoman communities (John Conrad Allen 1989). Rural revitalization strategies recognize that rural communities are exceedingly diverse in their organization, their capacity to initiate activities, and the willingness of their inhabitants to cooperate (Ryan 1987). For professionals concerned with initiating change supportive of rural communities, this diversity may appear daunting. However, the cultural systems described for the dominant Midwestern ethnic groups suggest that the range of diversity is not infinite.

The demise of village and community life is not necessarily bad for the family farm. Farms among Yankees have continued to prosper (especially those that triumph with consolidation) while their communities have deteriorated. It may not matter directly to entrepreneur families that their community declines—so what is lost? Yet, when communities die, families are deprived of intangible supports that they are unaware of until a crisis arises. Once social networks are weakened and little social capital exists, it is difficult to suddenly generate them when needs materialize. For yeoman farm families, the social capital they build and maintain through their community networks is there to be drawn on as a source of tangible support when times are tough.

Finally, the meaning of community—its place in the lives of families—differs between yeomen and entrepreneurs. For yeomen the meaning of life is found in the small, homogeneous, and ethnic nexus of their farming community. Because it is so important to yeomen to preserve links to the past, they work to sustain the community that provides that context. Entrepreneurs tend to think of the village more as a commercial center than as a locus for ethnic solidarity. When this function declines, an entrepreneur village loses its purpose. Their community is less important to their identity and judgments of worthiness; their lives are focused on a wider milieu. To entrepreneurs the yeomen's absorption in a tiny community is provincial. As their villages decline, entrepreneurs lose the center or core of the community; but it matters little, for identity is not dependent on this setting (Hatch 1979; Varenne 1977). Thus, groups have a responsibility for the type of community they live in, whether through the building of social capital or by default through negligence.

Conclusion

Midwestern farming had, from the outset, an almost split personality: it was pursued by some as a path to an agrarian way of life and by others as a business for capitalistic gain (Atack and Bateman 1987). This prototypical divergence still prevails and testifies to the critical importance of culture to agriculture. Both German and Yankee cultural systems maintain the asymmetrical relations of men over women and of owners and operators of larger farms over those of smaller ones. Yet, as a consequence of participation in very different domestic processes of management, succession, and inheritance to maintain a particular family relationship to land, yeomen and entrepreneurs engage in actions with distinctive outcomes for land tenure patterns and rural community life.

Midwestern agrarian society has relatively few communal rituals, and even more rare is a ritual concentrated on land, a resource pivotal to family and community social relations (Bloch 1985). However, the public land auction, a rare event enacted by both Germans and Yankees, ritually highlights the re-enactment of the asymmetrical social structure each group possesses (Ortner 1990). A community farmland auction tends to occur only every two or three years, so emotions are high when one is performed. When cultural guidelines for land transfer break down—no successor is ready, an owner does not write a will, heirs are too numerous or cannot agree on property division—a land auction often results. The auction drama throws into sharp relief inequalities of gender and status by re-creating publicly the intimate practices of daily family and community life. The ritual calls attention to taken-for-granted principles of inequality while simultaneously reendorsing them (Bloch 1985; Bruner 1986; Ortner 1984).

THE AUCTION RITUAL

Once the harvest is over, one is likely to see a land-auction notice in any Sunday newspaper in the rural Midwest. The date is announced, the seller's terms are listed, and a reason for the sale is described, such as a retirement or the settlement of an estate. The public announcement only formalizes ongoing community discussions organized by cultural notions about appropriate actions: why the family gave up land, who is expected to buy, what price the land should go for, and how the sale might change the existing social order. Auctions are emotionally charged because opportunities to buy land are relatively rare and not all tracts that come on the market are "good." Neighboring land is best; next best is that within the community; and families can wait a generation for the right tract to become available. Therefore families aiming to be auction participants are consumed by planning strategy.

Theoretically, anyone can buy the land and thereby improve his or her family's social standing. This possibility breeds a sense of chaos in which the normal social order is held in abeyance. From the time the auction is announced, those who intend to bid are in a state of limbo; status and gender are seemingly irrelevant (Turner 1969). In a society in which everyone normally knows everyone else's affairs, families become secretive. (Among my contacts an elderly farmer refused to talk on the telephone about his planned bid; evidently, he was still haunted by the former party-line system in the community.) An auction is the ultimate gamble, different from typical farm management gambles with weather or markets because it is played out in public by normally restrained and private people. The hope of being able to bid on land may have cost a family years of delayed gratification, yet all is won or lost in only a few moments. This state of standing on the threshold of change is central to the ritual enactment, for it clashes with the routines of daily life; yet it also emphasizes the status quo, which returns when the auction concludes (Bloch 1985).

Sales take place outside community territory in neutral, public arenas such as the county courthouse or a hotel meeting room. Removing people from the community where their status is well known to a place where rankings may be challenged or reordered heightens the drama and the latent possibility for upsetting the social order. On the ritual day a larger group than those intending to bid gathers. That they assemble to bear witness to an auction has a symbolic and financial impact beyond the act. Land values for estate and property taxes, for example, are tied to current market values. Absent are farmers of marginal status, both socially and economically, who "haven't the time to waste." Compelled to "know what's going on," the key people in the community hierarchy are always in attendance. There are also outside spoilers to worry about. Typically professionals seeking investment opportunities are visible at every auction. Their actions cannot be shaped through the ritual discussions, as are those of community members.

The actual auction contrasts with ordinary rural life by allowing usually suppressed emotions to surface. Farmers generally scorn braggarts, especially those who flaunt wealth or power. Democratic and egalitarian conformity is enforced by gossip, and a slow-talking deprecating wit is the accepted manner. The auction upends a community's taken-for-granted statuses by treating equally all bidders with money. Auctions are also inherently combative and assertive. The aggressive male, unless the audience judges his bid foolish or beyond the family's means, earns respect. A lifetime of humble behavior can be quickly overthrown by a winning bid that can improve a family's social standing in the community. Most bidders are mature farmers, unlikely to benefit fully from increased landed wealth, but by buying for a child's future, they can reinforce generational dominance.

Enormous tension is evident at an auction. A skillful auctioneer—an outsider, but frequently a community favorite—can knowledgeably manipulate the audience with his banter ("I see many of the fine folks from Heartland are here today to see the sale of this property that was once a showplace farm," one said, looking around the circle of assembled people). As the suspense builds during the competition, the auctioneer jokes to relieve the tension. If bids go higher than expected, he calls a recess to allow the participants to consult with their family or banker. Yet, despite the threat that chaos would ensue if the community social hierarchy were upended, order is typically maintained. Seldom does someone in the community have unexpectedly deep pockets. In one community, a lower-status man actually delegated a higher-status man to bid for him, perhaps to mask his audacity. Monitors of the land market agree with local opinion that the outcome of auctions leaves the established community hierarchy intact: "Those established here will hold on and buy anything that goes up for sale." For example, a farmer who paid a high price for a tract adjoining his homeplace was said to have been "sitting across the road from the piece for years just waiting. He can afford the price. He's never spent a dime on anything else."

Although gender distinctions are never discussed, they are fundamental to the ritual. An auction ought to be open to anyone, yet all the actors in the drama—bidders, auctioneers, and much of the audience—are males. Despite the crucial role that they play in the accumulation of wealth, women either keep to themselves or are kept from being public actors in this drama of family wealth distribution. In any event, they almost never bid. Thus, the auction ritual reinforces the female status of subordinate helpmate. This contradicts the daily reality of the family farm where the wife actively participates in the decision to buy and the act of planning. Community ritual discourse sanctions a sole actor: "he" bids, "he" can afford it, "he" waited, and "he" planned the act. It is typically a high-status, male bidder who comes out on top when the auctioneer shouts "sold." Community social and gender asymmetrical relations, which were threatened during the few minutes of ritual action, are publicly reinforced and endorsed when routine life resumes.

It is possible, however, that family interaction will someday become more of a struggle between actors asymmetrically related by gender. With more farm women contributing cash to the family economy from off-farm work, and with more off-farm female heirs inheriting land, women may not remain as willing to accept continuation of this system. They may no longer be inclined to retain relatively little actual control over a valued resource, the land they in fact already possess.

IMPLICATIONS OF CULTURE FOR
LAND TENURE AND RURAL COMMUNITIES

It is the central thesis of this book that culture structures family actions in important ways concerning land. Culture connects microlevel action among farm family households with the macrolevel of the regional land market and the fabric of Midwestern rural society. I chose land management, a concrete expression of family relations, as the window that provides insights on cultural contrasts between the ethnic groups and as a device for tracing cultural change (Ohnuki-Tierney 1990a). Family and land relations are key determinants in the evolution of local land tenure and whether a community's village remains viable.

Midwestern agriculture is still dominated by family farms. Family farmers are not anachronisms but are fully competitive, efficient producers (Reinhardt and Barlett 1989). Multiple types of family farms have persisted, and according to this measure, both yeoman and entrepreneur are successful strategies. Will the family-run, middle-sized farm eventually decline toward extinction, rendered uncompetitive by market forces (Friedland 1989; Penn 1979)? Many consider the continued consolidation of farms to be inevitable. Those who prophesy the disappearance of the medium-sized family farm, however, assume that all farmers are consummate entrepreneurs basing operation strategies entirely on profit maximization. This model for the farm enterprise is taught at land-grant universities to future agricultural economists, who go on to predict the long-term trends. The yeoman model of limited expansion and conservative management is largely ignored as a force that can affect the macrotrend of the distribution of farms. What will agriculture and rural life look like in the Midwest if each group continues to use its distinctive farming strategy to pursue the land and family priorities framed by each cultural system?

Over the years, entrepreneurs in Emerson, Libertyville, and Wheeler took gambles in their business choices, followed fluctuations in the land market, willingly sold inherited land, and negotiated succession—all to maximize profits. As a consequence, farm consolidation evolved at a rate predicted by the pundits of agricultural structure. According to an Emerson operator's reflections on farm consolidation during his career, "You don't make any more land. What there is is all there is. To farm more, you've got to push someone else out." Mean farm size in entrepreneur communities is higher than in yeoman communities; a bimodal divergence has developed between the few large operators and a number of smaller ones. Land tenure among the yeoman communities of Heartland, St. Boniface, and Freiburg has evolved differently. Yeoman families made risk-aversive business choices, rarely sold land, held on to inherited land shares, and managed succession in a way that assured continuity. Though some consolidation occurred, cultural constraints to an extent retarded that process. Mean farm size in yeoman communities is more narrowly clustered as a consequence of more similarly sized farms persisting with less consolidation. Even so, a very traditional Heartland retired yeoman voices apprehension about the future: "You know we don't know what's ahead in twenty years. The Germans may be gone. There might not be any family farms left. I wonder what people will work for then." His worries about the disappearance of German farmers are belied by demographic facts.

I showed that, according to the 1980 census, the Midwest farm population is over half German, the next most numerous group being of English origin. The German ethnic dominance of Midwestern farmers, coupled with the recent U.S. Department of Agriculture report that half the family farms are now located in the same region, means that German-Americans conservatively account for approximately one-quarter of the nation's family farms (Beale and Kalbacher 1989). If Midwestern German farm families possess even some of the yeoman characteristics that produce the persistent farms that gradually invade and succeed in Yankee territory, then an increasing proportion of medium-sized family farms can be expected to become German owned and operated. Assuming families aim to achieve the ideal goals of each cultural system, logic suggests that Midwestern industrial or agribusiness farms in the future will be dominated by entrepreneurs, while the medium-range farms are to be controlled by yeomen. The predicted increase of smaller, part-time or hobby farms should be a mixture of both types, including those unable to achieve viable operations or those seeking the land on which to farm on a larger scale.

The unheralded dominance of German ethnics I have uncovered in the Midwest, a region typified by family-run farms, indicates that predictions about the extinction of middle-range farms may be premature. High persistence is the hallmark of yeoman farms, and this trait suggests at the least a dampening effect on the foreseen trend toward fewer, larger farms or, conceivably, limits to the extent of eventual consolidation. Economists constructing farm trend models tend to leave out important cultural variables affecting how decisions are made. Nonfinancial, kinship, and ethnic beliefs all channel and shape choices made by family farmers. Pessimistic conclusions about farm structural trends—the vulnerability of the medium-range farm in particular—are drawn if critical social variables are not taken into account.

The environmental context for farming is rapidly changing as the public becomes increasingly concerned about such issues as food safety and agricultural runoff polluting the nation's water supply (Strange 1988). Sustainable practices more in tune with the environment are receiving attention. One can speculate about the adoption likelihood for a yeoman versus an entrepreneur of more sustainable farming systems. The yeoman strategy has traits resembling those associated with sustainable agrarian systems worldwide: small-scale, diversified farms that are owned and operated by independent proprietors (Netting 1989). Like sustainable farmers found cross-culturally, yeomen do not maintain the environment for its own sake, although they believe in this, but they practice stewardship of the land so that successors can farm good soils and maintain an agrarian way of life. The long-term planning strategies of yeomen should make them receptive to the adoption of sustainable practices on the basis of what is good for future generations. Entrepreneurial operators should be more amenable to financial arguments for adoption of sustainable practices—for example, how such systems are economically beneficial.

Persistence of more family farms in a specific locale and fewer in another affects which farm-dependent villages endure. Rural villages of under 1,000 inhabitants, dedicated to serving the middle-range Midwestern family farmers, are predicted to face hard times (Duncan 1989). If Main Street disappears as a consequence of competition from regional malls, discount stores, and supermarket chains, can communities reconstitute themselves as sustaining networks of social relationships among those who live in close proximity? Yeoman communities do not require a business center to link them—witness how tightly integrated Heartland is, which has never had a substantial business core. Yeomen typically have a strong ethnic identity and the community provided by a single church to support cohesion. Furthermore, yeomen dedicate themselves to working hard at the activities that build the social capital that reinforces communities, out of a commitment to continuity as strong as their commitment to continuity of the family farm. Entrepreneur communities have a more difficult time achieving cohesion and cooperation. However, they neither want nor are they willing to give up the privacy and autonomy required to attain the tightly integrated and supportive community of yeomen.

As the ideal farms for each operator type persist in agriculture, an ideal community has more likelihood of persistence. For yeomen this is a community that persists by maintaining a cohesive, ethnic enclave through rituals of sociability and religion that exclude those not sharing ethnic identity and traditions. Entrepreneurs, committed to economic progress, do not lament the decline of a community except, for example, when children must ride for hours on the school bus. Community quite simply is a place to live and farm; family social life, shopping, and religious experience are readily transferred elsewhere. Yet, among Yankees having a pride in their individual economic achievements, this was mixed with a sense of malaise and alienation. These feelings are attributed to Americans lacking an attachment to community that gives depth, meaning, and richness to life (Bellah et al. 1985). Prosperity does not always mean satisfaction. Germans complain about gossip and the price of land, but on the whole they are highly satisfied with their agrarian life led in the nexus of a community having "thick" culture where everyone knows everyone else's business and ethnic identity is rich (Waters 1990).

Families and culture matter to the making of economic and social trends. Land and ethnicity provide a window on the contribution at the household level to regional patterns. Therefore the Midwestern ethnic mosaic must be taken seriously in explaining the direction family farms and rural communities will take in the future. The entrepreneur model of aggressive expansion brought great efficiency and innovation to American agriculture, without much concern for the environment or social support. It may be that times are now ripe for the yeoman model to ascend. This model of controlled expansion, fiscal conservatism, ownership of what is farmed, and care for continuity may be a model more suited to sustaining family farms and a cohesive rural society in the 1990s and beyond.

Appendix
Methods for Farming Community Studies

My theoretical perspective is mainstream anthropology, but my methods are not typical of anthropological research. My methods of investigation evolved from the limitations and advantages of working with students whose applied professional goals led them to study for a master's degree in an interdisciplinary unit dedicated to human development and family studies. Master's students have a year to obtain data and write a thesis and are not trained in anthropology; these factors dictate close supervision. The procedures followed in each yearlong community study combined anthropological methods with those more typical of psychologists directing many graduate students on a large research project. I had an umbrella topic: farm families and their land. Students collected data to meet the project objectives, but they were free to pursue a unique family issue as long as it fit within the larger project. Some of these issues were women's changing status and the integration of the elderly in families.

Anthropologists typically carry out research by living among their subjects, interacting with people on a daily basis, and learning the rhythm of their subjects' lives by experiencing it. Although some (e.g., Oscar Lewis) have employed teams of fieldworkers, most anthropologists work individually. In the fourteen community studies I have directed, all but the Gray Prairie communities (studied by two anthropologists with Ph.D. degrees) were carried out with second-year master's degree candidates. To accommodate the supervision required of this group, I focused on central Illinois, where students could go to the field and return to campus daily. Although I did not do all the fieldwork personally, I chose the communities and subsample studied intensively, met many of the families, read all fieldnotes, guided what was asked and which issues were pursued, and discussed each interview as the work unfolded. Students typed fieldnotes (see below), and I read them immediately so that we could talk about findings before they returned to the field. Thus analysis took place virtually simultaneously with data collection, facilitating testing of working hypotheses with the families being observed (Denzin 1970).

At the beginning of a study, we visited with some key community members, who varied by community. If a single church, such as Catholic or Lutheran, anchored a community, we talked with the priest or minister and asked that he publicly announce our presence. If a religious leader was an inappropriate contact, we might talk with the mayor and place a story in the local newspaper. As a College of Agriculture faculty member at a land-grant university, I relied heavily on county-level Cooperative Extension agriculture and home economics agents. These people know their county well and served as background informants and provided introductions to families.

"Community study" is not an exact label for my research objectives. Typically a community study aims at fully describing all aspects of a community, with particular emphasis on the power, economic, and social structures. Because of these emphases, a community study does not generally reflect the lives of individual households. I chose the community as a target population but built it from the bottom up by household, and among all households I concentrated on those families with a link to farmland. With the exception of Wheeler (the last community studied) we contacted every household in the door-to-door survey but carried out the survey only with families who met the United States agricultural census criteria for a farm household: one or more adults who (1) work off-farm less than 150 days per year or (2) have farm earnings of over $2,500 per year and, by my additional criterion, (3) own more than ten acres of farmland. In reality we often ignored work off-farm; many farm families today practice pluriactivity; that is, they depend on a variety of income sources along with farming for a livelihood (Barlett 1986). Because the seven communities were farming-dependent, most households fulfilled the criteria. We also interviewed some nonfarm families who were related to local farmers and who lived in the community but commuted to work elsewhere.

THE SURVEY, HISTORIES, AND PARTICIPANT OBSERVATION

From the household survey, both demographic (family size, education level, mobility, occupation) and agricultural data (operation size, sources for rental and owned land, family labor involvement) were obtained. Farmers are besieged by salesmen hiding behind fake surveys to get in the door. They are reluctant to cooperate especially when suspicions are aroused that survey results might lead to higher taxes. Our in-person approach was therefore an advantage. We often won cooperation from the reluctant by saying that policymakers do not understand farmers. The sentiment was met with hearty agreement. Farmers, as firm believers in the work ethic, approved of graduate students working hard for a thesis. For this reason we met with success "to help the little girl out," as one farmer rationalized cooperation to his wife. Each survey required about an hour to complete. To facilitate the process and set people at ease, we provided a copy of the survey for the interviewee to read as we asked the questions. We also used an informed consent form on university stationery that explained the research and that participation was voluntary, and we included our phone numbers and address should further information be desired. No one contacted us, but the information helped to convince people that we were authentic.

The door-to-door survey produced an overview of the community, with much information emerging during nonformal conversations. Families often felt more free to visit after the interviewer put down her pencil and things were "off the record." Then, gossip, major concerns, and complaints were related, and recommendations were made for which families we "should see." Typically the largest landowners or the most prominent families—often the same people—were mentioned. We usually followed the recommendations, but the survey provided data for assuring that a community cross section—lifecourse phase, farm scale, type of farm operation, and social class—was covered. The interviewer explained that the survey was a first phase and that the second phase involved more intensive work with a few families, requiring the taking of family histories and observing daily life. Certain families obviously enjoyed the survey, were willing and open participants, and welcomed further contact with the project. The selection of families for the intensive phase struck a balance between the willing and the representative. Intensively studied families constituted approximately 20 percent of the households surveyed in each community.

We met with participants in the intensive phase from a minimum of six to as many as seventy-five hours, from three to as many as ten times, and over an average of three months' duration. The first two or three visits focused on constructing a genealogy and then compiling a land/family history, both ideal mechanisms for learning about relatives and the family's background. Furthermore, a genealogy provided something most families thought valuable that we could give in exchange for their time. The genealogies covered both husband's and wife's families from first settlement in Illinois. Many used family Bibles and mobilized relatives for assistance with forgotten facts. This process gave insights into the family's social network and the importance of such information. After collection of a genealogy, we were knowledgeable about kin relationships, and this was useful for the construction of family and land histories. Working together on the genealogy also allowed us to build trust so that people were at ease when we discussed the more emotional issue of family land.

The land history started with the ancestor who originally settled in Illinois, and it recorded all acreage ever farmed by the family, including rental land. We asked how owned land was obtained, and we ascertained the relationship between the family and the source. Families were less reliable about rental acreage although such acreage is an important indicator of how present families survive. Census data may show rental acreage, but the source of the land and the relationship of the owner to the operator is virtually undocumented. Qualitative methods are most useful to get at this ephemeral piece of the puzzle about how Midwestern families farm.

Stories always emerged as a land history was compiled. Family feuds, grudges over inheritance equity, pleasure about outsmarting a seller, and kinship jealousy all focus on land. When a story was related about cousin Joe being unhappy with how his father divided family land, we knew who Joe was because we had done the genealogy. One German farmer close to ninety still felt guilty about how he obtained some land from a relative almost sixty years ago. He waited until his wife left the room before telling the story. Land histories provided the data for determining cultural beliefs and practices: how much land people desired, who should inherit and what, how transfers should take place, and appropriate behavior. Land provoked the most emotion among families and was the topic about which farmers always had an opinion.

When families were willing, after the genealogy and land histories were completed, we observed them engaged in normal routines for at least a day. I developed the single-day approach after reading Oscar Lewis's field methods (Lewis 1965). Although Lewis was not particular about the day used, I found fall harvesting and spring planting days were especially good for uncovering the hierarchy and division of labor as families worked together at a busy time. If a full day's observation was not possible, we minimally asked to take a meal with the family. Mealtimes reveal a family's organization in ways about which they are unaware, and thus they are not self-consciously presenting "good" behavior (Bossard 1943, 1945; Kantor and Lehr 1975). Who sits by whom, who leads the conversation, how exchanges take place, and what topics are discussed all reveal family rules, concerns, and routines. In the course of the seven, year-long studies we attended a multitude of activities with families: church services, shopping trips, funerals and weddings, farm sales, visits with neighbors and relatives, land auctions, Bible study groups,

Cooperative Extension Homemakers' groups, 4H meetings, county fairs, community homecomings, and beer parties. We also worked at combining, disking, planting, castrating pigs, and milking cows. Some students were invited to spend several days with a family and stayed at their homes. They were then privy to visiting behaviors and time schedules. The participant observation aspects of the research contributed the most data about the networks that link families to the community and the community structure.

To not be biased toward one class of individuals in the family, we attempted to interview and observe males and females and parents and children, separately and together. Because my students were almost all female, we tried to begin fieldwork with the male head of household, although we indicated an interest in talking with the farm woman. Focusing on the entire family unit dictates obtaining a picture of multiple generations and extended family branches. This was a thorny problem when various linked households were involved in a conflict. Each household must be convinced that confidentiality will be preserved while, at the same time, the interviewer is expected to be a sympathetic listener.

Aside from the survey, genealogy, and land history little writing was done while with a family. I feel note taking interrupts the natural flow of behavior. The student research assistants had taken my family interaction seminar and were trained to observe verbal and nonverbal practices that disclose a family's organization and beliefs. Rules, they understood, are implied by what is rewarded or discouraged in families. They were trained to view stories related emotionally, repeated, and discussed as indicators of fundamental concerns. They observed how money was spent and the goal of earning from the appearance of the farmstead, home, equipment, cars, and the family's leisure activities. Inheritance rules were embedded in the land history—who had received land in each generation and why.

Notes were typed as soon after a field visit as possible to avoid losing details with much elapse of time. We attempted to record everything, from who uses the telephone to what is eaten for lunch, on the principle that one never knows what is data until the analysis is in process. The quotations are a close approximation of what was said; the memory improves as one learns to mentally play back a conversation that transpired. Students were constantly worried about forgetting something, and each devised methods for jogging the memory. Writing down key words during the observation and talking into a tape recorder during the drive back from the field were two useful devices. Some subtle factors are transient, but we found important issues generally recur. Critical factors, such as a person's core beliefs or long-felt bitterness about land, tend to be repeated at some, if not all, meetings. Those things that define a person or family were emphasized by them during interactions. Only after hearing or seeing the same thing three times in different contexts did we hypothesize a pattern. Most reported patterns were observed more frequently than the requisite three times.

A third research method employed was the investigation of archival materials. Ownership reflected in plat maps of county land (which show an owner's name and the size of the tract) provided community-level data to trace land tenure. These concrete facts provided a comparison for our informants' observations about community patterns. Illinois has a major rural map publishing firm and therefore the state's plat map record is among the best. For the entire state, maps were issued erratically until after World War II, when they began being published every three years. However, the more prosperous and heavily populated counties had more maps issued, and this difference dictated the communities chosen for in-depth analysis. Other archival sources used included county histories (issued for most Illinois counties in the late nineteenth century), local newspapers, church documents and histories, family mementoes, and community histories. It was fortuitous that the research began in 1976, for many Illinois communities undertook writing local histories as part of the national bicentennial celebration.

COMMENTS ON CONSTRUCTING
CULTURE FROM EVERYDAY FAMILY LIFE

The challenge of using the domestic setting for inductively determining a cultural system is to glean a sense of community from the actions and interactions of individual families. Several principles guide this process (Salamon 1990).

1. *The family is the primary arena for the socialization of neonates.* A high degree of consciousness of how to transmit, reinforce, and explain cultural practices exists in the family, a primary educational institution. The home is a context in which people are accustomed to teaching cultural rules, ideas, and beliefs. It is easy for the fieldworker as a neonate to be instructed about what family members take for granted.

2. *Everyday family behavior is not random.* Rules are necessary to allow family life to flow smoothly (Garfinkel 1972; Goffman 1971). All family rules are not evidence of patterned behavior shaped by culture; some are peculiar to the family as a consequence of history and personalities. What reflects a

shared culture are those factors duplicated, rewarded, or discouraged verbally, nonverbally, and spatially throughout the community. Stories concerned with inheritance or succession that are related emotionally, repeated, and widely commented on, for example, represent acts that either violate or re-create cultural structure.

3. *Culture permeates all aspects of life.* Beliefs are not matters easily obtained by asking people directly what they think or feel about behavior. What is most important to people, however, is present in a variety of communication channels. Often, for example, the nonverbal—where people sit, who imitates whom—reveals the family hierarchy. Everyday family life contains clues that allow a cultural system to be inferred from public behavior. I start with the public acts and evidence of family choices and work backward to get at the more private world. A reflection of priorities is found in the ordinary possessions of home or car: whether the barn or home is in better condition; whether the tractor or refrigerator is newer. Choices are clues to family goals and priorities and when widely replicated suggest aspects of a shared community culture.

4. *The family is larger than the sum of its parts.* The family system must be constructed from data gathered and observed of all its members. I argue it is best to observe families in their natural context going about activities they take for granted. They lower their defenses in familiar and comfortable surroundings, and how the group works emerges. Ideal versus real behavior can only be sorted out through actual observation of family interaction.

The research strategy had to accommodate constraints presented by farm families. Fieldwork had to fit into tight schedules dictated by the seasonal demands of farming and the active community and school involvements of family members. We made appointments that were often broken, or we were told, "Call me when it rains." Farmers would not allow the researcher to impose on them if it was inconvenient. This is not to say that we did not become intimate with families; I or my students were occasionally almost adopted. But most families wanted to know how long the interview was going to take, what it was to be used for, and whether confidentiality would be preserved. Unlike the subjects of traditional anthropology, the middle-class, educated farm families read the newspaper and are exceedingly well informed about research. Care had to be taken not to violate privacy while telling their story. I have given the communities pseudonyms and have altered details about people to make identification difficult without destroying meaning. Once I addressed a group of 4H leaders that included members of some communities I had studied. I explained that although they might choose to tell others about their participation, I would keep their identities confidential.

I felt an obligation to repay the families by informing others about their lives, as I had justified the research to them. Each professional journal article I published was translated—with the assistance of Gary Beaumont in the University of Illinois Agricultural Communications Department—into television and radio spots which were broadcast across the state and sometimes nationally. I have also written popular articles and done news releases about my findings. This book also contributes to my responsibility to make their lives known to policymakers and perhaps influence the policy-making process.

Bibliography

Allen, Graham

1977   Sibling Solidarity. *Journal of Marriage and the Family* 39 (1): 177–84.

Allen, John Conrad, III

1989   Against All Odds: Rural Community in the Information Age. Ph.D. diss., Department of Sociology, Washington State University.

Atack, Jeremy, and Fred Bateman

1987   *To Their Own Soil: Agriculture in the Antebellum North*. Ames: Iowa State University Press.

Barber, Bernard

1983   *The Logic and Limits of Trust*. New Brunswick, N.J.: Rutgers University Press.

Barlett, Peggy F.

1986   Part-time Farming: Saving the Farm or Saving the Lifestyle? *Rural Sociology* 51 (3): 289–313.

1989   Industrial Agriculture. In *Economic Anthropology*, edited by Stuart Plattner, pp. 253–91. Berkeley: University of California Press.

1991   Status Aspirations and Lifestyle Influences on Farm Survival. In *Research in Rural Sociology and Development*. Vol. 5, *Household Strategies*, edited by Daniel C. Clay and Harry K. Schwarzweller, pp. 173–90. Greenwich, Conn.: JAI Press.

Barth, Fredrik

1969   *Ethnic Groups and Boundaries*. Boston: Little, Brown and Co.

1984   Problems in Conceptualizing Cultural Pluralism, with Illustrations from Oman Somar. In *The Prospects for Plural Societies*, edited by Stuart Plattner and David Maybury-Lewis, pp. 77–87. 1982 Proceedings of the American Ethnological Society. Washington, D.C.: American Ethnological Society.

Beale, Calvin L.

1979   Demographic Aspects of Agricultural Structure. In *Structure Issues of American Agriculture*. Economics, Statistics, and Cooperative Service. Agricultural Economic Report 438, pp. 80–85. Washington, D.C.: U.S. Department of Agriculture.

1983   Agricultural Communities: Economic and Social Setting. In *The Interrelationship of Agriculture, Business, Industry, and Government in the Rural Economy*. U.S. House of Representatives, Committee on Agriculture, 88th Cong., 1st sess., October, pp. 90–104.

1989a   High Fertility in the Rural White Population of the Midwest. In *A Taste of the Country: A Collection of Calvin Beale's Writings*, edited by Peter Morrison, pp. 21–32. University Park: Pennsylvania State University Press.

1989b Personal communication.

1989c Race and Ethnicity. In *Rural and Small Town America*, by Glenn V. Fuguitt, David L. Brown, and Calvin L. Beale, pp. 139–55. New York: Russell Sage Foundation.

1989d Significant Recent Trends in the Demography of Farm People. *Proceedings of the Philadelphia Society for Promoting Agriculture* 1987–88 (February): 36–39.

Beale, Calvin L., and Judith Kalbacher

1989 Farm Population Trends: Shrinkage, Shifts, and Fewer Heirs. *Farmline* 9 (8): 19.

Beers, Howard W.

1937 A Portrait of the Farm Family in Central New York State. *American Sociological Review* 2 (5): 591–600.

Bell, Colin, and Howard Newby

1971 *Community Studies*. New York: Praeger.

Bellah, Robert, Richard Masden, Willam M. Sullivan, Ann Swidler, and Steven M. Tipton

1985 *Habits of the Heart: Individualism and Commitment in American Life.* Berkeley: University of California Press.

Bennett, John W., in association with Seena B. Kohl and Geraldine Binion

1982 *Of Time and the Enterprise*. Minneapolis: University of Minnesota Press.

Bennett, John W., and Seena B. Kohl

1981 The Agrifamily System. In *Of Time and the Enterprise*, by John W. Bennett, pp. 128–47. Minneapolis: University of Minnesota Press.

Berkner, Lutz K.

1976 Inheritance, Land Tenure and Peasant Family Structure: A German Regional Comparison. In *Family and Inheritance: Rural Society in Western Europe 1200–1800*, edited by Jack Goody, Joan Thirsk, and E. P. Thompson, pp. 71–95. Cambridge: Cambridge University Press.

Bidwell, Perry Wells, and John I. Falconer

1925 *History of American Agriculture in the Northern United States, 1620–1860.* Publication no. 358. Washington, D.C.: Carnegie Institution of Washington.

Bloch, Maurice

1977 The Past and the Present in the Present. *Man* 12 (2): 278–92.

1985 From Cognition to Ideology. In *Power and Knowledge*, edited by Richard Fardon, pp. 21–48. Edinburgh: Scottish Academic Press.

Bogue, Allan G.

1963a Farming in the Prairie Peninsula, 1830–1890. *Journal of Economic History* 23 (1): 3–29.

1963b   *From Prairie to Cornbelt.* Chicago: University of Chicago Press.
Bogue, Margaret Beattie

1959   *Patterns from the Sod: Land Use and Tenure in the Grand Prairie,*
            1850–1900. Vol. 34. Land Series, vol. 1. Springfield, Ill.: Illinois State His-
            torical Library.

Boorstin, Daniel

1965   *The Americans.* New York: Random House.

Bossard, James H. S.

1943   Family Table-talk, an Area for Sociological Study. *American Sociological*
            Review 8:295–301.

1945   Family Modes of Expressions. *American Sociological Review* 10:226–37.

Bossard, James H. S., and Eleanor S. Boll

1956   *The Large Family System.* Philadelphia: University of Pennsylvania Press.

Bott, Elizabeth

1971   *Family and Social Network.* 2d ed. New York: Free Press.

Bourdieu, Pierre

1979   The Kablye House or the World Reversed. In *Algeria 1960,* by Pierre
            Bourdieu, pp. 133–53. Translated by Richard Nice. Cambridge: Cam-
            bridge University Press.

Brengle, Marilyn S.

1981   Assessing Farm Wives' Involvement in the Family Farm. Master's thesis,
            University of Illinois at Urbana-Champaign.

Broderick, Carlfred B.

1990   Family Process Theory. In *Fashioning Family Theory,* edited by Jetse
            Sprey, pp. 171–206. Newbury Park, Calif.: Sage Publications.

Brooke, Michael Z.

1970   *Le Play: Engineer and Social Scientist.* London: Longman.

Brown, David L., J. Norman Reid, Herman Bluestone, David A. McGranahan,
and Sara M. Mazie, eds.

1988   *Rural Economic Development in the 1980's.* Rural Economic Research Re-
            port no. 69. Washington, D.C.: U.S. Department of Agriculture, Eco-
            nomic Research Service.

Brown, Kate

1990   Connected Independence: A Paradox of Rural Health? *Journal of Rural*
            Community Psychology 11 (2): 51–54.

Bruner, Edward M.

1986   Experience and Its Expressions. In *The Anthropology of Experience,* edited
            by Victor W. Turner and Edward M. Bruner, pp. 3–30. Urbana: Uni-
            versity of Illinois Press.

Brunner, Edmund De S.

1929   *Immigrant Farmers and Their Children.* Garden City, N.Y.: Doubleday,
            Doran and Co.

Buttel, Frederick H.
1983   Beyond the Family Farm. In *Technology and Social Change in Rural Areas: A Festschrift for Eugene A. Wilkening*, edited by Gene F. Summers, pp. 87–107. Boulder, Colo.: Westview Press.

Buttel, Frederick H., and Gilbert W. Gillespie, Jr.
1984   The Sexual Division of Farm Household Labor: An Exploratory Study of the Structure of On-farm and Off-farm Labor Allocation among Farm Men and Women. *Rural Sociology* 49 (2): 183–209.

Calhoun, Arthur W.
1918   *A Social History of the American Family.* Vol. 2. Cleveland: Arthur H. Clark.

Campbell, Rex R.
1985   Some Observations on the Deflation of Farm Assets in the Midwest. *Culture and Agriculture* 3 (Summer/Fall): 1–5.

Caplow, Theodore
1968   *Two against One.* Englewood Cliffs, N.J.: Prentice Hall.

Carroll, Edward V., and Sonya Salamon
1988   Share and Share Alike: Inheritance Patterns in Two Illinois Farm Communities. *Journal of Family History* 13 (2): 219–32.

Carter, Anthony T.
1988   Does Culture Matter?: The Case of the Demographic Transition. *Historical Methods* 21 (4): 164–69.

Chayanov, A. V.
1966   *The Theory of Peasant Economy.* Edited by Daniel Thorner, Basile Kerblay, and R. E. F. Smith. Homewood, Ill.: Irwin.

Chester, Ronald
1982   *Inheritance, Wealth, and Society.* Bloomington: Indiana University Press.

Clifford, William B., Tim B. Heaton, Paul R. Voss, and Glenn V. Fuguitt
1985   The Rural Elderly in Demographic Perspective. In *The Elderly in Rural Society*, edited by Raymond T. Coward and Gary R. Lee, pp. 25–55. New York: Springer Publishing Co.

Cogswell, Seddie, Jr.
1975   *Tenure, Nativity, and Age as Factors in Iowa Agriculture, 1850–1880.* Ames: Iowa State University Press.

Coleman, James S.
1988   Social Capital in the Creation of Human Capital. *American Journal of Sociology* 94 (Supplement S95–S120): 95–119.

Colman, Gould, and Sarah Elbert
1984   Farming Families: The Farm Needs Everyone. In *Focus on Agriculture: Research in Rural Sociology and Development*, edited by Harry K. Schwarzweller, 1:61–78. Greenwich, Conn.: JAI Press.

Conzen, Kathleen Neils

1980a   Germans. In *Harvard Encyclopedia of American Ethnic Groups*, edited by
            Stephan Thernstrom, pp. 405–25. Cambridge, Mass.: Harvard Univer-
            sity Press.

1980b   Historical Approaches to the Study of Rural Ethnic Communities. In
            Ethnicity on the Great Plains, edited by Frederick C. Luebke, pp. 1–18.
            Lincoln: University of Nebraska Press.

1985   Peasant Pioneers: Generational Succession among German Farmers in
            Frontier Minnesota. In *The Countryside in the Age of Capitalist Transfor-*
            mation, edited by Steven Hahn and Jonathan Prude, pp. 259–92. Chapel
            Hill: University of North Carolina Press.

1990   Immigrants in Nineteenth-century Agricultural History. In *Agriculture*
            and National Development: Views on the Nineteenth Century, edited by
            Lou Ferleger, pp. 303–41. Ames: Iowa State University Press.

Corner, Faye E.

1928   A Non-mobile, Cooperative Type of Community: A Study of the De-
            scendants of an East Frisian Group. *University of Illinois Studies in the*
            Social Sciences 16 (4): 505–70.

Coughenour, C. Milton, and Gregory S. Kowalski

1977   Status and Role of Fathers and Sons on Partnership Farms. *Rural Soci-*
            ology 42 (2): 180–205.

Coughenour, C. Milton, and Louis Swanson

1983   Work Statuses and Occupations of Men and Women in Farm Families
            and the Structure of Farms. *Rural Sociology* 48 (1): 23–43.

Crocombe, Ron

1974   An Approach to the Analysis of Land Tenure Systems. In *Land Tenure*
            in Oceania, edited by Henry P. Lundsgaarde, pp. 1–17. Honolulu: Uni-
            versity of Hawaii Press.

Danhof, Clarence H.

1969   *Change in Agriculture: The Northern United States, 1820–1870*. Cam-
            bridge, Mass.: Harvard University Press.

de Janvry, Alain

1980   Social Differentiation in Agriculture and the Ideology of Neopopulism.
            In *The Rural Sociology of Advanced Societies*, edited by Frederick H. But-
            tel and Howard Newby, pp. 155–68. Montclair, N.J.: Allanheld, Osmun.

Denzin, Norman K.

1970   *The Research Act*. Chicago: Aldine.

Dobbert, Guido A.

1967   German-Americans between New and Old Fatherland, 1870–1914.
            American Quarterly 19: 663–90.

Dovring, Folke

1962   European Reaction to the Homestead Act. *Journal of Economic History*
            22 (4): 461–72.

Dovring, Folke, and John F. Yanagida

1979   *Monoculture and Productivity: A Study of Private Profit and Social Product on Grain Farms and Livestock Farms in Illinois*. Urbana-Champaign: University of Illinois, Department of Agricultural Economics, AE4477.

Duncan, Marvin R.

1989   U.S. Agriculture: Hard Realities and New Opportunities. *Economic Review, Federal Reserve Bank of Kansas City* 74 (2): 3–20.

Dunham, A.

1962   The Method, Process and Frequency of Wealth Transmission. *Chicago Law Review* 30 (Winter): 241–85.

Ely, Richard T., and George S. Wehrwein

1940   *Land Economics*. New York: Macmillan.

Epstein, A. L.

1978   *Ethos and Identity: Three Studies in Ethnicity*. Chicago: Aldine.

Faragher, John Mack

1986   *Sugar Creek: Life on the Illinois Prairie*. New Haven: Yale University Press.

Farber, Bernard

1973   *Family and Kinship in Modern Society*. Glenview, Ill.: Scott, Foresman.

Featherman, David, and Robert Hauser

1978   *Opportunity and Change*. New York: Academic Press.

Fernandez, James W.

1990   Enclosures: Boundary Maintenance and Its Representations over Time in Asturian Mountain Villages (Spain). In *Culture through Time: Anthropological Approaches*, edited by Emiko Ohnuki-Tierney, pp. 94–127. Stanford: Stanford University Press.

Fink, Deborah A.

1986   *Open Country, Iowa: Rural Women, Tradition and Change*. Albany: State University of New York Press.

1987   Farming in Open Country, Iowa: Women and the Changing Farm Economy. In *Farm Work and Fieldwork: American Agriculture in Anthropological Perspective*, edited by Michael Chibnik, pp. 121–44. Ithaca: Cornell University Press.

Fischer, David Hackett

1989   *Albion's Seed: Four British Folkways in America*. New York: Oxford University Press.

Fisher, Claude S., Robert M. Jackson, C. Ann Steuve, Kathleen Gerson, and Lynne McCallister Jones, with Mark Baldassare

1977   *Networks and Places: Social Relations in the Urban Setting*. New York: Free Press.

Fitchen, Janet M.

1991   *Endangered Spaces, Enduring Places*. Boulder, Colo.: Westview Press.

Flora, Cornelia B.

1981   Farm Women, Farming Systems, and Agriculture Structure: Suggestions for Scholarship. *The Rural Sociologist* 1 : 383–86.

1985   Women and Agriculture. *Agriculture and Human Values* 2 (1): 5–12.

Flora, Cornelia Butler, and John Stitz

1988   Female Subsistence Production and Commercial Farm Survival among Settlement Kansas Wheat Farmers. *Human Organization* 47 (1): 64–69.

Flora, Jan L., and John M. Stitz

1985   Ethnicity, Persistence, and Capitalization of Agriculture in the Great Plains during the Settlement Period: Wheat Production and Risk Avoidance. *Rural Sociology* 50 (3): 341–60.

Fortes, Meyer

1966   Introduction to *The Developmental Cycle in Domestic Groups*, edited by Jack Goody, pp. 1–14. Cambridge: Cambridge University Press.

1969   *Kinship and the Social Order*. Chicago: Aldine.

Foster, Gary, Richard Hummel, and Robert Whittenbarger

1987   Ethnic Echoes through 100 Years of Midwestern Agriculture. *Rural Sociology* 52 (3): 365–78.

1989   Ethnic Echoes: A Rejoinder to Khawaja. *Rural Sociology* 54 (2): 256–61.

Freiburg Centennial Committee

1939   *Freiburg Centennial, 1839–1939*. Souvenir program. Freiburg, Ill.: Centennial Committee.

Friedberger, Mark W.

1983   The Farm Family and the Inheritance Process: Evidence from the Corn Belt, 1870–1950. *Agricultural History* 57 (1): 1–13.

1984   Handing Down the Homeplace: Farm Inheritance Strategies in Iowa, 1870–1945. *The Annals of Iowa* 47 (6): 518–36.

1988   *Farm Families and Change in 20th Century America*. Lexington: University Press of Kentucky.

1989   *Shake-out: Iowa Farm Families in the 1980s*. Lexington: University Press of Kentucky.

Friedl, Ernestine

1975   *Women and Men*. New York: Holt, Rinehart and Winston.

Friedland, William H.

1989   Is Rural Sociology Worth Saving? *The Rural Sociologist* 9 (1): 3–5.

Friedman, Harriet

1980   Household Production and the National Economy: Concepts for the Analysis of Agrarian Formations. *Journal of Peasant Studies* 7 (2): 158–84.

Fuchs, Victor R.

1983   *How We Live*. Cambridge, Mass.: Harvard University Press.

Fuller, Anthony M.

1984   Part-time Farming: The Enigmas and the Realities. In *Focus on Agriculture: Research in Rural Sociology and Development*, edited by Harry K. Schwarzweller, 1 : 187–220. Greenwich, Conn.: JAI Press.

Fuller, Wayne E.

1982   *The Old Country School: The Story of Rural Education in the Middle West*.
            Chicago: University of Chicago Press.

Gans, Herbert J.

1979   Symbolic Ethnicity: The Future of Ethnic Groups and Cultures in
            America. *Ethnic and Racial Studies* 2 (1): 1–20.

Garfinkel, Harold

1972   Studies of the Routine Grounds of Everyday Activities. In *Studies in So-
            cial Interaction*, edited by David Sudnow, pp. 1–30. New York: Free
            Press.

Gates, Paul W.

1932   Large-scale Farming in Illinois, 1850–1870. *Agricultural History* 6 (1):
            14–25.

1934   *The Illinois Central Railroad and Its Colonization Work*. Cambridge,
            Mass.: Harvard University Press.

1960   The Farmer's Age: Agriculture, 1815–1860. *Economic History of the United
            States*. Vol. 8. New York: Holt, Rinehart and Winston.

Geisler, Charles C., William F. Waters, and Katrina L. Eadie

1985   The Changing Structure of Female Agricultural Land Ownership. *Ru-
            ral Sociology* 50 (1): 74–87.

Gerlach, Russel L.

1976   *Immigrants to the Ozarks: A Study in Ethnic Geography*. Columbia: Uni-
            versity of Missouri Press.

Gerth, H. H., and C. Wright Mills, eds.

1972   *From Max Weber: Essays in Sociology*. Reprinted from a 1946 edition of
            translations. New York: Oxford University Press.

Gilbert, Jess, and Raymond Akor

1988   Increasing Structural Divergence in U.S. Dairying: California and Wis-
            consin since 1950. *Rural Sociology* 53 (1): 56–72.

Gilbert, Jess, and Craig K. Harris

1984   Changes in Type, Tenure, and Concentration of U.S. Farmland Owners.
            In *Focus on Agriculture: Research in Rural Sociology and Development*, ed-
            ited by Harry K. Schwarzweller, 1:135–60. Greenwich, Conn.: JAI
            Press.

Gjerde, Jon

1985   *From Peasants to Farmers: The Migration from Balestrand, Norway, to the
            Upper Middle West*. Cambridge: Cambridge University Press.

Glasgow, Nina

1988   *The Nonmetro Elderly: Economic and Demographic Status*. Rural Develop-
            ment Research Report no. 70. Washington, D.C.: U.S. Department of
            Agriculture, Economic Research Service.

Glazer, Nathan, and Daniel Patrick Moynihan

1970   *Beyond the Melting Pot*. 2d ed. Cambridge, Mass.: MIT Press.

Gleason, Philip

1980 American Identity and Americanization. In *Harvard Encyclopedia of American Ethnic Groups*, edited by Stephan Thernstrom, pp. 31–58. Cambridge, Mass.: Harvard University Press.

Goffman, Erving

1971 Insanity of Place. In *Relations in Public*, by Erving Goffman, pp. 335–90. New York: Harper Colophon.

Goldman, Robert, and David R. Dickens

1983 The Selling of Rural America. *Rural Sociology* 48 (4): 585–606.

Goldschmidt, Walter

1978 *As You Sow*. 2d ed. Montclair, N.J.: Allanheld, Osmun.

Goldschmidt, Walter, and Evalyn Jacobson Kunkel

1971 The Structure of the Peasant Family. *American Anthropologist* 73 (5): 1058–76.

Goody, Jack

1972 The Evolution of the Family. In *Household and Family in Past Time*, edited by Peter Laslett, pp. 103–24. Cambridge: Cambridge University Press.

1976 Introduction to *Family and Inheritance: Rural Society in Western Europe 1200–1800*, edited by Jack Goody, Joan Thirsk, and E. P. Thompson, pp. 1–9. Cambridge: Cambridge University Press.

Goody, Jack, ed.

1966 *The Developmental Cycle in Domestic Groups*. Cambridge: Cambridge University Press.

Goss, Kevin F., Richard D. Rodefeld, and Frederick H. Buttel

1980 The Political Economy of Class Structure in U.S. Agriculture: A Theoretical Outline. In *The Rural Sociology of Advanced Societies*, edited by Frederick H. Buttel and Howard Newby, pp. 83–132. Montclair, N.J.: Allanheld, Osmun.

Granovetter, Mark

1973 The Strength of Weak Ties. *American Journal of Sociology* 81: 1287–1380.

1983 The Strength of Weak Ties: A Network Theory Revisited. In *Sociological Theory*, edited by Randall Collins, pp. 201–33. San Francisco: Jossey-Bass.

Greeley, Andrew

1964 The Protestant Ethic: Time for a Moratorium. *Sociological Analysis* 25 (1): 20–33.

Greene, Jack P.

1988 *Pursuits of Happiness: The Social Development of Early Modern British Colonies and the Formation of American Culture*. Chapel Hill: University of North Carolina Press.

Handlin, Oscar

1980 Yankees. In *Harvard Encyclopedia of American Ethnic Groups*, edited by Stephan Thernstrom, pp. 1028–30. Cambridge, Mass.: Harvard University Press.

Haney, Wava Gillespie

1983 Farm Family and the Role of Women. In *Technology and Social Change in Rural Areas: A Festschrift for Eugene A. Wilkening*, edited by Gene F. Summers, pp. 179–93. Boulder, Colo.: Westview Press.

Hansen, Marcus Lee

1940 *The Immigrant in American History*. Cambridge, Mass.: Harvard University Press.

Hatch, Elvin

1975 Stratification in a Rural California Community. *Agricultural History* 49 (1): 21–38.

1979 *Biography of a Small Town*. New York: Columbia University Press.

Hawgood, John A.

1940 *The Tragedy of German-America: The Germans in the United States of America during the Nineteenth Century and After*. New York: Arno.

Heyman, Katy, and Sonya Salamon

1987 Kinship, Land Tenure, and Social Position in a Farming Community. Paper presented at the annual meeting of the Rural Sociological Society, Madison, Wis.

Hofstadter, Richard

1955 *The Age of Reform*. New York: Vintage.

Holbrook, Stewart H.

1950 *The Yankee Exodus: An Account of Migration from New England*. Seattle: University of Washington Press.

Hollingshead, A. B.

1937 The Life Cycle of Nebraska Rural Churches. *Rural Sociology* 2 (2): 180–91.

1938 Changes in Land Ownership as an Index of Succession in Rural Communities. *American Journal of Sociology* 43 (5): 767–77.

Hsu, Francis L. K.

1965 The Effect of Dominant Kinship Relationships on Kin and Non-kin Behavior: A Hypothesis. *American Anthropologist* 67 (3): 638–61.

1971 A Hypothesis on Kinship and Culture. In *Kinship and Culture*, edited by Francis L. K. Hsu, pp. 3–29. Chicago: Aldine.

Hudson, John C.

1985 *Plains Country Towns*. Minneapolis: University of Minnesota Press.

Hummon, David M.

1986 City Mouse, Country Mouse: The Persistence of Community Identity. *Qualitative Sociology* 9 (1): 3–25.

Illinois Department of Agriculture and U.S. Department of Agriculture

1990 *Illinois Agricultural Statistics 1990*. Bulletin 90-1. Springfield: Illinois Agricultural Statistics Service.

Jensen, Joan M.

1985   The Role of Farm Women in American History: Areas for Additional
            Research. *Agriculture and Human Values* 2 (1): 13–18.

Jensen, Richard J.

1978   *Illinois, A Bicentennial History*. New York: W. W. Norton.

Johansen, Harley E., and Glenn V. Fuguitt

1984   *The Changing Rural Village in America*. Cambridge, Mass.: Ballinger.

Johnson, Allen W., and Timothy Earle

1987   *The Evolution of Human Societies: From Foraging Group to Agrarian State*.
            Stanford: Stanford University Press.

Johnson, Bruce B.

1972   *The Farmland Rental Market: A Case Analysis of Selected Corn Belt Areas*.
            Farm Production Economics Division. Agricultural Economic Report
            235. Washington, D.C.: U.S. Department of Agriculture.

Johnson, Colleen Leahy

1989   In-law Relationships in the American Kinship System: The Impact of
            Divorce and Remarriage. *American Ethnologist* 16 (1): 87–99.

Johnstone, Ronald L.

1975   *Religion and Society in Interaction*. Englewood Cliffs, N.J.: Prentice Hall.

Jones, Calvin, and Rachel Ann Rosenfeld

1981   *American Farm Women: Findings from a National Survey*. NORC Report
            no. 130. Chicago: National Opinion Research Center.

Jones, John, and Charles H. Barnard

1986   *Farm Real Estate: Historical Series Data, 1950–85*. Statistical Bulletin no.
            738. Washington, D.C.: U.S. Department of Agriculture, Economic Re-
            search Service.

Jordan, Terry G.

1966   *German Seed in Texas Soil: Immigrant Farmers in Nineteenth-Century
            Texas*. Austin: University of Texas Press.

Jung, Karen

1980   Irish Identity: Its Influence on Farm Women. Master's thesis, Univer-
            sity of Illinois at Urbana-Champaign.

Kalbacher, Judith

1982   *Women Farmers in America*. Paper no. ERS-679. Washington, D.C.:
            U.S. Department of Agriculture, Economic Research Service.

1985   *A Profile of Female Farmers in America*. Rural Development Research
            Report no. 45. Washington, D.C.: U.S. Department of Agriculture,
            Economic Research Service.

Kamphoefner, Walter

1984   The German Agricultural Frontier: Crucible or Cocoon. *Ethnic Forum* 4
            (1–2): 21–35.

Kantor, David, and William Lehr

1975   *Inside the Family*. San Francisco: Jossey-Bass.

Keim, Ann

1976   The Farm Woman: Lifelong Involvement with the Family Farm. Master's thesis, University of Illinois at Urbana-Champaign.

Khawaja, Marwan

1989   Ethnic Echoes through 100 Years of Midwestern Agriculture: Commentary on Foster et al. *Rural Sociology* 54 (2): 246–55.

Kirschner, Don S.

1970   *City and Country: Rural Responses to Urbanization in the 1920s.* Westport, Conn.: Greenwood Press.

Kloppenburg, Jack R., and Charles C. Geisler

1985   The Agricultural Ladder: Agrarian Ideology and the Changing Structure of U.S. Agriculture. *Journal of Rural Studies* 1 (1): 59–72.

Kohl, Seena B.

1976   *Working Together: Women and Family in Southwestern Saskatchewan.* Toronto: Holt, Rinehart and Winston of Canada.

Kohn, Howard

1988   *The Last Farmer: An American Memoir.* New York: Summit Books.

Kollmorgen, Walter M.

1941   *The German Settlement in Cullman County, Alabama: An Agricultural Island in the Cotton Belt.* Washington, D.C.: U.S. Department of Agriculture, Bureau of Agricultural Economics.

Kramer, Mark

1977   *Three Farms.* Boston: Atlantic–Little, Brown and Co.

Lancelle, Mark, and Richard D. Rodefeld

1980   The Influence of Social Origins on the Ability to Attain Ownership of Large Farms. *Rural Sociology* 45 (3): 381–95.

Lash, Amy Marie

1990   Cultural Influences on Farm Family's Responses to Difficult Life Events. Master's thesis, University of Illinois at Urbana-Champaign.

Laslett, Peter

1984   The Family as a Knot of Individual Interests. In *Households: Comparative and Historical Studies of the Domestic Group*, edited by Robert McC. Netting, Richard R. Wilk, and Eric J. Arnould, pp. 353–79. Berkeley: University of California Press.

Laslett, Peter, ed.

1972   *Household and Family in Past Time.* Cambridge: Cambridge University Press.

Lebra, Takie Sugiyama

1984   *Japanese Women.* Honolulu: University of Hawaii Press.

Le Vine, Robert A.

1965   Intergenerational Tensions and Extended Family Structures in Africa. In *Social Structure and the Family: Generational Relations*, edited by Ethel Shanas and Gordon F. Streib, pp. 188–204. Englewood Cliffs, N.J.: Prentice Hall.

Lewis, Oscar

1965 Introduction to *La Vida*, by Oscar Lewis, pp. i–liii. New York: Random House.

Libertyville

1884 *History of Libertyville County.*

Lieberson, Stanley, and Mary C. Waters

1988 *From Many Strands: Ethnic and Racial Groups in Contemporary America.* New York: Russell Sage Foundation.

Lingeman, Richard

1980 *Small Town America.* Boston: Houghton Mifflin Co.

Litwak, Eugene

1965 Extended Kin Relations in an Industrial Democratic Society. In *Social Structure and the Family: Generational Relations*, edited by Ethel Shanas and Gordon F. Streib, pp. 290–323. Englewood Cliffs, N.J.: Prentice Hall.

Luebke, Frederick C.

1974 *Bonds of Loyalty: German-Americans and World War I.* DeKalb, Ill.: Northern Illinois University Press.

1980 Alsatians. In *Harvard Encyclopedia of American Ethnic Groups*, edited by Stephan Thernstrom, pp. 29–31. Cambridge, Mass.: Harvard University Press.

McCarthy, M., Patricia Salant, and William E. Saupe

1988 Off-farm Labor Allocation by Married Farm Women: Research Review and New Evidence from Wisconsin. In *Women and Farming: Changing Roles, Changing Structures*, edited by W. G. Haney and J. B. Knowles, pp. 135–51. Boulder, Colo.: Westview Press.

McGoldrick, Monica

1989 Ethnicity and the Family Life Cycle. In *The Changing Family Life Cycle*, edited by Betty Carter and Monica McGoldrick, pp. 69–90. 2d ed. Needham Heights, Mass.: Allyn and Bacon.

Mackintosh, Jette

1990 Ethnic Patterns in Danish Immigrant Agriculture: A Study of Audubon and Shelby Counties, Iowa. *Agricultural History* 64 (4): 59–77.

MacLeish, Kenneth, and Kimball Young

1942 *Culture of a Contemporary Rural Community: Landaff, New Hampshire.* Rural Life Series. No. 3. Washington, D.C.: U.S. Department of Agriculture, Bureau of Agricultural Economics.

McNall, Scott G., and Sally Allen McNall

1983 *Plains Families.* New York: St. Martin's Press.

Masuda, Kokichi

1975 Bride's Progress: How a *Yome* Becomes a *Shutome. Journal of Asian and African Studies* 10 (1–2): 10–19.

Maurer, Henrich

1924   Studies in the Sociology of Religion. *American Journal of Sociology* 30 (3): 257–86.

1925   Studies in the Sociology of Religion: II. Religion and American Sectionalism. The Pennsylvania German. *American Journal of Sociology* 30 (4): 408–38.

Meyer, Douglas K.

1976   Native-born Immigrant Clusters on the Illinois Frontier. *Proceedings of the Association of American Geographers* 8 : 41–44.

Michaelson, Evalyn Jacobson, and Walter Goldschmidt

1971   Female Roles and Male Dominance among Peasants. *Southwestern Journal of Anthropology* 27 (Winter): 330–52.

Miner, Horace

1949   *Culture and Agriculture*. Ann Arbor: University of Michigan Press.

Mingay, G. E.

1962   The Size of Farms in the Eighteenth Century. *The Economic History Review,* second series 14 (3): 469–88.

1989   Introduction to *The Unquiet Countryside*, edited by G. E. Mingay, pp. 1–8. London: Routledge.

Mooney, Patrick H.

1983   Toward a Class Analysis of Midwestern Agriculture. *Rural Sociology* 48 (4): 563–84.

1988   *My Own Boss? Class, Rationality, and the Family Farm*. Boulder, Colo.: Westview Press.

Moore, Henrietta L.

1988   *Feminism and Anthropology*. Minneapolis: University of Minnesota Press.

Morris, Richard M.

1927   Primogeniture and Entailed Estates in America. *Columbia Law Review* 27 : 24–51.

Nelson, Lowrey

1955   *Rural Sociology*. 2d ed. New York: American Book.

Netting, Robert McC.

1981   *Balancing on an Alp: Ecological Change and Continuity in a Swiss Mountain Community*. Cambridge: Cambridge University Press.

1989   Smallholders, Householders, Freeholders: Why the Family Farm Works Well Worldwide. In *The Household Economy: The Domestic Mode of Production Reconsidered*, edited by Richard R. Wilk, pp. 221–44. Boulder, Colo.: Westview Press.

Netting, Robert McC., Richard R. Wilk, and Eric J. Arnould, eds.

1984   *Households: Comparative and Historical Studies of the Domestic Group*. Berkeley: University of California Press.

Newby, Howard

1980   The Rural Sociology of Advanced Capitalist Societies. In *The Rural Sociology of Advanced Societies*, edited by Frederick H. Buttel and Howard Newby, pp. 1–30. Montclair, N.J.: Allanheld, Osmun.

Newman, Katherine S.

1986   Symbolic Dialects and Generations of Women: Variations in the Meaning of Post-divorce Downward Mobility. *American Ethnologist* 13 (2): 230–52.

Nicholls, William H.

1975   Industrialization, Factor Markets, and Agricultural Developments. In *Regional Policy Readings in Theory and Applications*, edited by John Friedmann and William Alonso, pp. 358–79. Cambridge, Mass.: MIT Press.

Office of Technology Assessment

1986   *Farm Structure, Technology, Public Policy and the Changing Structure of American Agriculture: A Special Report for the 1985 Farm Bill*. OTA Report F-285. Washington, D.C.

Ohnuki-Tierney, Emiko

1990a   Introduction: The Historicization of Anthropology. In *Culture through Time: Anthropological Approaches*, edited by Emiko Ohnuki-Tierney, pp. 1–25. Stanford: Stanford University Press.

1990b   The Monkey as Self in Japanese Culture. In *Culture through Time: Anthropological Approaches*, edited by Emiko Ohnuki-Tierney, pp. 128–53. Stanford: Stanford University Press.

Ohnuki-Tierney, Emiko, ed.

1990   *Culture through Time: Anthropological Approaches*. Stanford: Stanford University Press.

Ortner, Sherry B.

1984   Theory in Anthropology since the Sixties. *Comparative Studies in Society and History* 26 (1): 126–66.

1990   Patterns of History: Cultural Schemas in the Foundings of Sherpa Religious Institutions. In *Culture through Time: Anthropological Approaches*, edited by Emiko Ohnuki-Tierney, pp. 57–93. Stanford: Stanford University Press.

Ostergren, Robert O.

1981a   The Immigrant Church as a Symbol of Community and Place in the Upper Midwest. *Great Plains Quarterly* 1 (4): 225–38.

1981b   Land and Family in Rural Immigrant Communities. *Annals of the Association of American Geographers* 71 (3): 400–411.

1986   The Transplanted Swedish Rural Immigrant Community in the Upper Middle West. In *Scandinavia Overseas*, edited by Harald Runblom and

Dag Blanck, pp. 18–39. Uppsala Multiethnic Papers, no. 7. Uppsala, Sweden: Uppsala University.

Penas, Dwight J.

1983 Always Settling, Never Settled: Family Life among Contemporary Yankee Farmers. Master's thesis, University of Illinois at Urbana-Champaign.

Penn, J. B.

1979 The Structure of Agriculture: An Overview of the Issue. In *Structure Issues of American Agriculture*. Economics, Statistics, and Cooperative Service. Agricultural Economic Report 438, pp. 2–23. Washington, D.C.: U.S. Department of Agriculture.

Perkins, Kenneth B.

1987 Volunteer Fire Departments: Community Integration, Autonomy and Survival. *Human Organization* 46 (4): 342–48.

Perrin, William Henry, ed.

1885 *History of Freiburg County*. Chicago: O. L. Baskin and Co.

Peshkin, Alan

1978a *BRT. A Rural Case Study*. University of Illinois at Urbana-Champaign (NTIS PB-282 845).

1978b *Growing Up American*. Chicago: University of Chicago Press.

Pfeffer, Max

1983 Social Origins of Three Systems of Farm Production in the United States. *Rural Sociology* 48 (4): 540–62.

Pressly, Thomas J., and William H. Scofield

1965 *Farm Real Estate Values in the United States by Counties, 1850–1959*. Seattle: University of Washington Press.

Reinhardt, Nola, and Peggy Barlett

1989 Family Farm Competitiveness in United States Agriculture: A Conceptual Framework. In *Food and Farm: Current Debates and Policies*, edited by Christina Gladwin and Kathleen Truman, pp. 389–411. Lanham, Md.: University Press of America.

Reiss, Franklin J.

1967 *Farm Lease Practices in Western Illinois*. University of Illinois Agricultural Experiment Station Bulletin 728.

1976 Decision Making in the Farmland Market. *Journal of the American Society of Farm Managers and Rural Appraisers* 40 (1): 35–43.

1980 Personal communication.

1983 The Future of Farmland Leasing. In *Rents and Rental Practices in U.S. Agriculture*, edited by J. Peter DeBrael and Gene Wunderlich, pp. 117–26. Washington, D.C.: U.S. Department of Agriculture, Economic Research Service.

Reynolds, David R.

1990 The Restructuring of Social Relations in the Countryside: The School

Consolidation Movement in Iowa, 1895–1925. Paper presented at the Annual Meetings of the Association of American Geographers, Toronto, April.

Rhodes, Richard

1989   *Farm: A Year in the Life of an American Farmer*. New York: Simon and Schuster.

Rice, John G.

1977   The Role of Culture and Community in Frontier Prairie Farming. *Journal of Historical Geography* 3 (2): 155–75.

Ripley, La Vern

1985   Ameliorated Americanization: The Effect of World War I on German-Americans in the 1920s. In *America and the Germans*. Vol. 2, *The Relationship in the Twentieth Century*, edited by Frank Tommler and Joseph McVeigh, pp. 217–31. Philadelphia: University of Pennsylvania Press.

Rogers, Susan Carol

1975   Female Forms of Power and the Myth of Male Dominance: A Model of Female/male Interaction in Peasant Society. *American Ethnologist* 2:727–56.

1985   Owners and Operators of Farmland: Structural Changes in U.S. Agriculture. *Human Organization* 44 (3): 206–14.

1987   Mixing Paradigms on Mixed Farming: Anthropological and Economic Views of Specialization in Illinois Agriculture. In *Farm Work and Fieldwork: American Agriculture in Anthropological Perspective*, edited by Michael Chibnik, pp. 58–89. Ithaca: Cornell University Press.

Rogers, Susan Carol, and Sonya Salamon

1983   Inheritance and Social Organization among Family Farmers. *American Ethnologist* 10 (3): 529–48.

Rosenblatt, Paul C., Leni de Mik, Roxanne Marie Anderson, and Patricia A. Johnson

1985   *The Family in Business*. San Francisco: Jossey-Bass.

Rosenfeld, Jeffrey P.

1979   *The Legacy of Aging*. Norwood, N.J.: Ablex.

Rosenfeld, Rachel Ann

1985   *Farm Women: Work, Farm, and Family in the United States*. Chapel Hill: University of North Carolina Press.

Ross, Peggy J.

1985   Varying Roles for U.S. Farm Women. *Rural Development Perspectives* 1 (2): 22–24.

Royce, Anya Peterson

1974   Definitions of Ethnicity. *Ethnicity* 1:111–24.

1982   *Ethnic Identity*. Bloomington: Indiana University Press.

Ryan, Vernon D.

1987   *Research on Regional Economic Development Efforts in Iowa's Rural Com-*

munities. The Legislative Extended Assistance Group. Oakdale: University of Iowa.

Sachs, Carolyn

1983   *The Invisible Farmers: Women in Agricultural Production*. Totowa, N.J.: Fowman and Allanheld.

Sahlins, Marshall

1981   *Historical Metaphors and Mythical Realities: Structure in the Early History of the Sandwich Islands Kingdom*. Ann Arbor: University of Michigan Press.

Salamon, Sonya

1978   Farm Tenancy and Family Values in East Central Illinois. *Illinois Research* 20 (Winter): 6–7.

1982   Sibling Solidarity as an Operating Strategy in Illinois Agriculture. *Rural Sociology* 47 (2): 349–68.

1984   Ethnic Origin as Explanation for Local Land Ownership Patterns. In *Focus on Agriculture: Research in Rural Sociology and Development*, edited by Harry K. Schwarzweller, 1:161–86. Greenwich, Conn.: JAI Press.

1987   Ethnic Determinants of Farm Community Character. In *Farm Work and Fieldwork: American Agriculture in Anthropological Perspective*, edited by Michael Chibnik, pp. 167–88. Ithaca, N.Y.: Cornell University Press.

1989   The Uses of Ethnicity to Explain Agricultural Structure: A Rejoinder to Khawaja. *Rural Sociology* 54 (2): 262–65.

1990   Farming and Community from the Anthropological Study of Families. *The Rural Sociologist* 10 (2): 23–30.

Salamon, Sonya, and Karen Davis-Brown

1986   Middle-range Farmers Persisting through the Agricultural Crisis. *Rural Sociology* 51 (4): 503–12.

Salamon, Sonya, Kathleen M. Gengenbacher, and Dwight J. Penas

1986   Family Factors Affecting the Intergenerational Succession to Farming. *Human Organization* 45 (1): 24–33.

Salamon, Sonya, and Ann Mackey Keim

1979   Land Ownership and Women's Power in a Midwestern Farming Community. *Journal of Marriage and the Family* 41:109–19.

Salamon, Sonya, and Vicki Lockhart

1980   Land Ownership and the Position of Elderly in Farm Families. *Human Organization* 39 (4): 324–31.

Salamon, Sonya, and Kathleen K. Markan

1984   Incorporation and the Farm Family. *Journal of Marriage and the Family* 46 (1): 167–78.

Salamon, Sonya, and Shirley M. O'Reilly

1979   Family Land and Developmental Cycles Among Illinois Farmers. *Rural Sociology* 44 (3): 525–42.

Saloutos, Theodore

1976   The Immigrant Contribution to American Agriculture. *Agricultural History* 50 (1): 45–67.

Salter, Leonard A., Jr.

1943   *Land Tenure in Process*. Agriculture Experiment Station Research Bulletin 146. Madison: University of Wisconsin.

Schafer, Joseph

1922–23   The Yankee and the Teuton in Wisconsin. *Wisconsin Magazine of History* 21 (6): 125–45.

1927   *Four Wisconsin Counties*. Wisconsin Domesday Book 11. Madison: State Historical Society of Wisconsin.

Schertz, Lyle P.

1979   Farming in the United States. In *Structure Issues of American Agriculture*. Economics, Statistics, and Cooperative Service. Agricultural Economic Report 438, pp. 24–42. Washington, D.C.: U.S. Department of Agriculture.

Schneider, David M.

1980   *American Kinship: A Cultural Account*. 2d ed. Chicago: University of Chicago Press.

Schneider, David M., and Raymond T. Smith

1978   *Class Differences and Sex Roles in American Kinship and Family Structures*. Ann Arbor: University of Michigan Micro-Film Books.

Scholl, Kathleen K.

1983   Women Farm Operators. *Family Economic Review* 4 : 17–21.

Schulman, Michael D., Patricia Garrett, and Barbara Newman

1989   Differentiation and Survival among North Carolina Smallholders: An Empirical Perspective on the Lenin/Chayanov Debate. *Journal of Peasant Studies* 16 (4): 523–41.

Schwartz, Gary

1987   *Beyond Conformity or Rebellion*. Chicago: University of Chicago Press.

Scott, John T., Jr.

1985   Farmland Issues and Relationship to Credit in Agriculture. In *Financial Policies and Future Directions for Agriculture: Proceedings of a Seminar*, edited by Peter J. Barry, pp. 21–53. Urbana: University of Illinois, Department of Agricultural Economics.

Shammas, Carole, Marylynn Salmon, and Michael Dahlin

1987   *Inheritance in America: From Colonial Times to the Present*. New Brunswick, N.J.: Rutgers University Press.

Shannon, Fred A.

1945   *The Farmer's Last Frontier: Agriculture 1860–1897*. Vol. 5, *Economic History of the United States*. New York: Farrar and Rinehart.

Sherlock, Katy Heyman

N.d.   Land Access among Illinois Yankee Family Farmers: A Question of Social Status and Privacy. Master's thesis, University of Illinois at Urbana-Champaign.

Simmel, Georg

1898   The Persistence of Social Groups. *American Journal of Sociology* 3 (5): 662–98.

Simmons, Leo W.

1962   Aging in Primitive Societies: A Comparative Survey of Family Life and Relationships. *Law and Contemporary Problems* 27 (1): 36–51.

Smith, Elsdon Cole

1972   *New Dictionary of American Family Names.* New York: Harper and Row.

Smith, Page

1966   *As a City upon a Hill: The Town in American History.* New York: Knopf.

Smith, Thomas Lynn, and Paul E. Zopf, Jr.

1970   Some Salient Features of the Rural Family. In *Principles of Inductive Rural Sociology*, by Thomas Lynn Smith and Paul E. Zopf, Jr., pp. 300–320. Philadelphia: F. A. Davis Co.

Spillman, William J.

1919   The Agricultural Ladder. *American Economic Review Supplement* 9 (1): 170–79.

St. Boniface Bicentennial Committee

1976   St. Boniface Village History. Unpublished manuscript.

Stapp, K. E., and W. I. Bowman

1968   *History of [East Central] Illinois County.* Danville, Ill.: Interstate Printers and Publishers.

Strange, Marty

1988   *Family Farming.* Lincoln: University of Nebraska Press.

Sussman, Marvin B., J. N. Cates, and David T. Smith

1970   *The Family and Inheritance.* New York: Russell Sage Foundation.

Swanson, Louis E.

1988   *Agriculture and Community Change in the U.S.: The Congressional Reports.* Boulder, Colo.: Westview Press.

Swierenga, Robert P.

1989   The Settlement of the Old Northwest: Ethnic Pluralism in a Featureless Plain. *Journal of the Early Republic* 9 (Spring): 73–105.

Tambiah, Stanley J.

1988   Ethnic Conflict in the World Today. *American Ethnologist* 16 (2): 335–49.

Thernstrom, Stephan, ed.

1980a   *Harvard Encyclopedia of American Ethnic Groups.* Cambridge, Mass.: Harvard University Press.

1980b   Introduction to *Harvard Encyclopedia of American Ethnic Groups*, edited by Stephan Thernstrom. Cambridge, Mass.: Harvard University Press.

Tigges, Leann M., and Rachel A. Rosenfeld

1987 Independent Farming: Correlates and Consequences for Women and Men. *Rural Sociology* 52 (3): 345–64.

Truesdell, Leon E.

1960 *Farm Population: 1880 to 1950.* Bureau of the Census, Technical Paper no. 3. Washington, D.C.: U.S. Department of Commerce.

Turner, Victor

1969 *The Ritual Process.* Chicago: Aldine.

Tweeten, Luther

1983 The Economics of Small Farms. *Science* 219 : 1037–41.

Tweeten, Luther, and Wallace Huffman

1980 Structural Change. In *Structure of Agriculture and Information Needs Regarding Small Farms.* Paper VII of the Small Farms Project. Washington: National Rural Center.

U.S. Bureau of the Census

1975 *Consumer Price Index 1890 –1945.* Washington, D.C.: U.S. Government Printing Office.

1960 *Census of Population: 1960.* Vol. 1, *Number of Inhabitants.* Washington, D.C.: U.S. Government Printing Office.

1982a *1978 Census of Agriculture.* Special Reports, vol. 5, pt. 6, *1979 Farm Finance Survey.* Washington, D.C.: U.S. Government Printing Office.

1982b *Population Census of 1980.* General Social and Economic Characteristics. Table 60, *Selected Ancestry Groups.* Washington, D.C.: U.S. Government Printing Office.

1988 *1987 Census of Agriculture (AC87-A-17-000[A]).* Advance State Report. Illinois. Washington, D.C.: U.S. Government Printing Office, December.

1991 *Consumer Price Index 1950 –90.* Washington, D.C.: U.S. Government Printing Office.

U.S. Department of Agriculture

1986 *Agricultural Resources: Agricultural Land Values and Markets Situation and Outlook Report (AR-2.U.S.).* Washington D.C.: Economic Research Service.

U.S. Department of Agriculture, Crop Reporting Board

1962 *Number of Farms 1910 –1959: Land in Farms 1950 –1959, By States.* Statistical Bulletin no. 316. Washington, D.C.: Statistical Reporting Service, June.

U.S. Industrial Commission

1901 *Report on Immigration,* no. 15. Washington, D.C.: U.S. Government Printing Office.

Vanek, Joann

1980 Work, Leisure, and Family Roles: Farm Households in the United States, 1920–1955. *Journal of Family History* 5 (4): 422–31.

Varenne, Herve
1977   *Americans Together: Structured Diversity in a Midwestern Town*. New
            York: Teachers College Press, Columbia University.
Wall, Wendy L.
1984   New Breed of Farmers Focus on Bottom Line and Defy Traditions.
            Wall Street Journal, November 13.
Ward, E., and J. G. Beuscher
1950   The Inheritance Process in Wisconsin. *Wisconsin Law Review*
            25:393–422.
Waters, Mary C.
1990   *Ethnic Options: Choosing Identities in America*. Berkeley: University of
            California Press.
Weber, Max
1958   *The Protestant Ethic and the Spirit of Capitalism*. Translated by Talcott
            Parsons. New York: Scribner's.
1961   Ethnic Groups. In *Theories of Society*, edited by Talcott Parsons et al.,
            pp. 305–9. New York: Free Press.
Wheeler Centennial Committee
1984   Wheeler Centennial History, 1884–1984. Unpublished document.
Wheeler County Historical Society
1879   *Wheeler County History*.
1911   *Wheeler County History*.
Wilkening, Eugene A.
1981a   Farm Families and Family Farming. In *The Family in Rural Society*, ed-
            ited by Raymond T. Coward and William M. Smith, Jr., pp. 27–38.
            Boulder, Colo.: Westview Press.
1981b   *Farm Husbands and Wives in Wisconsin: Work Roles, Decisionmaking and
            Satisfaction, 1962 and 1978*. Madison: University of Wisconsin, R3147.
Wilkinson, Kenneth P.
1986   In Search of the Community in the Changing Countryside. *Rural Soci-
            ology* 51 (1): 1–17.
1990   Crime and Community. In *American Rural Communities*, edited by A.
            E. Luloff and Louis E. Swanson, pp. 151–68. Boulder, Colo.: Westview
            Press.
Wilson, Thomas M.
1988   Culture and Class among the "Large" Farmers of Eastern Ireland.
            American Ethnologist 15 (4): 678–93.
Wright, Harry Smith, Jr.
1969   The Principles of Setting Up a Special Extension Educational Program
            for Lady Landowners in Pike County, Illinois. Master's thesis, Univer-
            sity of Illinois at Urbana-Champaign.
Wunderlich, Gene
1989   Personal communication.

Yanagisako, Sylvia Junko

1977   Women-centered Kinship Networks in Urban Bilateral Kinship. *American Ethnologist* 5 (1): 15–29.

1984   Explicating Residence: A Cultural Analysis of Changing Households among Japanese-Americans. In *Households: Comparative and Historical Studies of the Domestic Group*, edited by Robert McC. Netting, Richard R. Wilk, and Eric J. Arnould, pp. 330–52. Berkeley: University of California Press.

Zuidema, Riener T.

1978   Personal communication.

Index